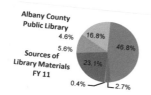

Albany County
Public Library

Sources of
Library Materials
FY 11

4.6%   16.8%
5.6%   46.8%
      23.1%
0.4%   2.7%

■ Donated Items
■ Individual Cash Gifts
■ Replacement Fees
■ ACPLF
■ City Sales Tax
■ County Sales Tax
■ Friends of the Library

NO WAY OUT

NO WAY OUT

A story of valor in the mountains of Afghanistan

MITCH WEISS AND KEVIN MAURER

BERKLEY CALIBER, NEW YORK

THE BERKLEY PUBLISHING GROUP
Published by the Penguin Group
Penguin Group (USA) Inc.
375 Hudson Street, New York, New York 10014, USA
Penguin Group (Canada), 90 Eglinton Avenue East, Suite 700, Toronto, Ontario M4P 2Y3, Canada
(a division of Pearson Penguin Canada Inc.) • Penguin Books Ltd., 80 Strand, London WC2R 0RL,
England • Penguin Group Ireland, 25 St. Stephen's Green, Dublin 2, Ireland (a division of Penguin
Books Ltd.) • Penguin Group (Australia), 250 Camberwell Road, Camberwell, Victoria 3124, Australia
(a division of Pearson Australia Group Pty. Ltd.) • Penguin Books India Pvt. Ltd., 11 Community
Centre, Panchsheel Park, New Delhi—110 017, India • Penguin Group (NZ), 67 Apollo Drive,
Rosedale, Auckland 0632, New Zealand (a division of Pearson New Zealand Ltd.) • Penguin Books
(South Africa) (Pty.) Ltd., 24 Sturdee Avenue, Rosebank, Johannesburg 2196, South Africa

Penguin Books Ltd., Registered Offices: 80 Strand, London WC2R 0RL, England

This book is an original publication of the Berkley Publishing Group.

Copyright © 2012 by Mitch Weiss and Kevin Maurer
Book design by Laura K. Corless
Front jacket photo: US Army photo by SPC Michael Carter
Maps by Travis Rightmeyer

FIRST EDITION: March 2012

Library of Congress Cataloging-in-Publication Data

Weiss, Mitch.
No way out : a story of valor in the mountains of Afghanistan / Mitch Weiss & Kevin Maurer. — 1st ed.
p.   cm.
ISBN 978-0-425-24526-2
1. Afghan War, 2001—Campaigns—Afghanistan—Shok Valley.   2. Afghan War, 2001—Commando
operations.   3. Special operations (Military science)—Afghanistan.   I. Maurer, Kevin.   II. Title.
DS371.4123.S56W45 2012
958.104'742—dc23
2011028877

PRINTED IN THE UNITED STATES OF AMERICA

10   9   8   7   6   5   4   3   2   1

For our wives and families

Theirs not to make reply,
Theirs not to reason why,
Theirs but to do and die . . .

"The Charge of the Light Brigade"
by
ALFRED, LORD TENNYSON

SHOK VALLEY
(April 6, 2008)

The mission, Commando Wrath, sent three Special Forces teams and a company from the 201st Afghan Commando Battalion to the Shok Valley to capture a high-ranking insurgent commander. Considered a sanctuary of the Hezb-e-Islami Gulbuddin terrorist group, the valley is far from any major American base.

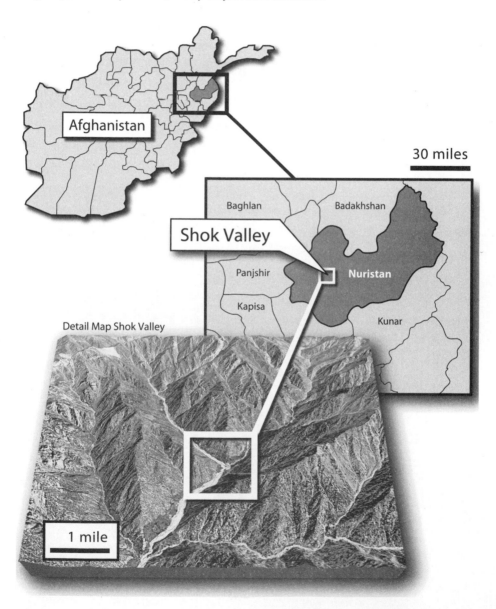

Afghanistan

30 miles

Baghlan

Badakhshan

Shok Valley

Panjshir

Nuristan

Kapisa

Kunar

Detail Map Shok Valley

1 mile

[Part 1]

PREMISSION

1

Captain Kyle Walton

It was still dark when Captain Kyle Walton stepped into the mist and bounded toward the B team's operations center. He was sure the drizzle would cancel the mission again. Maybe with another delay it would be scrapped for good—an idea he had been pushing for weeks.

Just a few days before, he and his team of Special Forces soldiers and Afghan commandos had been in helicopters on the way to a target in the Shok Valley. In midflight, they were ordered to turn around after they received word that the target was gone. Plus, everybody had concerns about weather, and this day didn't look any more promising.

Nothing about this mission looked promising.

Their target was Haji Ghafour, a high-ranking commander of the Hezb-e-Islami Gulbuddin, HIG, militant group. An extremist, Ghafour claimed to have three thousand fighters scattered in northeastern Afghanistan, and was threatening military-aged males in the Shok Valley with conscription. Ghafour was a tier-level-0 target—the military's highest priority. It was on the same level as Osama bin Laden.

Walton knew that by all accounts, Ghafour's men were heavily armed in well-fortified positions high above the valley floor. They controlled everything that moved in and out of the remote valley buried deep in Nuristan Province.

On paper, the mission was a logistical nightmare. Walton knew it. His team knew it. So did his commanders. Uneasy, Walton awoke just before 3 a.m. As the commander of Operational Detachment Alpha (ODA) 3336, he wanted to check in with the overnight staff at the operations center to see if the intelligence picture was any clearer.

The valley was a major HIG stronghold in the Hindu Kush—a picturesque five-hundred-mile mountain range that stretched between central Afghanistan and northern Pakistan with peaks topping twenty-five thousand feet. Isolated and surrounded by a wall of mountains, the valley was accessible only by pack mule. Intelligence sources said Ghafour had spent part of the winter in a compound in one of the villages in the valley. Several other nearby compounds were home to HIG subcommanders.

A source in one of the villages said Ghafour's fighters and supporters were armed with PKM machine guns and rocket-propelled grenades (RPGs). His men were stockpiling DSHK heavy machine guns, ZPU antiaircraft guns, and had collected eight surface-to-air missiles.

Walking into the headquarters at the sprawling Army base in Jalalabad, Afghanistan, Walton nodded to one of the support crew and moved to the flat-screen monitor hanging on a wall. On the screen was a black-and-white image of a village built into the cliffs possibly hundreds of feet above the valley floor. The Predator, an unmanned plane used for reconnaissance, circled high above, showing the thick mud houses. It made a long sweeping turn and shot video of the wadi—a dry creek bed that snaked through the valley.

On the white eraser board hanging next to the monitor were notes from the unit's source on the ground. Walton's eyes scanned the bullet points. It was mostly atmospherics stuff.

- They don't know you're coming.
- HLZ has no running water on it.
- There is no snow and running water.

Walton's eyes flicked back to the Predator feed. He could clearly see snow. On the spots where the helicopters were supposed to land, a river of melted snow raged like white-water rapids. To Walton, the water had to be at least waist-high.

He was worried. Not only did the intelligence reports seem unreliable, but the source knew where the helicopters were supposed to drop off his team. Not a good sign.

And he had no idea who the source was. As the ground force commander, he was uncomfortable basing so much on just one source, especially when the Predator feed in real time was telling him the source was wrong. Walton had been uncomfortable with the reporting from the start. Staring at the snow and water on the landing zones only reaffirmed his concerns.

Walton and his team were comfortable operating with uncertainty. But looking at the target and the intelligence made the hairs on the back of Walton's neck stand up. This was Walton's sixth combat rotation. He had been deployed to both Afghanistan and Iraq as a platoon leader in the 82nd Airborne Division. When the hair on the back of his neck stood up, he took heed.

Walton and his team sergeant, Master Sergeant Scott Ford, had clashed over missions in the past, but on this one they agreed: It was a shit sandwich. They had brought up the problems. The intelligence was bad. One source and, from what Walton could glean, inaccurate.

They had aborted an earlier attempt days before because it was reported that Ghafour had moved to another village, and it was unclear when he would return. So, when he popped back up in valley a few days later, commanders wanted to push forward quickly before he disappeared back into Pakistan.

In the end, Walton had no choice. They would hit the target in daylight and climb up the mountain and into the village.

The B Team's commander, Major Timothy Fletcher, and his chain of command seemed comfortable with it. They discussed the team's concerns with fighting up hill. But Fletcher and his boss, Lieutenant Colonel Lynn Ashley, believed that Ghafour's small group of bodyguards would only fight long enough for him to escape, and anyone else in the valley was probably just a part-time fighter.

And if the shooting started, Walton and the other Special Forces teams could pull back and call in air strikes. The soldiers often joked that they would rather be lucky than good—but that was easily said by guys who didn't have to go into the valley.

Walton knew when you were good you made your own luck. And that there was a fine line between sucking it up and doing the hard missions—like when the team took down several targets in Kandahar—and being reckless.

A few months before, the team had swooped into a village near Kandahar with the Afghan commandos, rounding up several Taliban commanders, destroying an opium-processing lab and a convoy of jingle trucks loaded with weapons and explosives. They had planned it for months, and even when the Taliban shot down a helicopter, the team was able to finish the mission.

But this operation, named Commando Wrath, didn't feel like that.

We're fucking awesome, but we're not fucking miracle workers, Walton thought.

The whole team's discomfort was palpable. He and Ford had several conversations. They had tried to hide their misgivings, but in private they all came out. Not only did the basic tactical plan of attacking up a mountain not work, but it was unclear how they would evacuate casualties or which unit was going to act as reinforcements if things went badly.

"There is no fucking medevac plan here. This is not good," Ford said.

Walton took his and Ford's concerns to Fletcher, urging him to take them up with Ashley and higher if necessary.

But at every level he got the same answer: You're going to do it.

Staring into the monitor at the village sitting on top of the mountains, he wasn't sure a Ranger battalion or a battalion of paratroopers from the 82nd Airborne could do this mission, let alone three Special Forces teams and one hundred Afghan commandos.

After rehearsing it again the day before, they all had the feeling that it was going to be a weather call again. They were prepared to go, but everyone, in the back of his mind, believed the mission would be halted.

But when Walton walked into the operations center and examined the Predator feeds—when he saw they weren't going to make a change off the live intelligence—the captain knew the mission was a go.

Grabbing Fletcher, who had walked into the operations center, Walton tried one more time to spike the mission.

"The intel you have is not fucking accurate. And now I have to contend with landing in a freaking river," Walton told Fletcher. "Hey, is this an abort call?"

All missions had abort criteria in place so commanders could halt an operation instead of moving forward just because they had assets in place—aircraft, men, and equipment.

He hoped to convince Fletcher to call Ashley and abort the mission. It was clear to Walton.

The intel was bad.

The weather was bad.

The whole thing felt like a setup.

Abort.

2

Staff Sergeant Luis Morales

It was dawn and a steady stream of soldiers at the base began getting dressed for the mission. As always, Staff Sergeant Luis Morales was one of the first to get ready. The night before, Morales, an intelligence specialist, had been sitting at a desk in the team's operations center. Leaning back in a chair, he had tried to stay awake. It was late and he was tired, but he had promised himself he would review the plans for the upcoming mission one more time.

Pulling a pack of Marlboro Lights from his pocket, he lit a cigarette and inhaled deeply. He glimpsed the bright maps of Afghanistan's eastern provinces—Nuristan, Kunar, Nangarhar, and Laghman—on the drab beige walls. A bank of black laptops on the tables was closed, and the only noise was the incessant humming of a clock on the wall.

Morales had been working tirelessly for weeks, collecting intelligence for Commando Wrath. That was a critical part of his job and he was passionate about his work. Now, on the eve of the mission, he had to make certain everything was right. No mistakes. Every detail was important. He knew preparation was the key to the success of any operation.

Morales had prepared an extensive report about the Shok Valley. It was important to let his team know what to expect. So he spent weeks studying Military Grid Reference System maps, intelligence reports, satellite imagery, and Predator feeds of the terrain and targets. Then he wrapped his findings in a PowerPoint presentation.

When he was ready, Morales stood in front of a room filled with Green Berets, clicking slide after slide, warning his men about the treacherous terrain: steep mountains that disappeared in the clouds, jagged ridgelines, boulders, loose rocks, and soft ground that, with the melting snow, made every step perilous. And their main target—Haji Ghafour—was located somewhere in a heavily defended compound high above the valley floor.

By the end of the presentation, he was confident that his team understood the dangers. Still, it was one thing to watch a PowerPoint. It was another to land in the middle of a wadi in the early morning, scale a mountain with more than sixty pounds of equipment strapped on your back, and surprise an enemy that had been defending the valley for generations. The valley was so dangerous that the Soviet Union, during its decade-long occupation of Afghanistan, had refused to go there. U.S. forces had never been there either. That's why Morales reviewed the intelligence one more time.

He learned this work ethic—paying close attention to details—from his father and grandfather, who'd had long and distinguished military careers.

His grandfather Luis Guillermo Morales enlisted in the Army in 1950, at the start of the Korean War. Growing up in Arecibo, Puerto Rico, a picturesque fishing village on the northern coast, he dreamed of one day emigrating to the United States. Only five feet four inches tall, Guillermo was proud and fiercely patriotic, telling recruiters at Puerto Rico's Fort Buchanan that he wanted to be an infantryman. He got his wish, fighting on the front lines. Even though he was wounded in action—shot in the hand—Guillermo stayed in the Army. He retired in 1975 as a sergeant major.

Morales's father, Luis Gilberto Morales, followed in his father's footsteps. After graduating from North Carolina State University in Raleigh, Gilberto enlisted in 1976 and attended officer candidate school. As a young second lieutenant, he served as an artillery officer in the 82nd Airborne.

His early days in the military were hectic. He had married his college girlfriend, Sharon Weers, a Colorado girl with bright red hair, and started a family. Like many military families, Gilberto's moved from base to base. His first child, Luis Geraldo Morales, was born while Gilberto was stationed at Fort Sill, Oklahoma.

During his early childhood, Morales and his younger brother spent a good deal of time at Fort Bragg, a sprawling military base in Fayetteville, North Carolina. One of the largest military complexes in the world, Fort Bragg was home to the 82nd Airborne and Special Forces, including the John F. Kennedy Special Warfare Center and School, which trains Green Berets.

It also was where his grandparents had retired. They bought a house near Fort Bragg in Spring Lake and his grandfather became an important figure in Morales's life. He filled young Morales's head with stories about his exploits in the Korean War. And when he visited the base, Guillermo always seemed to be greeted warmly by soldiers who would laugh while they reminisced about their days in his unit.

Morales was proud of his father—especially during "All-American Week," when soldiers of the 82nd Airborne would conduct public training demonstrations on the base. Holding his mother's hand, young Morales was spellbound at the sight of his father and other paratroopers dropping from the sky during training exercises. He knew from that moment he wanted to be in the Army.

When he was a teenager, his father landed a job at the Pentagon and moved the family to Fredericksburg, Virginia. For Morales, it meant starting over. But shortly after enrolling at James Monroe High School, he met Katherine Barksdale—and his life changed. She was outgoing, a perky, pretty blonde. Morales was quiet but handsome, with thick biceps and powerful legs from running and playing soccer. He had a bright smile, and loved fast cars and action movies. They would sit in the bleachers and talk for hours about their friends and family. They dated off and on for the rest of high school, but inside, Morales knew she was "the one."

As he was nearing graduation in 1996, Morales had to decide about his future. There was no pressure from his family. They were always supportive. In his heart, he knew he didn't want to go to college, and when a recruiter who had been trying to get him to enlist for years called, he knew it was time.

Morales decided that if he was going to enlist, he wanted to be part of something special: an Army Ranger. While training would be long and arduous, Morales welcomed the challenge and was confident he could excel. He told himself over and over again that a Morales never quits, never fails.

To get ready, he trained hard. He began running longer distances and lifting more weights. He wanted to be in the best shape of his life.

He was eighteen when he reported to basic training in September 1996. And after basic, he joined the Rangers for even more training. The whole time, though, he thought of Katherine. Before he left, they had started dating again. And during the Ranger Indoctrination Program, known as RIP, he kept a photograph of her pinned inside his patrol cap. He didn't have it laminated, so he covered the picture with Scotch tape to waterproof it. Whenever things got rough—whenever he felt so exhausted he couldn't move—he would lift his hat and take a peek at the portrait of Katherine. And this would give him the inspiration to keep going.

Ranger school was divided into three phases—each one three weeks long—and during his downtime, he daydreamed of Katherine. One day, he reached a conclusion: He wanted to spend the rest of his life with her. So a few months after graduating Ranger school and joining the 1st Ranger Battalion, Morales headed with a buddy to a mall in Savannah, Georgia, where he was stationed. When they arrived, Morales told him he was going to buy Katherine an engagement ring. He picked out a gold band with a half-carat diamond, which he financed. If he was going to do it, he wanted a ring that stood out.

On a chilly October night in 1998, he took Katherine on a dinner cruise on the Savannah River. Before he left the base to pick her up, he made sure he stuffed a small box with the ring in his pocket. During dinner, they made small talk, but the tough young Ranger was uncharacteristically nervous. Would she say yes? What if she said no? It would be embarrassing, especially in front of everyone on a cruise ship. As the boat slipped under the Savannah River Bridge, with the brilliant night skyline of the city in the background, he pulled out the box with the ring, reached for her hand, and knelt. When she saw the glittering stone, she jumped up and wrapped her arms around him. It was yes. They were married a few months later.

It was an exciting time in his life. He was married to his high school sweetheart and was being deployed overseas for training missions. In a three-year span, he was deployed to Botswana, Germany, and Egypt. He loved being a Ranger. They were a band of brothers; all young, in top physical shape, and poised for action. Eventually Morales moved up in rank to sergeant.

But the terrorist attacks on September 11, 2001, changed his life.

He watched news accounts of hijacked planes smashing into the World Trade Center and the Pentagon. He was outraged when the buildings collapsed, killing thousands. He was angry when he saw a hijacked plane slam into the Pentagon. He knew that building—his father had worked there for years and he had visited many times. He was riveted to the television when newly elected president George W. Bush visited Ground Zero and promised to avenge the deaths of innocent Americans.

And Morales began hearing the names Osama bin Laden, Al Qaeda, and Afghanistan over and over again. Like many Americans, he learned that Afghanistan had been taken over by the Taliban—Islamic extremists—and the Taliban allowed Al Qaeda to set up training camps for the extremists that attacked the United States.

Morales knew it was a matter of time before the United States would strike back. So he began prepping about Afghanistan, because he was certain that one day, he would be deployed there to fight terrorism.

He knew this conflict—the one the president called the War on Terror—was a noble one, much like World War II, where the "greatest generation" fought against evil. Unlike Vietnam, a conflict with no clear-cut objective that became more and more unpopular with the public as casualties mounted, the War on Terror had a clear goal with villains straight out of central casting. The most notorious: Osama bin Laden, a sullen, bearded, rifle-toting Islamic revolutionary who created the terrorist network known as Al Qaeda, which planned the attacks. In the aftermath of the destruction, America was united in a way that it had not been in years, and overwhelmingly supported invading Afghanistan to kill bin Laden and his terrorist followers and dismantle the Taliban government.

If there was an invasion, Morales wanted to be part of it. That's what soldiers do—fight in wars. It took a while, though, for Morales to be deployed to a war zone.

In 2003, Morales was sent to Korea. As his yearlong deployment was winding down, he received orders to return to Fort Benning, Georgia. Disappointed, he bumped into a Special Forces recruiter in Korea who asked him if he wanted to join the Green Berets. Morales didn't hesitate. He knew they were an elite group of soldiers who specialized in unconventional warfare, and that much like the Rangers, only a few were selected. More importantly, they were always being rotated in and out of Iraq and Afghanistan.

To join Special Forces would be the ultimate challenge. He understood the rich history of the Green Berets, and the role Special Forces played in stopping the spread of communism, and how the focus had shifted to battling terrorism.

In the late 1950s and early 1960s, Soviet- and Chinese-sponsored Communist insurgencies flared up against Western governments in Asia, Africa, and Latin America. Numerous failures by the CIA to counter these revolutions led President John F. Kennedy to turn to Special Forces, which was formed in 1952.

Kennedy was elected in 1960, in part because of his cold war stance. A hard-liner, Kennedy claimed the United States was losing the arms race to the Soviets in what the Democratic candidate characterized as a "missile gap."

A war hero and student of military affairs, Kennedy had developed an interest in counterinsurgency—the art and method of defeating guerrilla movements. He knew Special Forces soldiers were the ideal vehicle for implementing such missions, and began sending them to problem areas. One of the first places they were deployed: South Vietnam, where they were used to help fight North Vietnam guerrillas, known as the Viet Cong, who were threatening to topple the U.S.-supported regime in Saigon.

Kennedy's interest in Special Forces led to the adoption of a green beret as the official headgear of Special Forces. Preparing for a visit to the Special Warfare Center at Fort Bragg in October, 1961, Kennedy sent word to the center's commander for all Special Forces soldiers to wear green berets as part of the event. The president believed that since they had a special mission, Special Forces should have something to set them apart from other fighting units.

Kennedy called the green beret a "symbol of excellence. A badge of courage. A mark of distinction in the fight for freedom." Soon it became synonymous with Special Forces and, with Kennedy's support, new outfits began to emerge, including Morales's unit: 3rd Special Forces Group.

Special Forces had become an iconic symbol of battle-hardened soldiers fighting communism, thanks in part to Barry Sadler's hit song, "The Ballad of the Green Berets," in 1966. With lyrics like: *Fighting soldiers from the sky. Fearless men who jump and die,* the tune became a recruiter's dream. The same year, John Wayne starred in a movie about Green Berets "fighting commies" in the jungles of Vietnam. It was based on the best-selling nonfiction book by Robin Moore, *The Green Berets.*

The group's stellar reputation continued to grow over the years, and with wars in Afghanistan and Iraq, the military was depending more and more on Special Forces to hunt insurgents and train Afghan and Iraqi soldiers. But constant deployments were taxing what was a relatively small force, making it imperative that more Special Forces soldiers be trained more quickly.

At the heart of Special Forces were the small, twelve-member teams known as Operational Detachment Alpha (ODA). Each team had a commander who was an officer, an assistant commander who was a warrant officer, and a noncommissioned officer in charge. In addition, the teams usually had two weapons sergeants, communications sergeants, medical sergeants, engineering sergeants, and an intelligence sergeant.

Designed to spend months deep within hostile territory, the units had to learn how to survive on their own without extensive resupply from the outside. They were cross-trained in one another's specialties, and many spoke at least one foreign language.

So picking the right men was critical.

To even be considered, Morales had to prove he was worthy. The only way to do that was by attending Selection at Fort Bragg. Selection was brutal. It was a series of exhaustive tests over a three-week period to determine which soldiers had the physical and mental toughness to wear a green beret. Morales knew he would be tested for strength, endurance, intelligence, and if he showed that he could handle the pressure, would be picked and move on to Special Forces training known as the qualification course.

Morales sailed through Selection, and spent a year in training before being deployed to Afghanistan in 2006. During that nearly yearlong tour, he saw little action—just one firefight when insurgents launched an RPG at Humvees in a convoy.

Most of the time, 3rd Special Forces Group and Morales's ODA were stationed at a forward operating base in Gardēz, helping train the Afghan National Police. Gardēz was a city of seventy thousand inhabitants built along a river in a mountain valley at an elevation of about 7,600 feet. Like most of Afghanistan, the area was poor. The population was overwhelmingly Pashtun, and Gardēz was a stronghold of the Taliban. In addition, the inhabitants were divided into tribes—many of which were involved in feuds with each other that dated back generations. Rival warlords still maintained private armies in the area.

To Morales, it seemed that his team had spent most of the year visiting villages, trying to collect intelligence, and quelling potential tribal disputes. Keeping the peace. Not the most exciting deployment. He was surprised that the team wasn't going out on missions to hit targets.

But that all changed during his second tour, which began in September 2007. The makeup of ODA 3336 changed. Scott Ford had become the non-commissioned officer in charge. He was a no-nonsense, tough-as-nails leader—just what the team needed. He preached the basics: Be prepared. Do things the right way during training and maneuvers. It will keep you alive in the field. And he was quick to get in your face if you fell out of line. Kyle Walton was the new team captain. Like Ford, he was aggressive. A West Point grad-uate, he had served several tours in Iraq.

Now the team had a new philosophy: They were going to be aggressive. They were going to plan missions to go after the bad guys.

That's why they were in Afghanistan in the first place.

Kick ass.

Take no prisoners.

Morales liked the new tone.

First, though, they had to train Afghan commandos who would accompany them on missions. For two months, Morales's team taught the commandos the basics of warfare. It was an accelerated course that covered everything from intelligence gathering to driving Humvees in convoys. His unit had taken the commandos on several missions, and they faced some resistance. But no one was killed or wounded.

Morales knew those missions paled in comparison to the planned Shok Valley operation. This would be a real test for the commandos—maybe even for his team. He knew how Ford and Walton felt about Operation Commando Wrath: It was a potential death trap.

And so after all these years, here he was, at the airfield surrounded by his fellow soldiers and commandos. Waiting for word about whether the most dangerous mission of his career was a go. He was ready to light up a cigarette when he saw Walton heading in his direction. And as soon as he glimpsed Walton's face, he knew the answer.

3

Specialist Michael D. Carter

Rummaging through his camera bag, Specialist Michael D. Carter wanted to make sure he had all the equipment he needed for the mission.

His Nikon D2X?

Check.

His Sony PD170 video camera?

Check.

His batteries?

Check.

It was all there, but he just couldn't shake the feeling that something was missing. Maybe it was because the Special Forces guys had forced him to "strip down" his bulky equipment bag filled with cameras. They laughed when they spotted it, and told Carter he didn't need all that gear—not where he was headed. Not when he was going to be climbing up a mountain to reach an enemy compound built on top of a cliff.

Carter wasn't exactly sure where he was headed. He only knew it was someplace called the Shok Valley. But he could tell from glancing at the guys—the way they were pacing and chain-smoking cigarettes—that this was no routine mission. He could sense it was dangerous, and it just figured. This was his last assignment before heading home. That's just the way it goes sometimes. The luck of the draw, Carter thought as he stood near the flight line waiting to board a CH-47 Chinook, a twin-engine, heavy-lift helicopter used to move troops, artillery, supplies, and equipment on the battlefield.

He had been in a "homeward-bound state of mind" when another combat cameraman, Staff Sergeant Corey Dennis, contracted pinkeye. Carter was his replacement, and he didn't mind accompanying troops one last time. He had been in Afghanistan for nearly a year, and enjoyed his job. He had gone on dozens of missions, taking photos and videos of soldiers "at work in the field," and providing pictures and video to help combat commanders plan missions.

Carter was hardworking, and his commanders thought highly of the tall, wiry, quiet, clean-cut Texan with the round glasses. With cameras dangling around his neck, he looked like a throwback to another era—not someone from the digital age. But Carter was part of a lineage of photographers whose roots stretched back more than 150 years.

Photographers had been on battlefields since the Civil War when Mathew Brady supervised a corps of shooters to follow troops and document the war on a grand scale. In the 1860s, photography was still a relatively new art form, and many of his photographs captured the "terrible reality and earnestness of war" with stark, sobering shots of corpses rotting in farm fields after battles. At the time, it was startling for the public to view such images.

After the Civil War, the military discovered that photography could be a useful tool. To many, combat cameramen are the unseen frontline warriors and their work can be viewed on nightly news shows or while watching one of the many documentaries containing archival combat footage.

But Carter's job was more than just documenting history. It was dangerous. A member of the 55th Signal Company, Carter knew each embed was risky. Since 2003, nearly a half-dozen combat cameramen had been awarded the Purple Heart, and more than thirty soldiers had received the Bronze Star during missions in Afghanistan and Iraq. Carter had been lucky. He hadn't been in any major firefights and he didn't want his luck to change now. Not when he was so close to the end of his tour.

He took a deep breath and sighed, then snapped a few frames. He had arrived at the base a day earlier, and didn't get much sleep. Now, with all his nervous energy, he was trying to find a way to kill time before boarding the Chinook. His job was nothing like the movies, where combat cameramen always seemed to be jumping on helicopters or riding in Jeeps, darting from village to village, taking photos of firefights that would somehow end up on the front pages of major American newspapers. In contrast, Carter rarely said a word as he snapped pictures in relative anonymity.

And he liked it that way.

It all stemmed from his upbringing in a small Texas town where people were taught to be polite, humble, and praise God for their blessings. Carter was born in Smithville, Texas, a hardscrabble, former railroad town in the southeastern part of the state near the Colorado River. A flyspeck on the map, Smithville, about forty-five minutes south of Austin, had only 2,500 people. It was a place where fathers would take their sons hunting in the woods and fishing in the river, or would watch them play football on Friday nights. It seemed like most of the inhabitants drove pickup trucks—mostly Fords and Chevrolets—and worked on farms, where they raised cattle or toiled in the hundreds of oil fields that dotted the landscape from Corpus Christi to Beaumont.

Carter's father, Mark Carter, worked in those oil fields, while his mother, Anna, was a teacher and later a principal in private schools. But there was little stability at home. His family moved all over southeastern Texas from Smithville to Bowie to Katy as his father took a series of oil jobs, including one on an offshore rig in the Gulf of Mexico.

When Carter was a boy, his father would sometimes take him to the refineries—giant playgrounds of pipes and pumps and big metal buildings that turned black crude oil into liquid gold. He would tousle his hair as he told young Carter stories about growing up in south Texas. At night, the sparkle of refinery lights would illuminate the pitch-black sky. To approaching motorists, it would appear as if they were driving toward a magical city. It was more Las Vegas, Nevada, than Lake Charles, Louisiana.

The more his family moved, the more his parents' relationship began to dissolve. When Carter's father worked on an offshore oil rig in Lafayette, Louisiana, he would spend two weeks at a time away from home. It was too much for his mother. When Carter turned fifteen, his parents separated. His mother moved the family back to Smithville and filed for divorce. A few months later, his father died of a heart attack. The sudden death hit Carter hard. His father was a mentor, someone he could talk to.

After his father's death, his mother struggled to make ends meet. She was unemployed for a while. Then she took a job in a nursing home. Her life began falling to pieces. She began drinking heavily. It all began to take a toll on Carter and he turned inward. He kept everything inside. He would find solace in hunting and fishing. And guns were his passion. He could tear them apart and put them back together. He knew everything about guns. Maybe that's why he enjoyed action movies so much—everyone had guns and the action heroes knew how to use them. One of his favorites was Rambo, a former Special Forces soldier who battled a crooked sheriff and later the Soviets after they invaded Afghanistan in the 1980s. Rambo was big and tough and smart and wasted bad guys without thinking. In fact, it was Carter's love of guns and action movies that sparked his interest in the military.

At Smithville High School, he was unsure about his future. He knew he didn't want to go to college or follow his dad into the oil fields. The military was appealing. He had two uncles who were in the Army and his grandfather was a Marine.

When he told his mother what he wanted to do, she didn't stop him. She already knew, telling him she had "figured it out." When he was a boy, she would stare out the kitchen window and there, in the backyard, she would watch him as he ran around with his friends, playing war games in a thicket of woods.

After the September 11, 2001, terrorist attacks, he became passionate about enlisting. He was a sophomore, sitting in English class, when the planes hit the World Trade Center towers. His English teacher, Robert Duke, escorted his class into the library to watch history unfold on television. Other classes followed, and they mostly sat there in silence. When the buildings collapsed, Carter had one thought: *These motherfuckers are going to get paid back.* He remembered looking around the library and spotting some students who were laughing and joking. They weren't paying attention, and Carter became angry at their indifference. *They are attacking your country,* he thought.

When Carter told his uncle he was going to enlist, the older man made a suggestion: "If you're going in, go for a job that you can take with you when you get out." That idea clicked. He loved guns, so why not learn how to repair them? With a knowledge of small-arms armament repair, he could become a gunsmith and work with guns for a living.

So he called up his recruiter and enlisted for six years. All set, Carter said his good-bye to his aunt Raymeh Davis, who helped raise him after his father died, and to all his other relatives. He was excited and couldn't wait to get to basic training.

But days before he was scheduled to leave, his mother was hospitalized with pneumonia. She told him to go, but he was worried about her. She was growing weaker and weaker. Carter stayed with her at the hospital, monitoring her condition and praying. But she continued to deteriorate and soon passed away. Carter was heartbroken. He loved his mother and to see her die so young was heartbreaking. Now, as a young man, he had no parents. His aunt Raymeh stepped in and promised to help his younger brother. She encouraged Carter to go.

So on an autumn day in 2003, Carter boarded a plane in San Antonio and flew to Louisville, Kentucky, then took a bus to Fort Knox.

But there was a problem. He had missed the beginning of basic training. That meant he would be late for the small-armament repair program—and he had to be there for the first class. So Carter had to find another military occupation specialty, or MOS. He was disappointed, but there was nothing he could do. As he sat in an office at the base flipping through a book of possible specialties, nothing seemed to grab him. Sometimes, Carter asked the sergeant what a certain MOS entailed. But when he heard the details, he would shake his head no.

He was searching for an MOS that would allow him to split time between the field and the office. When someone mentioned a combat cameraman, he paused for a moment and asked the sergeant to explain. When Carter heard the fine points, he perked up. He had never thought about becoming a photographer. Sure, in high school, he had a few "happy snap cameras." But it never crossed his mind that he would do something like that for a living.

He accepted the MOS, but it didn't take Carter long to discover that there was more to taking pictures than squinting through a lens and pressing a button that trips the shutter release. There was a real skill—and science—to shooting good photos.

When he arrived at photography school at Fort Meade, Maryland, he quickly realized that most of the people in his class had some photographic background. They had owned digital cameras and studied the art. For them, it had been a calling. But Carter struggled.

He had to learn how to use the shutter speed, which controls the length of time the shutter remains open. Not only did he have to understand the terminology, he had to deal with math and science. (Typical shutter speeds are measured in fractions of a second, such as 1/30, 1/60, 1/125, 1/250, 1/500, and 1/1000 of a second.) Then there was the theory of prisms—how, when light passes into a material at an angle, the light beam is bent or refracted. And when beams are refracted, they can cause problems with camera lenses.

At first, Carter had a hard time grasping the concepts, calling it "fucking stupid." But once he started going out in the field to shoot, the concepts clicked. And he soon discovered that he could be at peace with his cameras. He could be an observer and fade into the background. And he discovered that he was pretty good at shooting video—a critical part of his job.

After his graduation, the Army gave him a thirty-day leave before he was deployed to Germany, to join the 7th Army Training Center. He flew back to Smithville and visited his aunt and brother, who was considering becoming a corrections officer.

While he was there, he stopped by the recruiting office to help a local recruiter. It was early 2004 and the war in Iraq had entered a new phase. It had morphed from "shock and awe" when U.S. troops quickly dispatched

Saddam Hussein from power, to Al Qaeda and insurgents attacking soldiers and planting improvised explosive devices, known as IEDs. Still, it appeared to Carter that people in his hometown wanted to enlist. The country was in the middle of a patriotic boom, still angry at the terrorists' attacks.

At the end of his leave, Carter boarded a plane and headed to Germany. Inside, he was a little apprehensive. He knew he still had a lot to learn about photography and Germany would be a perfect place to train. It was better to learn his craft in a peaceful country than in a war zone.

And he was right.

He worked with the training support center, and shot stills and video of companies conducting training exercises. But Carter quickly grew bored. The job just plain sucked. Here he was, documenting everyone else prepping to go to war while he was left behind. He felt like he should be going, too.

After two years in Germany, he returned to Fort Meade. A few months later, he was told he would deploy to Afghanistan. Now he was stoked. This is what he had been looking for all along. He wanted to prove his mettle in firefights. Finally, he was going to be a real combat cameraman. He felt inspired and invigorated.

Transferred to Fort Benning, Georgia, for more training, Carter was informed that he would be assigned to Special Forces. He smiled when he heard a commander tell him, "Don't fuck up. You'll have to be able to do what they do. You need to train with these guys so you don't stand out. So you all look the same."

Carter took the words to heart. For several weeks, it was like he was back in basic training. He knew the commander was right: He would have to be in the best shape of his life if he was going to be embedded with Special Forces.

The night before he shipped out to Afghanistan, his friends threw a big party in the barracks. Carter and his buddies drank all night—Jack Daniel's, beer; whatever they could get their hands on. They swapped stories and laughed at the frat-house jokes. And at dawn, Carter showered and got dressed, and boarded a plane for the first of a series of flights that would end at the Bagram Air Field in Afghanistan.

When he landed, it was unlike anyplace he had ever seen. He gazed at towering mountains with snowcapped peaks in the distance. When he opened his mouth, he could taste the gritty blowing sand. The temperature was hotter than a typical southeastern Texas day in the summer, but with less humidity, which made it somewhat bearable. He actually liked it.

Over the next year, Carter traveled with 7th Special Forces Group, and then 3rd Special Forces Group. He would go from firebase to firebase, talking to soldiers and taking photos. He enthusiastically tackled each assignment and, thankfully, he didn't see serious action.

And he was packing his bags, getting ready for the long trip back to the United States, when he heard that his friend Dennis was sick. The next thing he knew he was packing his gear and heading to Jalalabad to hook up with Walton's team.

Now here he was, waiting to board a helicopter with the other soldiers for an operation to hunt and kill a top terrorist—a mission that seemed straight out of *Mission: Impossible.* And for a moment Carter couldn't help wondering if his final mission in Afghanistan would be his last.

4.

Master Sergeant Scott Ford

Even though he'd been fighting to stop the mission, Commando Wrath was a go. Master Sergeant Scott Ford knew that. The commanders had been pushing too hard. So Ford promised to make sure his team and the Afghan commandos were ready and pumped up for the mission.

Pulling his tan desert uniform shirt over his lean, muscular body—minus the undershirt because he would have to hump sixty pounds up a mountain—Ford headed to the team's operations center.

It was still drizzling, and if it was sprinkling in Jalalabad, he knew it was worse in the mountains.

"Zach, call over to the airfield and see if the birds are going," Ford said to Senior Airman Zach Rhyner, the Air Force joint terminal attack controller or JTAC. It was Rhyner's job to call in air strikes when the shooting started.

Ford wanted to tell the guys to be ready, but he also wanted to manage the stress. The mission had been a series of starts and stops for the past several days, and the team all believed it was going to be canceled again.

"It's socked in. This thing isn't going to happen," said Rhyner, a twenty-two-year-old from Medford, Wisconsin. This was his first combat deployment.

Ford looked at Master Sergeant Jim Lodyga, the team sergeant for ODA 3312. His team was supposed to set up a support position and cover Ford and his men as they climbed up the mountain. Both men shook their heads.

"Get your shit. That way we're ready," Ford told his team.

The sun was starting to rise when the soldiers all made it to the flight line. They waited as usual, and just as they were getting ready to board the Chinooks, the departure time was pushed back. But the mission was still on. Sitting by the helicopters, Ford reflected back to when he took over the team. They had come a long way.

When Ford joined the team in July 2007, the unit had already been through three team sergeants in three years. They were a very young team, and in Ford's opinion, they hadn't been guided in the right direction. There were no team standard operating procedures (SOPs). They hadn't done a thing in the seven months since their last Afghanistan rotation. Ford knew he had his work cut out for him. He had until October—three months—to get the team ready before they deployed again to Afghanistan. They needed a "team daddy" in Special Forces lingo, to whip them into shape.

And Ford was that guy.

In a way, Ford's upbringing had prepared him for the military.

He grew up in rural southeastern Ohio, about twenty minutes down the road from Ohio University. The Fords were family oriented. Every weekend there was a cookout or some kind of gathering at an uncle's house. When his parents got married, they bought his mother's family's farm.

Ford learned about hard work on the family farm, where they kept cattle, hogs, and horses. He would get up in the morning before dawn, do his chores, eat breakfast, and catch the bus to school. When he arrived home, he had more chores and sometimes would have a little time to hunt squirrels before dinner.

School just wasn't Ford's thing. He did well enough, but he didn't enjoy it. Sports were the only reason he even attended—and they forced him to study. If you didn't keep up your grades, you were off the team. He played football—both offense and defense—and basketball. His was the type of school where everybody had to come out in order to field a full team. His graduating class only had sixty students.

Ford knew college wasn't an option. He just wasn't disciplined enough—at least not at that point in his life. There was no future in southeastern Ohio. The area had few good jobs—unless you worked for Ohio University in Athens.

So at the end of high school, he decided to join the military, following his father, who had served in the Air Force just after the Vietnam War.

Ford enlisted in the Army—but not until he'd checked out the Marine Corps. When Ford asked the Marine recruiter what the service had to offer, he was given a smug answer.

"You can be in the Marine Corps or you can't. It's up to you," the recruiter said.

It didn't matter. Ford had always wanted to join the Army so that he could be a Ranger. Ever since the invasion of Panama, an attack the Rangers had spearheaded, he figured that was his best chance to do the high-speed missions. He was planning to go for infantry, when his uncles pulled him aside and told him to get a skill. So he chose communications and went to Fort Jackson in Columbia, South Carolina, for basic training.

It was a breeze. For someone who'd grown up on the farm, it wasn't difficult to get up early and work hard all day. He was used to being told to do something and getting it done correctly the first time. Plus, once he started playing sports, he barely had time to sleep, what with his chores, practice, and schoolwork. If it was sports season or harvesttime, he rarely got eight hours of sleep. Some guys just weren't used to a little sleep deprivation. Ford thrived on it.

After basic training, he finished jump school at Fort Benning, Georgia, and was assigned to the 319th Airborne Field Artillery at Fort Bragg. There, he was surrounded by a bunch of gun bunnies who spent their days firing howitzers.

Ford figured he would do the Army thing for a few years, then get out and maybe go to college. But when he was ready to leave the military, his neighbor talked him into checking out Special Forces. His Army hunting buddies were all Green Berets and encouraged him to go to Selection. At first, Ford hesitated. He had never failed at anything and he didn't want to try and not get selected.

"Don't worry," they told him. "You fit the mold perfectly."

They were right. He made it through easily. The whole time, he wanted more. He just loved the fact that he was getting some real Army training. Knowing that he was going to join a team and would be soon traveling around the world.

Selected as an engineer, Ford was excited: He wanted to blow shit up.

After training, he went straight to 3rd Special Forces Group. His team spent most of their training missions in the islands—the Dominican Republic, Grenada, and Saint Vincent. He found the guys on the team were a lot like him. Most had a rural background. They came from small communities in Michigan, Ohio, Pennsylvania. They hunted. Fished. They appreciated home and had matured in the Army.

During the months leading up to the Afghanistan deployment, Ford tried to beat the bad habits out of the new team like his old teammates did to him. He drove them in training, making them come in early for physical training (PT) in the mornings and keeping them late. Everything Ford did was met with resistance until the team realized that they were only going to lose.

On his first day as the team sergeant, he laid down the law. His first move to change the culture: He told the guys to clean up the team room. It was cluttered. Junk was stacked up on all the desks and tables. The top of the refrigerator was covered in papers and binders, and in Ford's eyes the room looked trashy. It lacked pride.

Part clubhouse, part office, the team room was the one part of Fort Bragg that the soldiers owned. Each team room was unique. They were often decorated with mementos from past deployments. "I want everything off the top of the fridge. If you have clutter on top of everything, it looks like shit," he told them.

Pulling open the door to the refrigerator, he saw a massive turkey, leftovers from Thanksgiving. It was July, and the picked-over bones had inches of thick mold on them. Ford was sure they had spores that hadn't been discovered yet.

"Clean the fridge," he barked.

But the team blew him off. Nobody owned up to bringing in the turkey.

"You all own the fridge," Ford said. "One, you need to be able to put your lunch in there because you're not going home every day for lunch. You're going to be training. Two, I want that thing full of beer."

Beer in the refrigerator was technically forbidden. They had all been given counseling statements saying they couldn't keep beer in the team room. So Ford rummaged through all of their folders and tossed all of the statements in the trash.

"I said put beer in there. If I tell you to do something that is illegal, I am accepting the responsibility for it. If you get called out on it, I am going to take that heat round personally," he told them.

Beer was currency in the Special Forces. And Ford used it to help make his points. If you say you're doing something for the first time, that was a case of beer. If you made a mistake, that was a case of beer. At the end of most training shoots on the range, there was a "beer shoot." Each soldier saved a magazine and the worst shot, well, that was a case of beer.

The team had been accruing beer debt, so when the refrigerator was finally clean, Ford told the soldiers who owed beer to stock the fridge before they went home. They came back with twelve-packs. Ford was shocked.

"Did I say you owe half a case or a case? I don't do half cases. It is either a full case or none," Ford said.

So Ford broke out the marker and drew a box with twenty-four circles on it.

"Now you have a pictorial view of what a case of beer looks like," he said. "If you have any questions, come back to this dry-erase board to make sure you know if you have a case or not."

It was hard for Ford at first. He had come from a team of senior sergeants who knew their job and had been doing it for ten years. On his new team, the most senior guy was Karl Wurzbach. Some of the men had never been in the Army until they joined Special Forces. Ford would often explode because they didn't know their job. But he soon realized that it wasn't all their fault. They just hadn't been given the right guidance.

One time, two soldiers didn't show for PT. They stayed home and put their kids on the school bus. Ford understood it—but they hadn't asked him first. The soldiers said they had cleared it with Walton. In Ford's view, he was the only one who could excuse a soldier from physical training. That was how he ran his team. Old-school. But he knew what the guys were doing. They were playing the "mom and pop" game. If Ford said no, they would go to Walton. That had been going on a lot—and it had to end. Walton was an officer—and was responsible for planning missions. Ford's job was to whip the team into shape—mold them into a cohesive unit that could tackle any assignment. And physical training was an important part of that process. He knew the mountains in Afghanistan were no joke.

Ford's relationship with Walton also was a work in progress. They were both type A personalities who wanted to do things *their* way. Walton was used to being a platoon leader and wanted to micromanage the daily activities. But in Ford's view, that was the team sergeant's duty. It made sense. Most team sergeants were rolling with a decade's worth of experience in Special Forces, while many team leaders rotated in and out of units quickly, and some, like Walton, were brand-new to the job.

So that day, Ford decided to talk to Walton to close that fissure.

"Listen, you stay out of their business," Ford told Walton. "I am going to change it. I am going to fix it. That is what I do. It is my job to keep you out of our business. If you have an issue, you can come to me.."

So, while the team showered up after PT, Ford took out a marker again and began drawing on the dry-erase board. He started by sketching a stick figure for each team member. Then he drew a stick figure above everybody. That was him. Lightning bolts led to him, and over his figure he wrote in block letters: THE MAN. When the guys arrived in the team room, the message was clear.

"The only guy that relieves anybody from PT, or any other training on this team, is me," he told them.

Some of the soldiers weren't used to it. He heard their complaints. Their wives were upset that they weren't home. Two guys even had the balls to approach Ford to gripe about it. He detonated on them.

"I give a shit what your wife thinks? The reality is you guys sat here and didn't do anything for seven months," he said. "You got paid for the extra seven months you didn't do anything and now you're paying for it."

Plus, he knew that if something happened to his men, he wouldn't be able to look at their wives and families knowing that he hadn't done everything he could to prepare them for the mission.

Ford had already been to Iraq and Afghanistan. He knew what combat was like and knew this team just wasn't ready. Not yet. They had a lot of work to do, especially after the team's previous deployment, in which they didn't conduct a lot of missions. Ford was set on making sure the team had the skills to survive because he didn't plan on sitting on his ass in some firebase. They were going after the bad guys.

Soon after taking over the team, he sat down with Walton and came up with the tasks they needed to accomplish. The training ranged from shooting to land navigation to just driving trucks at night.

Thinking back to their premission training in Savannah, Georgia, he recalled one of the first live fire drills. It was a convoy exercise. That's where a team driving trucks is attacked. He wanted to see how his team would react.

"Upon contact," Ford told the guys huddled around his truck, "everybody is going to shoot. I want a high volume of fire. If you can shoot in the direction of the contact, you will have a gun out and it will be shooting until I tell you to stop."

Ford explained that after the initial burst there was nothing but confusion.

"Your truck might be the only one left alive," he said.

Gaining fire superiority was essential. A few minutes later, the team started down the path in their trucks. One of the instructors placed a smoke grenade on the lead truck, signifying that it had been hit. Then a machine gun fired a few blanks. But his team only responded with a short burst and then silence. Guys with their rifles were just sitting there. Then another gun opened up after a minute.

Pathetic, Ford thought.

He had given the team basic instructions. Everybody shoot.

Jumping out of his truck, he stopped the convoy. His rage was practically palpable. Grabbing his helmet, he threw it onto the road. It hit and skidded onto the shoulder.

"Get the fuck out," Ford yelled. "Get out."

The team climbed out of the trucks and gathered up.

"We are going to redo this exercise if it takes us the next three days until you get it right," Ford shouted at them. "We were going to train to standard and not to time. We can either get this done in a matter of six hours or twenty-four hours."

Ford had to very quickly teach them how to operate as a team. He didn't want to come down too hard, but that's what happened. He didn't want to see guys trying to learn it in Afghanistan. He owned them from Tuesday through Thursday. They would go to the range, driving in convoy formation, and they would stay out past sundown reacting to ambushes all night. That was when the team really bought into his leadership style. At first they thought that he was a prick.

But after premission training, things clicked. The team understood what Ford was doing and their hard work paid off. The team's old mentality was buried.

When Ford was growing up in Special Forces, if you screwed up, you found your rucksack in the hallway. It sent a simple message: Find another team. Ford told them if he heard them talk about the last deployment, he was going to throw their rucksacks out of the team room. That's because during the last trip they'd done nothing. This trip, they were going to do something.

A few weeks before the team left for Afghanistan, Ford discovered that his team was getting the battalion's most important mission. The battalion's operations officer had gone to Selection with Ford and respected him. He knew Ford was a badass team sergeant who could get the job done.

"You're going to mentor these commandos," the officer told him at Fort Bragg.

Ford was excited. "We can run with it," he said.

His team was going to build Afghanistan's first special operations force from the ground up. But he knew it came with a risk. The commandos were the Afghan Ministry of Defense's "shiny new toy," and Ford knew that training them would involve a lot of politics. He expected Afghan officials to showcase the unit, and use them as a symbol of the country's new military prowess. But if his team broke that toy—if the training went poorly or if they were attacked and many commandos were killed in combat—his team would be the embarrassment of the regiment. *We have to execute this well,* he thought.

The officer tried to ease Ford's fears. "With what you did in Iraq, this should be a piece of cake," he said.

But Ford knew it wasn't going to be easy. His team was young and still subscribed to the idea that Special Forces was like a SWAT Team, rescuing hostages and killing terrorists. *Yeah, that's part of the mission,* Ford thought. But training host-nation soldiers was the real work. He had done it in the Caribbean before 9/11. He had trained Iraqis after the attacks. Now he would be back in Afghanistan doing the same thing.

Back in the team room, he gave the team the good news. They had earned it. In a short few months, they had transformed themselves into the best team in the company and probably the battalion. But this mission was going to be hard. Few of the guys had trained foreign soldiers before. They'd been taught how to do it, but lacked experience. Ford knew it would require a lot of hands-on work.

Walton ordered the team a bunch of manuals and each soldier received a copy of 7-8, the Army's basic infantry skills guide.

"As long as you and the commandos can operate under this book, then we're going to be fine. Nothing sexy," Ford said. "I don't want them to think about sexy. Basic 7-8. Because if you can't master that, we can't go on to anything sexy."

But most of all, he stressed that the team had to buy into the commandos and their mission, or the whole thing would fail.

Right before they deployed, Staff Sergeant John Wayne Walding and Staff Sergeant Matt Williams showed up right out of the qualification course. Ford would have to get them up to speed in-country because within two weeks, they would be on a plane going to Afghanistan.

Wheels up, baby. Here we go, Ford thought.

When the team landed in Afghanistan, Ford pushed them hard the first few months. His team killed themselves getting the commandos ready for operations. The chain of command on both the Afghan and U.S. side kept pressing to get the new unit onto the battlefield, but Ford and Walton pushed back. The Afghan commandos weren't ready yet. The team was already working eighteen-hour days training them.

Eat. Sleep. Train on infantry tactics.

Ford knew he had to keep morale up. So when he discovered that team members had been stalking and smashing each other with three-foot fluorescent-tube lightbulbs, he let it go. But Ford added his own twist, of course.

No one was injured except for a little cut on the hand from the glass. Ford didn't want to take the fun away from the guys, even though it was a bit unsafe. It was a way to relieve stress. Plus, he viewed it as training.

So, one day, Ford sat down and created rules and a name for the game: Punisher Sword, named after Marvel comics most famous vigilante. And in typical Ford style, he put together a PowerPoint presentation. After one team meeting, Ford walked the team through the rules of engagement.

"I can put out any rule. I could tell you not to do it and I know it is going to happen. So rather than make a bullshit rule I can't enforce, I will make a rule we can respect and live by it," he told the team.

The rules were simple. All attacks had to take place in the team house and the mess had to be cleaned up afterward. Nothing below the belt. Nothing above the breast line and each ambush had to be recorded. If it wasn't videotaped or the "sword" didn't break, the victim got to take the bulb from the attacker and, in front of the team, smash back. After each team meeting, Ford would ask if there were any "Punisher Sword" violations.

Soon the team house became a war zone. Typically, it would involve five or six guys. It got to the point that when a guy called someone over to talk, the other guy would walk the other way. The soldiers began setting up ambushes around corners. Guys would come into the house, even coming from the shower, and surreptitiously find their way down the hall and back to their rooms. It was a game, but it also meant that the unit was using skills they would need to enter houses in a combat situation, clearing the corners and doing it better than they'd have been able to do if Ford had taught them on a range.

Because now it meant a blow to the ego and the curse of a video showing you getting beaten down with a lightbulb.

5

Staff Sergeant John Wayne Walding

Wandering out of the barracks wearing just his uniform and a pair of flip-flops, Staff Sergeant John Wayne Walding glanced at the sky. It was overcast again and felt like rain. *No mission today,* he thought. It was going to get pushed back again. He just knew it.

So Walding headed back to the tiny room he shared with Morales and Wurzbach. It was empty and Walding began to get ready. The three had been sharing the closet-size room with two sets of bunk beds since they arrived at Jalalabad. The room was so tight that Walding could sit on the edge of his bed, extend his arm, and touch the wall on the other side.

The tight quarters made it feel like they were teenagers having a sleepover. Sometimes, they would stay up most of the night bullshitting, talking about family, friends, and their lives. Walding was the new guy. This was Morales's and Wurzbach's second tour with ODA 3336. But this was Walding's first deployment with Special Forces—and he fit right in.

He was young and tough and smart. With his high cheekbones, soft but rugged features, soft blue eyes, wavy black hair, and lean runner's body, he looked like a young Brad Pitt. He had an innocent, boy-next-door look. But when he flashed his infectious wide smile and gritted his white teeth, you could tell he had a playful mischievous side. He was charismatic and handsome enough to be a movie star, or a regular on a television show. But Walding had no interest in acting. He just wanted to do his job, and do it right.

Before heading to the flight lines, Walding began inspecting his gear. He had an M4 carbine, pistol, combat load of magazines in pouches on his body armor, and a tourniquet. He had a survival kit, a knife, and an assault pack with food, water, socks, night vision, and batteries. Ford had pressed them to carry batteries. Just in case. Walding had thought briefly about bringing some music—his iPod—but didn't want it to get damaged.

Before every mission Walding would pump himself up by listening to some heavy metal. It wasn't unusual for him to back an SUV up to the flight line about 150 feet from the helicopters and crank up one of his favorite songs—"Die Motherfucker Die" by the group Dope. It would get him ready for the mission:

With helicopter rotors spinning and the flight crew running through their checks, Walding's head would bounce up and down to the pounding rhythm and screeching guitars. At that moment he was in the zone, primed and ready to go. Songs provided background music for his tour. Sometimes when he was running hard and fast on the base, the song "Indestructible" by the group Disturbed would play on his iPod, and it would give him a boost like an extra shot of Red Bull.

The twenty-seven-year-old would run faster and faster and pump his fist in the air. The tune would amp him up so much that he would begin thinking: *Go ahead and shoot me. I'm going to get back up again. I've become indestructible.* During his tour in Iraq, Walding had a major who loved classic rocker Bob Seger. Every time they had a night mission—when a convoy of Humvees was rolling down some remote pockmarked road—the major would pop a Seger CD into a boom-box and play "Night Moves." It helped the major relax.

But Walding knew there would be no night move for this mission. This operation would take place in daylight—something that worried him and other members of the team. He hoped they wouldn't be discovered, because if they were, they would be easy targets.

Walding just wanted to "do something bad to bad people" and come back alive. He wanted to see his wife and children. He thought about them before missions—that he was making their world a safer place. But what kind of life would they have if he was killed in action? He tried not to think about that, although those thoughts did cross his mind.

Walding slipped into his uniform and body armor, and swapped his flip-flops for boots. He took a deep breath and headed to the helicopters. If anything, today would probably be another rehearsal. But if it were up to Walding, his team would go and "get it done." Hunt down the insurgents.

Walding viewed Commando Wrath as a challenge, and he never backed down from a challenge—a reason he joined the Army in the first place.

Born on the Fourth of July in Victoria, Texas, about two hours southwest of Houston, Walding was a tough kid from the start.

His mother and father were "hippies"—they named him after the iconic actor because his father said if he was born on July 4, he had to have a "cool name"—who were busted for selling marijuana when he was six years old. After they headed to jail, he and his older brother, Mark, went to live with their paternal grandparents in Groesbeck, Texas, about forty miles east of Waco.

His grandfather, Sam Walding, was an oilman, a wildcatter, a disciplinarian who believed that hard work built strong character. And his grandmother, Gracia, was a southern Baptist who taught Sunday school.

Before he lived with his grandparents, there was little discipline or structure in Walding's life. Once he and his brother arrived, his grandfather made them get up in the morning and work on the farm. He taught the boys to treat people with respect and dignity, and never prejudge anyone. You judge a man by his actions, his character—not by his looks, not by whether he was rich or poor.

After his grandfather retired, he moved to four hundred acres his family owned outside of Groesbeck, a farming and mining town. He had a cattle ranch with two hundred acres of pasture—Walding's grandparents owned fifty head of cattle—and the rest was woods, where his grandfather would take young Walding hunting. On weekends, he would take his grandson fishing at Lake Limestone, where they would catch bass and catfish.

His grandparents were supportive of everything Walding did. They encouraged him to follow his dreams. They never tried to impose their own on him. Sure, he had to do chores around the ranch, bale hay and feed the animals. That was expected and Walding never complained.

He remembered on his sixteenth birthday, he loaded over eight hundred bales of hay. Dripping with sweat, Walding was tired and just wanted to hang out with his friends. But he stuck with it, and when he was finished, his grandfather handed him four hundred dollars. Walding hadn't known he was going to get paid. That wasn't the point. He hauled the hay because his grandfather asked him to, and he always did what his grandfather asked. He respected and loved the old man.

Sam Walding didn't have more than an eighth-grade education, but he had a strong work ethic. It rubbed off on his grandson. Walding never complained, even when it came to pain. Once, when he was horsing around, he fell out of a second-floor window at the house and broke his arm. He didn't say a word. Didn't cry. He had a high tolerance for pain. *Real men don't cry,* he thought. That's not the way he was raised.

In a way, Walding was the quintessential East Texas boy: He played football and baseball—he was on the all-district baseball team—and dated a lot of girls. He had one serious relationship: Lane Neil. They would spend long hours making out in his car or under the bleachers. She had the picture-perfect life. Her father was the president of a local bank. Their house looked like something out of a TV sitcom of the 1950s, and Walding liked to call her family the Brady Bunch. Everyone was happy and cheerful, not a chair or picture out of place in the house.

Walding knew that when he graduated high school he wanted to make money. While he was a good student, he had no plans to go to college right away—not like Lane, who was accepted at Texas A&M in College Station.

So after graduation, he took a job with a company laying cable lines. Walding and his cable crew traveled all over the state, and the company put them up in hotels. It was a great gig. He was pulling down about a thousand dollars a week, and he was spending every penny.

Every once in a while he would visit Lane at Texas A&M, but that wasn't working out. The turning point in his young life came when he took a trip to Las Vegas with a few buddies. All weekend long, he drank and gambled, and returned home with no money in his pockets. He was broke. He looked at himself in the mirror and was brutally honest with himself: He had to find another job. He had to do something else. He didn't want to continue with that lifestyle. That's not the way he was raised.

A day after he returned from Las Vegas, he ran into a friend who had joined the Army. The friend told him about traveling and shooting guns, and Walding thought it would be a good gig. He needed that kind of structure again. Plus, the military was a job where you can "lay down your head at night and be proud of it." So he told his grandparents his plans.

As usual, they were supportive, and encouraged him to work hard. So Walding enlisted. A month before basic training, he decided to go to Las Vegas for his birthday. He asked his best friend in high school, Jackie Don McKinley who was in the Air Force stationed at Edwards Air Force Base in California, to join him. Jackie said he would, and asked if he could bring along his cousin Amy Stovall, who lived in Waco.

Walding agreed, and Jackie gave him his cousin's number. Walding had never met Amy, and when he called, they hit it off. They talked every night for a month. They had that same East Texas background and friends and experiences. As they talked, they began to flirt. When he picked her up at her house to take her to the airport, his heart melted. She was pretty and funny. And by the end of the long weekend in Las Vegas, he asked her out. She said yes, even though he was headed to basic training and they didn't know when they would see each other again.

So on August 16, 2001, Walding began basic training at Fort Sill, Oklahoma. But everything changed less than a month later, on 9/11. That morning, they were learning about hand-to-hand combat when a sergeant interrupted training and marched them back to a classroom. The sergeant sat them down and told them what happened. Then he carried a television into the classroom and they watched the events unfold. Walding couldn't believe it. How could terrorists do that? And like most of the soldiers in the room that day, he became angry. He wanted to quit training right there and hunt down the people who were responsible.

The next day, the base was the same—but it had changed. Concertina wire surrounded the installation. The entire Army had gone into high alert. Even the focus of the training changed. The Army had a new mission. All the drill sergeants gave the recruits the "we're going to war" speech. He knew it was every drill instructor's wet dream to give that speech. It helped the recruits focus. But now they knew it was serious. No bullshit. And the irony wasn't lost on Walding.

When he joined, there was no war. But less than a month after he started basic training, the United States was on the cusp of a major military action. His mind-set had changed. He thought he would join the Army, maybe get some college in the future, and serve his country. For a moment he wondered if he had made the right move.

After basic training, he learned how to work radar and light maintenance on Patriot missiles, and was sent to Iraq for the invasion in 2003. His unit provided air cover for troops, who were leapfrogging from Iraqi city to city. And by July, the war was over—at least for him. He remembered watching Special Forces soldiers, how they operated, how they always seemed to be in the middle of action, and decided that he wanted to be one of them. He wanted to be the best of the best. He didn't want to be sitting in the rear again. If he was going to stay in the Army, why not? It made sense. He never took any shortcuts.

When he returned home that summer, he asked Amy to move in with him. She agreed. While he was in Fort Gordon, a recruiter came into the office one day and asked who wanted to join the Green Berets. He jumped at the chance.

Walding brought home a video they had played at the recruiting station to show Amy what he was getting into. He knew it was dangerous. But it would be fulfilling, he thought. He was afraid that if he didn't try, he would regret it. As he told Amy, he didn't want to be that guy at sixty years old on the front porch saying, "Man, I wonder if I could have done that."

He married Amy in August 2004 and they had a son—the first of their three children. After making it through Selection, he headed to the qualification course.

It was grueling, but Walding thrived. And when he joined the 3rd Special Forces Group, it was one of the proudest days of his life. He finally made it. Before he headed to Afghanistan in October 2007, he promised Amy he would be careful. That he would do everything to return home safely.

Walding had fully bought into the concept that Special Forces were force multipliers—a few men training many to become cohesive fighting units. He enjoyed training the Afghan commandos. He knew that it was making the commandos better soldiers. They were more prepared to fight and die for their country. If they were ever going to defend their country, they had to learn to do it themselves.

But he discovered that many commandos didn't have his work ethic or a sense of urgency. Sometimes in the middle of a training exercise, they would stop for prayer. That was frustrating and sometimes hard to understand. Walding believed that if his people were being waxed by the Taliban, he was going to concentrate more on training than on praying. But he understood that the Afghan commandos didn't see it that way. They had to pray to Allah. And who was he to say they were wrong? That's their life. And he made sure he articulated that it was okay to stop training for that purpose.

But there were other problems, including the Afghans' "intelligence level." Walding and other team members had to teach them basic math. If you're telling them to add five plus five, what good is it if they don't understand what it means. And throw in night vision and lasers and it was just overwhelming. They were never taught life skills that Americans take for granted.

And it was a hard sell to get the commandos to use the high-tech equipment. The Afghans hated using their night vision. They would always use the flood lamps to "see better." Walding would tell them that they might be able to see better but "you can also be seen better." He would say they couldn't be naive to think the Taliban didn't have night vision. If you just walk around with a flood lamp, it's just going to give away your position. It took time to get them to understand basic concepts. When you put it all together—the training—it was a long day's work. And he wasn't sure they understood everything.

But he couldn't think about that now. Not when he was standing on the flight lines, wondering if the Shok Valley mission would even take place, and if it did and they hit resistance, how would the commandos react?

He knew that training was one thing, and real combat was another. He had been in battle before and you had to keep your wits. You had to stay calm under fire. It was a lot of pressure and he didn't know how the commandos would handle it.

6

Staff Sergeant Dillon Behr

As a seasoned combat veteran on this third deployment, Staff Sergeant Dillon Behr was ready. He had been in fierce firefights. He had been on sweeps through insurgent strongholds in Iraqi cities, and on patrols through mountainous passes in Afghanistan where danger lurked behind every ridge.

The Special Forces communications sergeant had the experience to tackle just about any crisis in the field. But it was unclear how the Afghan commandos would react in a firefight. And that's what worried him as he prepared to deploy to the Shok Valley.

Within an hour or two, three teams of Green Berets and a company of Afghan commandos would be in the heart of the valley, struggling to find a clear and unobtrusive path to an enemy compound on top of a cliff overlooking the basin. In a firefight, Behr knew he could depend on his fellow American soldiers. They were Special Forces. They knew what to do. The Afghan commandos? They were a wild card. They had performed fairly well on previous missions with a lot of American help. But this mission was tougher. They were going after an HVT—a high-valued target, which meant bodyguards, often Arab fighters, ready to fight to the death. How would the commandos react if they made contact with that kind of enemy? Would they run? Stand their ground and return fire? Would they be able to even hit their targets? Behr had spent months helping train the commandos in the basics and intricacies of modern warfare. But training was one thing; execution under intense enemy fire was entirely different.

The bulk of Behr's time during this deployment—and even the previous one—was spent training Afghans. While he preferred combat operations—rooting out terrorists—he understood that training was a critical part of the Special Forces' mission. And Behr was a good teacher. He was patient, understanding, and found creative ways to explain complicated skills to a largely uneducated battalion of Afghan soldiers. It all stemmed from his midwest childhood, where he was more of a "nerd" than a jock, a quiet teenager who was on his high school Scholastic Bowl team and found solace in the confines of a Pentecostal church.

He was born in Rock Island, Illinois, where five cities straddle the Mississippi River on the Iowa-Illinois border. The metropolitan area is home to three hundred thousand residents, but outside the city limits, there was nothing but rich farmland.

While he lived in a rural area, his parents were blue-collar. Behr's parents divorced when he was two, and he lived with his father, who was a Rock Island firefighter. At the time, his mother gave up custody so she could go back to college, and when she graduated she became a police officer. His father had remarried and had three children with his new wife; two girls and a boy. His house was always filled with activity. His stepmother was a stay-at-home mom and shuttled the children back and forth to school-related events. That included Behr, who was active in baseball. A third baseman, he played in Little League and summer leagues. While he loved the game, he excelled more in academics, and was a fixture on the honor roll.

His parents didn't have a lot of money—they were public servants and his father took a construction job on the side to make ends meet. Still, his father and stepmother's was a loving, tight-knit household. On most days, passersby would see Behr and his siblings playing in the backyard.

When he turned sixteen, Behr began working after school and on weekends to earn money—bagging groceries at the Hy-Vee store in Rock Island, working concessions at a movie theater, or helping his father in construction.

During high school, Behr had a few good friends, but he was mostly the quiet kid. Probably the last person anyone thought would become a Green Beret. He was an important member on the Scholastic Bowl team—a *Jeopardy!*-like game for high school students. He also spent time at the Pentecostal Assembly of God in youth groups. That's where he felt most comfortable. During high school, he hung out in a church recreation room, playing games and listening to music. He spent most of his free time there.

When he graduated in 1998, he attended North Central University, a Bible college in Minneapolis, with plans of becoming a missionary. He took a job at an American Eagle clothing store in a mall to help support himself in school. But he decided to leave North Central after two years. He became disillusioned and decided that he "didn't want to follow that path." In a way, his job at American Eagle changed his life. He started hanging out with a "different group of people." He began "getting exposed" to the world.

His childhood had been somewhat sheltered. It was all focused on school and church and small-town values. His new friends had a different perspective—they partied and smoked and drank—and it influenced him. Behr didn't like the old philosophy of "God's way or the highway." He wanted to have fun. He wanted a change.

After dropping out of Bible college, he returned home, moved in with his biological mother, and started attending Scott Community College in Bettendorf, Iowa. He took general courses, but was lost. In high school, he had taken a drafting class in hopes of becoming an architect. He had even thought about applying to the University of Illinois or Southern Illinois University in order to major in architecture. But even that didn't interest him anymore.

After taking an acting class at the community college, he decided on a whim to become an actor. Behr received a scholarship to attend Waldorf College in Forest City, Iowa, a liberal arts school with just 650 students. But he dropped out after one semester, in part so he could continue dating a girl he met just before he left. That girl, Amanda Emmert, was bright and funny.

But in order to make the relationship work, he felt he had to be in Rock Island. He didn't want a long-distance relationship.

When he returned, Behr was at a crossroads. He had spent four years in colleges, but didn't even have an associate's degree. He was, by his own account, "screwing off." He had no idea what he wanted to do with his life. He was smart. But so what? He certainly wasn't living up to his potential. So he did the unthinkable: He decided to enlist. He had the "idealistic view" that the military would somehow "straighten him up," give him structure. Maybe it would give him a sense of purpose in his life.

His father, who had served in the Navy in the 1970s, was opposed. It was a dangerous time to join the military, he told his son. It was 2002 and the United States was fighting in Afghanistan. President George W. Bush and his advisers—Vice President Dick Cheney and Secretary of Defense Donald Rumsfeld among others—were beating the war drum to invade Iraq to topple Saddam Hussein. They claimed the Iraqi dictator had played a critical role in the terrorist attacks, and also had weapons of mass destruction.

Amanda also was less than thrilled about his decision. But at that point, Behr stood firm. His mind was made up. He was enlisting. It was time to leave the Quad Cities and do something meaningful with his life. If he hung around there too long, who knew what would happen? Before too long, twenty could turn into twenty-five. What then? Would he still be bagging groceries at the Hy-Vee? He had to leave, and explained to Amanda that he wanted to continue dating her. After some trepidation, she agreed to the plan. They would try to make the long-distance relationship work—even though Behr would probably be away for months, maybe even years.

When Behr enlisted, he didn't know much about the Army, and had no idea what kinds of jobs were available in the military. After discovering the Army had multimedia editor's jobs, he told a recruiter he would like to pursue video editing. But first he had to pass a test.

Every recruit has to take the Armed Services Vocational Aptitude Battery test. It gives recruiters a snapshot of the recruit's intelligence. When Behr's results came back, the recruiter was stunned. Behr had scored extremely high and the recruiter told him to forget about multimedia. Instead, he pushed Behr toward Special Forces.

Behr had never heard of Special Forces and that night took home a promotional video. It changed his life.

In the video, he saw a soldier hiding in a thicket of trees and then, without warning, the soldier disappeared. He became one with nature. The video explained how Green Berets were elite soldiers. The presentation was so impressive that when the credits rolled at the end, Behr knew he would join. It was his chance to actually live up to his potential. Do something great.

But first he had to pass a basic physical training test. To his surprise, he failed. Given a chance to take it again, he trained like a boxer for a championship fight. Endless push-ups and pull-ups. He ran several miles a day. When he retook the test, he aced it and was inducted in the Army. It was the beginning of his two-and-a-half-year journey to Special Forces.

In Special Forces training, he learned the skills that turned him into a communications expert. He was trained to build and operate computers, and set up networks and satellite communications in the field. He could do the little things, too, like make an antenna out of anything that conducted electricity, including trees and people. Behr also learned how to speak Arabic. It was difficult—and there were days he felt so tired that he could collapse on the spot—but for the first time in his life, he felt good about the direction he was headed in.

Just before he graduated Special Forces school, he asked Amanda to marry him. She said yes, and moved to North Carolina. It was one of his proudest moments. He accepted his Green Beret with his family and Amanda in the crowd watching the ceremony.

After training to be a communications sergeant, Behr finally got to 3rd Special Forces Group in July 2005. But the barracks at Fort Bragg were empty. His team was already in Iraq. After getting his equipment ready, he was deployed, but he didn't have time to get acclimated. The day he showed up in-country and met the team, he was told they were going on a combat mission to Tal Afar.

At the time, the city was controlled by Al Qaeda insurgents who had been launching attacks against U.S. and Iraqi positions in the area. The offensive was launched on September 1, 2005, and the initial fighting was heavy. It was classic urban warfare, with troops fighting from building to building, door-to-door. Although most of the city was secured in a few days, Tal Afar was still a dangerous place. There were pockets of snipers who would pick off soldiers before disappearing in a building or alleyway. It wasn't until the end of the month that all the fighting ceased and the Army declared the mission accomplished.

Behr learned fast that there was a difference between training and real combat. Everything moves faster. There is more chaos, and your adrenaline rises to the point where your senses are heightened. You can hear every sound. Every movement. You can see clearer. And you understand that you can't make any mistakes because if you do, you could end up dead. It was sobering to see the death and destruction, rubble and body parts. There was the stifling heat exacerbated by their heavy equipment—rucksacks, body armor, and weapons. And then there was the stench. It smelled like a landfill. A shithole. It was so thick you could almost taste the rotting garbage.

After they secured Tal Afar, his team was assigned to train Iraqi troops. But they became bogged down in jurisdictional infighting between the "Big Army" and Special Forces over who did what and in what parts of the city. There were days when his team did nothing. They were bogged down by the military bureaucracy. In the end, his team may have helped capture Tal Afar, but they accomplished little else for the rest of the operation.

When he returned to the United States, he shared some of his experiences with Amanda. He told her about terrain and people, but couldn't bring himself to talk about the death and fear.

His next deployment with ODA 3336 was to Gardēz, Afghanistan, where, unlike in Iraq, he saw almost no action. It was mostly a training mission. The team worked with the Afghan National Police (ANP), and for Behr, it turned into a frustrating operation. Training indigenous forces was a key Special Forces' mission, but it's not always the "coolest thing in the world." A team would rather be patrolling, searching for the enemy. Any combat MOS would agree. If you're sitting at an FOB, you feel like you're being wasted.

In Gardēz, Behr got his first taste of training Afghans—and the difficulties associated with trying to get them to grasp basic military concepts. He taught advanced combat maneuvers—tactics that would be challenging to Americans who had never been exposed to the military. But with the Afghans, Behr was dealing with police officers who had the intelligence of third graders. So he had to figure out a way to break down the lessons like he was teaching a child. He knew he had to be very clear and concise and simple. Break it down into small parts and work your way up to the more complex ideas.

If you're talking about room clearing—barging into a room with your gun drawn looking for the enemy—you start by drawing a big square in the dirt. You tape off the area so that it's completely open. You place an imaginary door is in the middle. Then you run your guys through that door a hundred times with their guns in position. Turn left. Turn right. Shout "all clear" if no one is in there. Sometimes you have to show them how to hold their rifles so they don't end up shooting everybody in the room. Once they have that principle down, you move to the next step. You might change the position of the imaginary door. You might add a person in the room. Behr discovered that you had to be patient with the Afghans. He knew that they would master the concept one day, only to forget it the next. It was two steps forward, one step back. For the entire mission, it seemed like the team was "handcuffed" to the ANP.

When they returned to Fort Bragg, his team was disappointed—and somewhat fractured. There were disputes and bickering among the team leaders about the direction of the mission—some wanted to go out on more combat missions—and that caused a wedge among the team members. You put twelve hardheaded individuals together long enough, and without a strong team leader, there will be disputes. Team members came away from the deployment feeling disenchanted. There was no sense that they had accomplished anything.

That all changed when Ford took over.

He molded the men into a cohesive unit. Together with Walton, he told the team in no uncertain terms: This is the way we're going to roll. Check your egos at the door. This is how we're going to handle training. Deal with it or else. At first, some of the team grumbled. But soon the bickering stopped, and the team began preparing in earnest for its next deployment.

Behr's team knew their assignment before they left Fort Bragg for Afghanistan in October 2007. They were going to train seven hundred would-be commandos in the very first Afghan *kandak,* or battalion, of Special Forces soldiers. (A small group of commandos had graduated in May 2006 and had gone on a few missions.) The team only had a few months to accomplish the task. The 201st Commandos would have to be in the field by the end of the year. It seemed like a daunting assignment. How were twelve men going not only to train seven hundred troops, but to equip them, teach them how to plan missions, and, in effect, turn them into a self-sustaining force?

It would be difficult but not impossible. These were the types of operations that jumped off the pages of Special Forces training manuals. In Vietnam, ODAs would sneak deep into the jungles along the Cambodian and Laotian borders to establish outposts to train the Vietnamese and track the enemy. During the U.S. involvement in the conflict, which lasted from 1965 to 1973, Special Forces trained thousands of Vietnam's ethnic tribesmen in the techniques of guerrilla warfare. They took the Montagnards, the Nungs, and others and molded them into the sixty-thousand-strong Civil Irregular Defense Group. Those troops became the Special Forces' most valuable ally in battles fought in faraway corners of Vietnam, out of reach of conventional U.S. fighting units.

In Afghanistan, the Special Forces had the commandos. Born from the Afghan Army, the commandos had been chosen by military planners to become the country's elite force. They would hunt high-profile targets like Al Qaeda and other terrorist groups, like the Hezb-e-Islami Gulbuddin whose core members had been together for nearly thirty years.

Behr knew the HIG was causing major problems in Afghanistan, especially in the northeastern part of the war-torn nation.

First, the HIG fought the Soviets. Then they focused on fellow Afghans in a brutal, internecine struggle. Now they had turned their attention to Coalition forces led by the hated "infidels." And the HIG had their own arsenal: RPGs, AK-47s, and even SAMs. They were well equipped, blended into the population, and didn't care who got in the way. With the HIG, there were no rules of engagement. No Geneva Conventions. They ruled by sheer terror. And the HIG had another advantage: They knew the land. They were fighting in their own backyard. They knew every ridgeline, every stream, every cave. They built fortresses that blended into mountains. This was no cakewalk. Behr and his team knew that.

During this period in the fall of 2007, U.S. policy was focused on Iraq. Most of the casualties were in Iraq—primarily because of IEDs and snipers—and the nation was precariously close to falling into all-out civil war. Some experts said it was already in a civil war, though the Bush administration disputed that assertion. For the most part, Afghanistan was relegated to the inside pages of newspapers while Washington focused on Iraq. But the Bush administration knew—and so did commanders—that Afghanistan would become a major problem. There weren't enough U.S. and Coalition troops deployed there to hunt down the HIG and pockets of Taliban insurgents who were threatening the Kabul government. And at that point, there was little hope that the administration would increase the number of troops in Afghanistan to counter the growing threat. If the country was ever going to be stabilized, Afghans had to help. Under U.S. guidance, the Afghans were going to have to handle more of the fighting. And the only way to do that was to train more Afghans. But finding Afghans willing to do the job—and who also had the intelligence to master basic techniques—was difficult.

The team understood the dilemma from the day they landed for their second deployment. But going into this important mission, Behr's team had a goal and a clear plan. Each team member would train a group of commandos in a different specialty. They would go slow to make sure the commandos understood every concept. Then they would take their team of commandos out on training missions. It was all about repetition. The more they practiced, the more the commandos would, hopefully, "get it."

Behr's job was to teach the reconnaissance unit—a group that collects intelligence and spies on the enemy. But he knew it would take time, which he didn't have. There was pressure from commanders to get the commandos in the field. He knew the commandos were commandos in name only. They didn't have the education or training. The vetting process to select commandos hadn't been followed. All candidates had to read at a certain level. But about two-thirds could barely read at all. They had to pass a physical fitness test, but most of the trainees couldn't do a push-up or sit-up. They had to know how to shoot and drive a vehicle. But that wasn't the case either. In most cases, they were just regular guys "right off the streets." Behr guessed that if the criteria had been strictly enforced, his team probably would have been training a company rather than a battalion. It made the job that much more difficult.

On the positive side, he knew that the commandos wanted to be there. They had all volunteered. It was different from training the Afghan National Police. With the ANP, the team had a hodgepodge of officers who regularly missed training exercises. They were always making excuses for not showing up or training hard. The commandos, though, were in camp every day and trying their best to be good soldiers.

Behr was told he would get some of the brighter guys in the commandos. And he did, but decided that wouldn't be fair to the rest of the team. They had to divide up the soldiers with above-average education so they would have strong leaders in all the platoons. That was a critical step to building cohesive units. They had to spread out the smart soldiers so those commandos could help train others.

Behr began by teaching his unit the basics of collecting intelligence. He wanted to get the commandos thinking forward. He knew that a lot of the soldiers were from towns and villages in mountainous places where Special Forces and U.S. forces might need to go. So Behr wanted to develop a network through which the commandos could help the Special Forces gather intelligence—information that could help them plan missions, help them find out where the insurgents were hiding.

But teaching the commandos how to gather information without people knowing what they were doing was challenging. You just didn't walk up to someone and ask if they knew where the Taliban guys were living. You asked people in the village about their own families. How were things going? Was anything new going on in the village? Look around the village like a tourist and don't be suspicious. Be friendly and pump the locals for information gently. You just don't blurt it out. There were other basic training, issues, too. The commandos learned how to pack a rucksack and shoot and maintain their weapons.

After a week or two, it reached a point where Behr believed his commandos were ready to learn how to use a GPS. They had the most basic GPS unit available—an eTrex, a lightweight navigator that could fit in the palm of a hand. Simple to operate, the GPS could run a day on just two AA batteries. While roaming, it could store up to five hundred waypoints in memory for easy retrieval—a plus when you were humping over rough terrain, in places with no street or terrain maps. The devices were so basic that they looked like a child's toy. And they were set up to play basic navigation games, so an eight-year-old could learn how to use the device. After explaining how they worked, Behr told his commandos to take the units home over a weekend and practice with them.

But when they returned to the next formation, the commandos told Behr their GPS units were broken. The screens were black. He shook his head in disbelief. How could they be broken? They were brand-new. Right out of a box. He'd put the fresh batteries in himself. So Behr started playing around with the units. Still nothing. Then he opened the back and noticed something strange: the batteries had bite marks—like they had been crunched between somebody's teeth.

Behr lifted the batteries and asked the group, "Please tell me why there are bite marks in these batteries?"

A soldier raised his hand. "That makes the batteries last longer. We thought they were out of juice so we bit them."

He noticed that most of the soldiers in the unit bobbed their heads up and down in agreement. Behr was dumbfounded. Almost to a man, the soldiers believed that the way you extended the life of batteries was by biting them.

He took a deep, cleansing breath and told the unit, "Don't do this anymore. This does not make a battery last longer."

Behr played around with the GPS devices and discovered that the commandos had accidentally turned the brightness of the screen all the way down. There was nothing wrong with them at all.

That was a "wow, really?" moment for Behr. And it taught him a good lesson: Don't assume the commandos know anything. Expect the unexpected. That lesson was hammered home when he began a session on how to draw targets, including buildings. On paper, it seemed like a simple assignment. But there's nothing simple in Afghanistan, and it turned into an elementary school lesson on shapes.

One of the things Behr had wanted the commandos to do was to learn how to sketch targets, mostly buildings. This skill would help them on missions. That way they could not only describe a target, they could draw it. His lesson began when he hung a picture of a house in the training room. He had studied drafting in high school and drew 3-D images all the time. For Behr, it was routine. But that wasn't the case with the Afghans. He was shocked at some of their drawings. Many of the pictures were just amorphous shapes. Scribble. Nothing that even closely resembled a house. At that moment he knew what he had to do. He had to teach the men basic shapes. Even more rudimentary, he started by showing them how to draw a straight line. Then he moved up to a square, then a triangle, then a circle. He did this for a few days, and when they showed they were grasping the concepts, he had them begin sketching cylinders and cones. Soon they started on 3-D images—tables, chairs—and Behr took them out on the base, where they sketched buildings. Some soldiers grasped the ideas quicker than others. But by the end of the weeklong session, most of the commandos understood it. With all the drawing and teaching, though, Behr felt more like an elementary school teacher than a soldier.

Other training proved just as difficult.

Few commandos knew how to drive. But the team had to show them how to drive a Humvee, the U.S. military's all-purpose, modern-day jeep. With four-wheel drive and automatic transmission, this diesel-powered off-road beast is among the most capable all-terrain vehicles in the world. Like the versatile jeep it replaced, the Humvee has many configurations, including troop carrier, command vehicle, ambulance, and weapons platform (Stinger, .50 cal, MK19 automatic grenade launcher). Giving the commandos

Humvees was part of the plan to separate them from the rest of the Afghan fighting units. The commandos were the only unit to have Humvees. They were given body armor and had helmets like the Special Forces wore. They actually looked special compared to the rest of the military. They even had different patches. But what good was all that equipment if they didn't know how the use it?

The Humvees helped illustrate that point. They are relatively easy to drive. They all have automatic transmissions. No shifting gears. They're easy to use—if you know how to drive and have been doing it your whole adult life. But not only did the commandos have to learn how to drive, they had to be taught how to maneuver the vehicles into tight places, and the correct way to position-park them on a convoy. When you are out on a mission and need to stop somewhere, you want to place your vehicle in a prime location. You want the vehicle to have good cover and your gunner to have the best field of view so he can defend the troops properly. That's the case even when you park in a big open area and you have several vehicles in the convoy. You place the vehicles in a circle or some kind of shape facing outward with even lines of fire. Getting the commandos to understand this was mind-blowing at times.

And forget about night driving. That is a critical part of moving troops in any operation. It's all about the element of surprise. There's no surprise if you have a convoy of thirty Humvees moving with their lights on. But to maneuver at night, soldiers have to use night-vision goggles. The Afghans did not like using them. At times, that training seemed like a scene straight out of a slapstick movie. Humvees were running into each other. They were running off the road.

So the team began discussing how to teach the commandos these key concepts. They came up with a plan. Instead of teaching everyone to drive, they designated a few drivers—the ones who seemed to have an aptitude for driving—and made them Humvee drivers. As part of the training, the team would stand in front of a Humvee and walk the vehicles into place. The drivers would follow the team as they guided them into position. After a while they could move them into position without fear of getting run over.

Sitting in his barracks, Behr smiled when he recalled the breakneck training sessions. There were incredibly long days and nights, and the few missions they had embarked on since training ended saw little or no contact. The reality was this was the 201st Commandos first real mission, and it was important. At least that's what the commanders told them. That's why they were given such a high-priority target: Haji Ghafour.

The publicity machine for the Afghanistan Ministry of Defense and the U.S. Army had been touting the commandos. They said the commandos were nicknamed the "Wolves," and that they were feared by the Taliban and the HIG and Al Qaeda and every other terrorist on the planet. The touters were embellishing, of course. While the commandos were better trained and equipped than regular Afghan fighting units, Behr and others on his team knew the truth.

7

Staff Sergeant Ron Shurer

Staff Sergeant Ron Shurer packed and repacked his medical kit.

He had more than enough bandages, syringes, scissors, tourniquets, morphine, and a portable intravenous system, or IV, with lifesaving fluids to treat the wounded. While every team member carried a first-aid kit with bandages, tourniquet, and morphine-filled needles, known as syrettes, to ease the pain, it was nothing like his. As the team medic, it was Shurer's responsibility to keep soldiers alive until a medevac arrived to whisk them away to a field hospital. It was an awesome responsibility, and as unlikely as it was where they were headed, Shurer hoped he wouldn't have to use his skills on this operation.

Still, as he reviewed his kit, he knew he had to pare it down. Carrying his gear up a mountain would be difficult enough under normal circumstances. Whatever he didn't absolutely need had to go. He decided against taking a Skedco—a heavy-duty fold-up stretcher—because it weighed twenty-five pounds. Instead, he took a poleless litter—a lightweight fold-up stretcher made of cloth. For a moment Shurer thought about tossing out a green tubular nylon rope. He didn't think they would need it. But Ford required everyone to carry it. He didn't know why. It seemed pretty useless in the field.

Shurer had requested this role. Nothing was more important—and challenging—than taking care of wounded soldiers in the field. It took more than a year of intense training to become a Special Forces medic, and medics usually had to perform their duties in desolate, dangerous areas, where medical help wasn't readily available. It was a pressure-filled job. No doubt. But it was one that Shurer embraced.

When he enlisted in 2002, Shurer had told the recruiter he wanted to be a medic. Not just any medic, but Special Forces. He knew Special Forces teams were among the Army's most specialized combat forces, and the medical sergeant was a critical member of the team. They were considered the finest first-response/trauma medical technicians in the military. Though their training emphasized trauma medicine, they also had to have a working knowledge of dentistry, veterinary care, public sanitation, water quality, and optometry.

When they were not in the field, their duties included maintaining medical equipment and supplies, and providing examination and care to detachment members. They also ordered, stored, cataloged, and safeguarded medical supplies.

It was a big workload and every ODA usually had two medics. But on this mission, Shurer was the only one. The other medic had been sent home a month earlier after he was injured in a truck crash. If Shurer's team was caught in a firefight, this might pose a problem. If too many soldiers were wounded, would a single medic be able to take care of them all? And what happened if he was hit? Then who would take care of the wounded? These were more than hypothetical questions, and not unreasonable ones. In firefights, shit happens. Always does. That's why teams prepared and planned for the worst. But in this case, it seemed that the commanders were being overly optimistic in thinking that a second medic wouldn't be necessary.

When Shurer studied a mission, he analyzed every possible scenario to make sure he had everything covered. He learned that in the Green Berets, and it was an extension of his major in college: economics. Explore every aspect of a deal so you know what you're getting into. One mistake could cost you your business, or an investor millions of dollars. Here, though, the stakes were higher.

He understood the way the military worked because he was a military brat. By the time he was three years old, he had lived in Alaska, Idaho, Illinois, and the state of Washington.

His parents met while they were in the Air Force. After they were married, his mother left the military to raise Shurer, who was an only child. They settled in a small community about fifteen miles south of Tacoma. His father, Ron Shurer Sr., worked in the Air Force Office of Special Investigations at McChord Air Force Base. Tacoma was Washington's third largest city, with approximately 203,400 residents, but it seemed like everyone there had a military connection.

With no siblings, Shurer spent a lot of time by himself. He would run and cycle—he would later compete in triathlons—and spent a lot of time outdoors in the shadow of Mount Rainier. He went to Rogers High School, and when he graduated, he attended Washington State University, a school with twenty-five thousand students in nearby Pullman, Washington.

As he was getting ready to graduate, he thought about joining the Marines. He even enlisted and was accepted to officer candidate school in August 2001. But at the last minute, he was rejected when the medical board discovered that he had pancreatitis. There were only three ways to get it: trauma, diabetes, or alcoholism. He told the board it was from an injury—a car smashed into his bicycle in 1995. But in the pre-9/11 mentality, the board didn't want to take a risk.

Disappointed, he applied and was accepted in Washington State University's master's program in economics. But he never stopped thinking about the military, especially after the 9/11 terrorist attacks.

Shurer finished one year of graduate school and, in August 2002, enlisted in the Army, a move that surprised his parents. Growing up, he had model airplanes and played war games in his backyard, but it wasn't until later in life that he thought about the military as a career option.

His parents tried to persuade him to join the Air Force. The United States was engaged in one war in Afghanistan, and a conflict with Iraq loomed on the horizon. The Air Force was a safer choice. But Shurer wanted to be a medic, and if he was going to do that, it made sense to join the Army. Its soldiers were on the front lines in the War on Terror. He could use his skills to help save wounded soldiers. So Shurer enlisted in Spokane in 2002. He turned twenty-four while he was in basic training.

When he enlisted, a recruiter asked him if he ever thought about joining Special Forces. Shurer was the perfect candidate. He was athletic and smart. He asked if they could guarantee that he would become a medic. They said no. So he stayed in the Regular Army and trained to be a medic.

After basic training, he decided to take matters into his own hands. On his first day with his new unit, he told his sergeant he was going to try out for Special Forces because he wanted to be around a "different group of people." Not that the soldiers in his new unit were slackers. It was just that they didn't have the same mentality as Special Forces.

So Shurer went to Selection. It was brutal, much harder than he thought, but he became friends with Seth Howard, and they would later serve together in ODA 3336. In Selection, Shurer, like all the candidates, endured three weeks of hell. There were times when he wondered why he was doing it. But that's when his stubbornness kicked in. He told himself over and over: *I'm not going to quit. Keep going.*

He did keep going and was offered a position as a medic. And that was when Shurer's real training started. He spent a year in the medic program, and it covered everything from treating gunshot wounds to veterinary medicine. He did an internship in an emergency room and completed a nationally accredited paramedic program.

The goal was to get the soldiers as much experience as possible and give them the confidence to treat everything from severe wounds to an Afghan villager's cough.

It was just the kind of training Shurer was looking for. He threw himself into it and excelled. After Special Forces training, he joined ODA 3336 in June 2006. He had done everything he had set out to do in the military, but he was lonely.

His girlfriend had broken up with him when he decided to join the Army. At the time, they had been going out for a year and a half. They reunited briefly, but they kept fighting, and after Shurer had been in the Army for six months, they broke up for good.

Shurer wanted someone to share his life, but he hadn't met anyone while he was stationed at Fort Bragg. So he turned to eHarmony, an online dating service. That's where he met Miranda Lantz.

She was a graduate student at James Madison University in Harrisonburg, Virginia, about five hours north of Fayetteville, North Carolina. Originally from West Virginia, Miranda had graduated from the Illinois Institute of Technology in Chicago.

Their first date, he drove up to Harrisonburg and they went to the movies to see *The Incredibles*—an animated film about a family of superheroes. Shurer was quiet and shy, and had just come out of a bad relationship. Miranda was supportive. It was a long-distance relationship, but one that they both wanted to pursue.

When he found out he was being deployed to Afghanistan in August 2006, he asked her to marry him. She said yes—even though there was some apprehension about Shurer being in the military.

About six months before she and Shurer met, Miranda's brother-in-law died in Iraq. She definitely knew what she was getting into with Shurer. Soldiers always face danger during a deployment. But Special Forces soldiers seemed to always be in the thick of things. He told her not to worry. He assured her that his job was to save lives. He wouldn't be in danger.

And during his first tour with ODA 3336, he hardly saw action at all. His team mostly trained Afghan National Police. But it was a real eye-opening experience. He was surrounded by natural beauty. Ice-capped mountains and deep valleys and crystal-clear, clean, fast-flowing rivers and gorges. But he was shocked to see the abject poverty. The Afghans didn't have paved roads and people lived in mud huts. No one had money. The way of life—with bartering and using donkeys for transportation—probably hadn't changed much in hundreds of years. The only difference was the technology. Even though they had few material possessions, many people owned cell phones.

And they were quick to use them to call tribal leaders to settle disputes over money, land, or with American troops. As a medic, Shurer provided health care services to the people—shots and examinations. He also was responsible for training the Afghan police medics.

At times, it could be frustrating. Shurer was a no-nonsense soldier. He expected everyone to train like him. Stay long, until you get it. No excuses. And he was patient as long as people were trying. He would stay late and explain concepts and techniques. But he found that he had no patience for the Afghans who didn't take their training seriously. He would snap at them. By the time his deployment was over, he was glad to go home. His wife was pregnant with their first child.

His second deployment with the team was vastly different. Ford was their new team sergeant, and he was strict, a disciplinarian with an aggressive philosophy. Shurer liked Ford and his approach. He toughened up the team. No doubt about it. There were no more cliques. Everyone worked together for the benefit of the team. It was all about the unit—something that had been missing during his first deployment. It seemed that his friends during the first mission—Howard, Morales, Wurzbach, and Behr—all respected the new team sergeant. Ford worked them hard because he wanted them to be prepared for every obstacle they could possibly encounter in the field.

And so now, sitting on the helicopter headed to the Shok Valley, Shurer was confident his team was ready. There was nothing his team couldn't handle, he thought. He just hoped he had enough supplies—and enough time to treat everyone—if the team hit a shitstorm.

8

Sergeant First Class Karl Wurzbach

Usually outspoken, Sergeant First Class Karl Wurzbach was quiet as he prepared to board the chopper. At thirty-four, he called himself the "old man" of the team. He had seen just about everything the Army could throw at him. He had become a sage, a person the younger soldiers could talk to for advice. In the Army for fifteen years, he also was the one who knew how to cut through all the bureaucratic bullshit to get things done. But with this mission, he knew something was wrong. From the time Ford had presented it to the team, he had voiced his objections. A good soldier always follows orders. But they will also speak their mind when they see bullshit, and he knew this mission—the way it was laid out—was total bullshit.

They were fighting uphill. They were landing in the daylight, far from their objective. And, if they made it up the mountain, they weren't even sure that Haji Ghafour, their objective, would be there. Intelligence was sketchy, so why put so many men at risk?

Wurzbach expressed his concerns to Ford, who listened intently. He knew Ford was on his side. One of Ford's roles as the lead noncommissioned officer on the team was to sell the mission, get his men pumped up before battle.

But Wurzbach sensed that Ford felt the same way he did: They were headed into a goat fuck.

At the end of the conversation, Ford told him that they were going. End of conversation. Wurzbach only hoped that if they were ambushed, the commandos would exceed expectations. This was far from certain. His team had taken the commandos on a few missions and they performed well. But those operations were relatively easy. They were well planned and the soldiers didn't encounter intense enemy fire. That was key because Wurzbach knew that not everyone behaved the same when bullets start flying. Under fire, soldiers behave differently. Some men lift their weapons and run toward the fire, while others hide.

Wurzbach knew how his team would react. They would stand and fight. But he was worried about the commandos. Would they participate or cower? It was hard to tell. No man really knows how he is going to react to war until he is placed in a life-or-death situation. And the commandos were far from battle tested.

Wurzbach had already warned his wife that he was going on a dangerous mission. Before each operation, he would phone home just to let his wife know he was going on a "camping trip." That was his code to let her know he was about to go in the field. He made sure he talked to her and his three children. While he didn't disclose details, he urged her to pay attention to the news. He wanted her to be prepared just in case the phone rang in the middle of the night, or if someone from the military showed up at her door. At least she would know why. Before he hung up, he told her he loved her.

This was a different kind of war for soldiers—they could keep in close contact with family members. Soldiers stayed in touch with their families and friends through the Internet, cell phones, and Skype. It made the war seem less dangerous. It was almost like the soldiers were at the base instead of ten thousand miles away in a war zone.

At that moment Wurzbach wished he was home with his family.

Born in Syracuse, New York, he grew up in Erie, Pennsylvania, a drab, gray city on the banks of Lake Erie. At one time the city had 140,000 inhabitants, but when Wurzbach was growing up, the population had declined to about 108,000. When the steel mills and other manufacturing jobs dried up, people left. The weather didn't help either. During the winter, winds swept off the lake, and snow blanketed the city.

His father was a supervisor for Roadway Express, and his mother was a nurse. They lived in a ranch-style house in a close-knit neighborhood with houses stacked next to one another, a place with side streets and kids riding bicycles, and parents decorated their homes in grand style for Halloween and Christmas.

But across the street was a big field with acres of land and woods and trails. And with all his restless energy, that was a good place to spend time with his friends. Wurzbach was good at soccer and played some hockey, but he was always restless. Sometimes at night, he would sneak out of his house and jog for miles. No reason. He just couldn't sit still. He wanted to explore.

His father had been in the military and served in Vietnam, but he rarely talked about his Army experience. When Wurzbach began high school, he joined the ROTC. But by the time his senior year rolled around, he knew he wanted to leave Erie. There were no jobs. So when he graduated high school, Wurzbach enlisted in the National Guard. College was out. He knew he didn't have the money to go "experimenting" in college before he found himself. That wasn't for him.

He excelled in the National Guard. But even with that, his life was in a rut. Outside of his two weeks in the summer and one weekend a month with the Guard, he only worked part-time jobs in Erie. In the summer, he toiled at a lumberyard, and around Christmas he would usually land a position with Toys "R" Us. He was stuck in Erie, going nowhere. He was twenty and could barely afford to fill up his car with gas. He wanted to move out of his parents' house, but had no money for rent or food. He was totally dependent on his parents.

So in the summer of 1992, Wurzbach decided to enlist in the Army. If he liked the National Guard, the Army would be more fun—and he would make some money and travel, he thought.

In January 1993, he was sworn in and was deployed to Berlin, Germany. He bypassed basic training because of his National Guard experience. He returned to Fort Campbell, Kentucky, in 1994, and met a woman who also was in the military. After they married, she left the Army while he tried to decide what to do with his career.

He had thought about joining Special Forces, but had put it off. One day his wife challenged him: She was tired of him talking about it and encouraged him to go to Selection. He did in 1996, but he just wasn't ready. While Wurzbach had no problems with the physical part of Selection, when instructors started talking about patrols and what to do on patrols, it was "all Greek" to him.

He stayed in the military, but not making Special Forces bothered him. So in 2004, he tried again. This time he made it. He graduated from Special Forces training in October 2005 and was assigned to 3rd Special Forces Group.

He was with the team when they were deployed in August 2007 to Afghanistan. But he was unhappy with the direction. He liked his fellow soldiers, but the team leadership wasn't aggressive enough. They weren't planning enough missions. Like the others, Wurzbach spent most of his time training members of the Afghan National Police.

When he arrived, the Afghans had minimal training. They knew how to carry their rifles and "march around in a square for show." But there was no driver training—and few, if any, knew how to operate a car. And if they did, they had taught themselves. They learned by driving a tractor on a farm or they bought an old vehicle, jumped in, put the key in the ignition, and just drove.

He also realized quickly that they had a very leisurely approach to how they spent their day. They didn't train like a U.S. fighting unit, which would get up in the morning and have the day planned out in advance. They were not even real soldiers. They were all young, looking for a paycheck, a means to survive. They didn't have a clue about warfare.

Wurzbach knew much of the training would have to start with basics. He conducted marksmanship training—firing at targets, teaching them how to use their guns. They had to break bad habits. They were used to lying on the side of a cliff, shooting from their hip up into a mountainside with no cover. That had to change fast.

The hours were long and tough and often frustrating.

Wurzbach was more disappointed in the philosophy of his team. On the only mission where they received fire—when insurgents fired an RPG at a patrol—they didn't plan a follow-up maneuver to track them down. He believed they should look for the insurgents. Instead, they "tucked their tails between their legs" and never went back.

At a meeting a few weeks later, the commanders asked Wurzbach's team what they wanted to focus on. His response: "Let's go back and get the bad guys." It didn't happen. The mind-set was different and members of ODA 3336 were disgruntled. *This was not what we signed up for,* Wurzbach thought.

But things changed when the team returned to the United States, in part, because team leadership was switched out. Ford and Walton came in, and as soon as they began training, Wurzbach could see that the unit was going to have a new mentality. He could tell that the team was starting to become cohesive again—and it felt good.

As the new team sergeant, Ford quickly took ownership of the ODA. He expected his team to be prepared. They were going to do the little things well—keep their areas clean, plan, get administrative paperwork taken care of on time. It was back to basics. Get on board or get out, and everybody was willing to practice what he had to preach. Including Wurzbach. Ford was selling a philosophy that was basic: Learn your goddamn job so we can go out there and kick some ass and come home alive.

At first, though, Wurzbach, like everyone else, had to figure out what Ford was looking for. It was often difficult to ask Ford to articulate what he expected. At times, he could be sarcastic. He came across as: "Seriously. You're asking me that? What the hell is wrong with you? You know the answer to that?" And Ford was right. Deep down, the team knew the answers. This band of highly trained soldiers—"quiet professionals"—was afraid to take charge. Once the team began to figure out what Ford wanted and understood why they were doing it, everything began to click. Wurzbach realized that Ford was trying to train them to think on their own.

When they returned to Afghanistan, they knew in advance that the mission would be different—they would be training Afghan commandos. But Wurzbach also knew that the public was more interested in Iraq than Afghanistan.

By late 2007, most of the U.S. military policy was focused on Iraq, where the war had not been going well for years. Insurgent attacks and a growing civil war had led to total chaos. And U.S. troops were having a difficult time getting things under control. Several thousand U.S. troops had been killed in the conflict and tens of thousands more were injured, mostly by hidden road-side bombs and ambushes, leading to calls back home to withdraw from Iraq.

Meanwhile, military leaders were pressing President George W. Bush for more troops to help stabilize the country. But the president was in a quandary. The extended wars in Iraq and Afghanistan had left the military scrambling to find soldiers for deployments. As a result, the military had become more dependent on National Guard units, and leaders were extending deployments, causing more unrest back home. It was a crisis, and with the upcoming 2008 presidential election, it was surely to become a major campaign issue. Bush was prohibited from running for a third term, but he knew the situation could hurt the GOP's chances of retaining the White House.

But the war in Afghanistan seemed to be flying under the radar. U.S. and Coalition forces had been in the country since 2002. While most of the fighting units were stationed in remote outposts to prevent Al Qaeda and the Taliban from making inroads, a large contingent of them was in Kabul and major population centers.

And that's what worried Afghan leaders the most: Major terror networks were still operating freely in remote areas like Nuristan and posed a major threat to the stability of the entire country. The biggest thorn in the side of the government was the HIG, which, along with the Haqqani Network and Mullah Omar's Quetta Shura, made up the three strongest terror groups in Afghanistan. All three had close ties to Al Qaeda and other jihadist groups based in Pakistan and Central Asia.

The HIG was led by Hekmatyar, a notorious opportunist who had links with Al Qaeda, Iran, and Pakistan's military and intelligence establishment. Hekmatyar had been a key player in the Soviet-Afghan war and led one of the biggest insurgent factions against Soviet and Afghan Communist forces.

But Hekmatyar's brutal battlefield tactics and wanton destruction of Kabul following the collapse of the Afghan Communist regime in the early

1990s led to the demise of his popularity. The Taliban overran his last stronghold south of Kabul in 1995 and forced him into exile in Iran, where he stayed from 1996 to 2002, when the Taliban government fell to U.S. forces.

Since he returned, HIG forces had been conducting attacks in northern and northeastern Afghanistan and maintained bases in Pakistan's Swat Valley as well as in the tribal areas of Bajaur, Mohmand, Kuram, and North and South Waziristan.

Then in May 2006, Hekmatyar swore his alliance to Al Qaeda's top leader, Osama bin Laden. "We thank all Arab mujahedeen, particularly Sheikh Osama bin Laden, Dr. Ayman al-Zawahiri, and other leaders who helped us in our jihad against the Russians," he said in a recorded message broadcasted by the news agency Al Jazeera. "They fought our enemies and made dear sacrifices. Neither we nor the future generations will forget this great favor. We beseech Almighty God to grant us success and help us fulfill our duty toward them and enable us to return their favor and reciprocate their support and sacrifices. We hope to take part with them in a battle which they will lead and raise its banner. We stand beside and support them."

And since that message, he had been leading brutal attacks in Nuristan and other areas. The attacks were destabilizing provinces. His chief lieutenant was Haji Ghafour, who was particularly brutal. He would personally behead villagers for disobeying Islamic law. It seemed that the only way to stop the HIG was to kill Ghafour. And the Afghan commandos—at least in the eyes of U.S. commanders and the Afghan Ministry of Defense—had to be part of that operation.

So when Wurzbach's unit arrived in Afghanistan in 2007, its main job was to train the commandos. The Ministry of Defense had devoted a large amount of time and energy to promoting the unit. They called them the "Wolves" and hoped the unit would strike fear into the heart of the Taliban and Al Qaeda. With a sense of pride, the ministry wanted insurgents to know that the Wolves could be unleashed anytime, anyplace in Afghanistan, and that the elite team was composed of Afghans, not Americans.

The reality, though, was that the commandos had a long way to go before they could be even called commandos, Wurzbach thought.

But in their favor, the commandos all wanted to be there, which would help with training. They all wanted the prestige and mystique of being commandos, too. And they seemed like they were willing to become a cohesive fighting unit. Wurzbach discovered they actually cared about the job.

So Wurzbach and other members of ODA 3336 had to make sure the commandos understood the basics of missions. They had to build a structure so they could learn how to plan and conduct operations on their own. It was like the old proverb: Give a man a fish and he'll eat for a day. Teach a man to fish and he'll eat for a lifetime. In a way, they were teaching the commandos how to fish. And to do that, they had to teach them basic skills, just like they did with the Afghan National Police.

But as it had been with the ANP, Wurzbach found that he had to "physically walk them through training." If they were on patrol, he would show them "Crayola style" how to do things—literally drawing pictures on a piece of paper.

Several times, Wurzbach stopped convoys, dismounted, and literally walked every commando truck into position. He would often engage in fierce battles with the leader of the Afghan commandos about the way to do things. It would sometimes reach a boiling point, where Wurzbach would finally tell him, "Dude, we're not going to sit on the side of the road anymore."

Then he would give the commander a choice about the way to proceed: He could listen to Wurzbach and order his men to do it the right way. That way he would save face. Or Wurzbach would take over right there, and the commander's men would know he fucked up. It usually worked.

Throughout training, the reputation of the commandos continued to spread throughout Afghanistan—even though they had not been tested in a single major battle. They appeared in parades and other government functions. Afghan children cheered and said they wanted to be commandos. The Taliban and Al Qaeda were gun-shy of picking a fight with the commandos, in part because they knew U.S. Special Forces was paired with them. And that meant the commandos had air support.

In a short time, Wurzbach thought his team had whipped the commandos into shape. The Wolves had a real sense of who they were and what their jobs were. The problem was that the Ministry of Defense rarely let them go on missions. They were afraid they would fail. But Wurzbach's team knew the commandos needed to go out on operations. That was the only way to get true combat experience. To see what they could do and learn from any mistakes. Still, getting approval to take them along was tough sledding. They had to have permission, and almost every planned mission kept getting overruled by the Afghan government.

While the commandos had gone out on a few operations with Wurzbach's team, they faced little resistance. He had no idea how they would react on a mission like the one in the Shok Valley, where there would be no room for mistakes. The plan was to kill or capture Haji Ghafour. But Wurzbach had some serious reservations about the plan.

Standing on the flight lines, Wurzbach remembered his conversation with Ford after he heard about the mission. How they argued.

"Seriously, Scott, we're going in a helicopter to the low ground? Why?"

"Dude, don't you think I argued this point?" Ford snapped.

"Okay. I got it. But seriously, this is what we're doing? Come on, now. This is nuts. We're going to get killed."

Wurzbach knew they had no clear way into the objective area.

But Wurzbach's biggest concern was finding a way to get everyone on the high ground so they didn't have to fight their way up a mountain. That was the biggest thing when it came to the plan—no matter how Wurzbach skinned it, that was the biggest headache. He knew you can't fight up a hill—even if it's just two insurgents, you're still fighting up a hill. That gave the enemy a major advantage. They had the cover. They had the buildings.

It didn't make sense when Wurzbach first heard the plan, and as he got ready to board the helicopter, it still didn't make sense.

He just wanted to get back from this "camping trip" alive.

9

Walton

Walton had never balked at any mission.

But something didn't feel right about this one. Sitting on the back ramp of the Chinook, he plugged his Peltor headphones into the jack and listened as the pilots went through their preflight checklist.

In his mind, the problems were clear. Rough terrain. Intel gaps. *Shit, now we're socked in by bad weather,* he thought. Before heading to the helicopters, Walton had to try one more time to stop the mission.

Along with a team leader from ODA 3325, which was in charge of searching a nearby Shok Valley village code-named Panther, he went looking for Fletcher.

They found him near the helicopters.

"We're not going to do this fucking mission," Walton said. "Unless you order us to do it, I am not going to do this fucking mission."

Fletcher didn't flinch: "I order you to do it."

Fletcher knew that only Ashley could abort the mission. He had called his boss and discussed the weather in the valley and how it was clear in nearby Nangarhar and lower Laghman provinces. They also talked about the intelligence. Their source confirmed that Ghafour was in Kendal, another Shok Valley village, and both agreed the risk was worth it. It was their one chance to get the HIG commander.

Walton snapped a salute, in more of a smart-ass than a respectful way.

"Roger," Walton said, turning to head toward the helicopters.

Walton knew in a few hours he would be at the bottom of the valley looking up. And that wasn't a good feeling.

Missions in Special Forces weren't supposed to be planned like this. From the beginning, teams are drilled on planning a collective effort that includes every member of the unit. And once a plan was set, it traveled to the B team for approval, then the battalion, and a final inspection by the headquarters in Bagram. But at its core, a Special Forces mission is almost always planned by the team.

But not Commando Wrath. Almost from the start, the teams had been told how to operate. Where they would land. When they would go.

The mission had been in the works for months.

It started after a platoon of paratroopers from the 173rd Airborne Brigade Combat Team was ambushed in October 2007, heading back to their base camp in Afghanistan's Korengal Valley, the site of some of the war's most fierce fighting.

All day, there had been warnings of an attack. Stretched along a goat trail on a spur near their outpost, insurgents ambushed the paratroopers with RPGs and PKM machine guns. The ambush lasted three minutes, and when the fighters retreated, they tried to carry off Sergeant Joshua Brennan, a twenty-two-year-old fire team leader from Ontario, Oregon, who was gravely wounded.

Specialist Salvatore Giunta ran through enemy fire to push back the fighters who were close to overrunning his squad. When he saw the two insurgents carrying away Brennan, Giunta chased after them, killing one and wounding the other. They dropped Brennan, who was evacuated but died in surgery the following day.

Giunta, who left the Army in June 2011, was awarded the Medal of Honor, the U.S. military's highest award for valor under fire.

Major General David M. Rodriguez, commanding general of Combined Joint Task Force 82, was in charge of all the forces in eastern Afghanistan. It had been his men who were ambushed in the Korengal Valley. An ambush that was well coordinated and executed almost to perfection. If not for Giunta's actions, the fighters would have escaped with a captured American soldier.

Weeks after the ambush, Rodriguez and Brigadier General Joe Votel, the officer in charge of operations for the task force, called Colonel Christopher Haas and Ashley. Haas was in charge of all special operations forces in Afghanistan and Ashley's battalion operated in the eastern provinces of Afghanistan.

"We've got good information that Haji Ghafour's fighters were behind this ambush," Rodriguez said. "We want you guys to target him."

The mission fell to Ashley's battalion. But Ashley and most of his staff had never heard of Ghafour. So they spent the next few months tracking the elusive Afghan commander. Ghafour seemed to survive by moving only on foot or donkey and did not use a cell phone. So there was no way to track him using satellite phone transmissions.

Iraq was the main effort in 2008. Afghanistan was still only a support effort. Almost all the assets commanders now enjoy, from unmanned drones to elite special operations units, were fighting in Iraq. That meant intelligence resources were sparse, too.

But Ashley's staff slowly started to piece it together with the help from the Federal Bureau of Investigation and the Central Intelligence Agency. Ghafour was the main facilitator for the HIG in Afghanistan. He had amassed a massive weapons cache of machine guns and RPGs, and he had thousands of recruits.

All of his operations were financed by his massive gem-smuggling enterprise. It alone had been bringing in millions of dollars for the insurgents—money his network used to kill U.S. troops. Some of the gems—emeralds and rubies—were even found in a shop in Arizona.

Soldiers on Ashley's staff watched a documentary, *The Gem Hunter in Afghanistan,* to learn more about the routes used to move the gems, and even interviewed the filmmaker, Gary Bowersox, in hopes of gleaning enough information to track down Ghafour.

By March 2008, they had a good idea of how the gem-smuggling operation worked. They also had a source where Ghafour was operating. That was all they needed to start writing up an operation they would call Commando Wrath.

But they didn't have enough information on the exact location of Ghafour. They only knew he could be in two villages: Kendal (code-named Patriot 1 and 2) or Shok (Panther).

So, they called the mission a "cordon and search," not a raid. With these missions, teams surround a village and then search each building, talking to villagers and building rapport in hopes of rooting out the insurgents. The idea is that villagers will lead the soldiers to enemy fighters and weapons caches and provide information about operations in the area.

Captain John Bishop, who was a team leader in the previous rotation, was the point man on the staff, and shuttled between Bagram and Jalalabad, to make sure everything was in place.

The plan was fairly straightforward. Three ODAs with Afghan commandos would swoop into the valley. ODA 3336, led by Walton, would hit Kendal, called objective Patriot 1, and ODA 3312, led by Master Sergeant Jim Lodyga, would hit objective Patriot 2, a row of buildings that ran parallel to Kendal village on the other side of the wadi. ODA 3325 would hit Shok village, called objective Panther. Shok village was smaller than Kendal and at a significantly lower elevation. An air reaction force made up of Special Forces soldiers on Fletcher's B team would act as reinforcements.

The operation called for helicopters to fly to a spot above the villages and hover while the Green Berets and commandos fast-roped in. There, they would set up and sweep into the villages, fighting from the high ground down into the village.

The intelligence picture was unclear at best. Ghafour and his fighters hadn't been challenged, creating a safe haven for his men and his gem operation.

While planners believed there would be some resistance, they thought most of the men in the valley were workers in the gem mines. While they expected them to fight, they discounted the danger. The commanders believed they wouldn't be any match for well-trained soldiers like the Special Forces and commandos. Plus, two sets of Apaches were going in with the assault force and a pair of A-10 and F-15 fighters were positioned nearby, ready to attack if there was trouble.

The operation was approved by Ashley and he took it to Haas in late March. Because of weather and illumination, the first window to do the operation opened April 1. Haas approved the operation, but only after making a critical adjustment. He nixed the fast roping and instead ordered the helicopters to land in the wadi, out of range of machine guns in the village.

When Ashley pressed Haas for a reason, the colonel said he didn't feel the pilots from the 101st Airborne Division, who had just arrived in Afghanistan, were ready to fly such a difficult mission high in the mountains. It also would have been too difficult at those altitudes to have the commandos fast-rope onto rough terrain.

Once approved by Haas, the operation went to Votel for coordination and was sent back to the teams.

No one liked the changes, most of all Walton and Ford, since their team was the main effort. They wanted to fight from high to low, basic tactics, instead of landing in the valley and climbing up the mountain. If they had to land, they wanted to do the mission in the dark.

"We have to hit this at night," Walton said.

"Well, the pilots can't fly in this level of illumination at this time," Fletcher said.

"Then let's wait until they can," Walton said.

"The target will be out of there by that time," Fletcher said.

Back in the helicopter, Walton could see the commander of the commando company, Captain Mateen. Walton remembered how the Afghan commander hadn't liked the plan either.

Walton had brought him into the operations center a few days before. A series of unclassified images of the villages and the wadi were on the table. Nearby was a map. They had learned that the more the commando leadership knew about the mission, the easier it would be for them to do it because they had a stake in it. As Walton outlined the plan, Mateen, a skinny Afghan with a thick black beard, picked up the images and the map. He examined them closely. When Walton was done, Mateen looked at him.

"This is not a good plan," the Afghan said.

Walton, of course, tried to tow the party line.

"Hey, listen. We'll be okay. We just have to do what we have to do," Walton said. "It will be over quick."

But the Afghan didn't respond to the pep talk.

"This is not a good plan, my friend," Mateen said. "We are fighting from low to high. And they have the high ground around us."

The Afghan captain was right. Walton figured there was no reason to lie. No more bullshit.

"Listen, we don't have a choice. We have to go," Walton said.

Finally, he reverted to what he had been told.

"The aircraft can only land here," Walton said, pointing to the landing zones in the wadi.

He couldn't have the commandos refuse to go, or worse, turn on his team. Mateen just stared at Walton and shrugged his shoulders.

"Okay. If you want to do it that way," the Afghan said.

Walton didn't want to do it that way. But sitting in the Chinook, he knew he had no choice. He was going over the mission in his head when a message in his earphones caught his attention. The pilots in the medevac Black Hawks lifted off and turned north toward the valley. Walton could hear the pilots talking. Everyone was worried about the weather, so the commanders sent a recon bird up to see if they could find a path through the clouds.

Ford broke in.

"Hey, Kyle, what if those clouds move and we take casualties, we can't get the aircraft in to get our casualties out?" he asked over the radio.

Walton agreed.

Walton also knew that if the helicopters flew into the valley, the mission could be compromised. Ghafour had asked the locals in a village at the mouth of the Shok Valley to provide early warning to him if they heard or saw Coalition forces. They were also instructed to fight any Coalition attempt to enter the valley. Walton didn't want to be compromised when the team landed in broad daylight. He was still hoping that they could catch Ghafour off guard and go fast up the hill. But they couldn't count on luck if bad guys knew they were going to show up.

Climbing off the back ramp of the Chinook, he pulled out his Roshan cell phone and called Fletcher. The blades of the helicopter were turning, and he could feel the hot exhaust on his face. Walking to the edge of the concrete pad, he pushed his headphones up on his head and pressed the phone hard into his ear to mute some of the noise.

"We cannot fucking send those helicopters in there. If you send those helicopters and if they make that turn, we have to launch no matter what because we're blown," said Walton, practically screaming into the phone over the rotor wash.

"If they find a path, you're going," Fletcher said.

Discouraged, Walton walked back into the helicopter and plugged his headphones back into the radio feed. He had never been one to question orders.

When Walton was in the fourth grade, he told his teacher that he was going to West Point. He had wanted to be a soldier like his father for as long as he could remember.

The Indianapolis-born Walton's father was a sergeant in the 82nd Airborne and his mother was a nurse. When he was an infant, the family moved to Howe, Indiana, a small town on the border between Indiana and Michigan.

Walton's father enlisted as the Vietnam War was winding down. After leaving the service, he worked as a manager, more than two hours away, in Kalamazoo, Michigan. His mother continued working as a nurse at Sturgis Hospital in Michigan.

Walton had two brothers—Cory and Cole. Cory was three years younger and Cole was two years younger. His extended family lived within an hour of his home, and after his mother's sister died of breast cancer, his two cousins, Eric and Layne, moved in. They were older and became like brothers to Walton.

As a kid, Walton was obsessed with being in the Army or being a doctor. He and his brothers used to play hospital. His mother would bring them medical supplies and bandages. If they weren't saving lives, they were taking them as soldiers.

Walton's family moved across the state to Carmel, Indiana, when he was in fifth grade. For Walton and his brothers, it was big change. They were now going to large public schools.

Walton started playing football in the eighth grade. He was fast. Real fast. He was always a guy who never half-assed things. Even in practice, during conditioning sprints, he tried to outrun everybody.

Sports made him popular and soon he was getting the attention not only of his fellow classmates, but of colleges looking for a speedy wide receiver. Every day, he looked forward to opening his locker to see if he'd gotten any letters from interested programs.

When he received a letter from West Point, everything came into perspective. Up until his junior year, he figured he would be a criminal justice or psychology major or a professional photographer. But the letter from the military academy brought him back to his childhood goal. He was going to be a soldier. His goal was to follow his father into the 82nd Airborne, and ultimately the Special Forces.

For the rest of his junior and senior years, he focused on the goal. While his grade-point average was decent, he took the SATs five times in order to get the best score he could and signed up for every extracurricular activity he could find. After months of cajoling the staff of Congressman Dan Burton, a Republican, he earned a nomination to West Point and was accepted in 1997.

Walton went to West Point to play football, too. It helped him get in. In high school, he could run past defenders, but when he got to Highland Falls, New York, he couldn't. In college, everybody was fast. Before he arrived, he sat outside of his house in Indiana and read about West Point's football program. He expected not only to make the team, but to be one of its stars. He had more yards in two games in high school than any of West Point's receivers.

He soon learned that college football was about the X's and O's. It was about execution.

On the first day of practice, the coaches handed Walton a thick playbook. As he studied it, he tried to pick up the idiosyncrasies, like where to line up if the defense is in "Cover 2."

But looking at the playbook, Walton knew he was over his head. He didn't know how to read defenses.

At West Point, there were a bunch of other receivers. Usually, freshmen are red-shirted and get a chance to learn. Not at West Point.. During one of the scrimmages, Walton ran the wrong route. It was one of many mistakes he committed. He just wasn't getting it and the coaches knew it. They pulled him aside after practice and told him he wasn't at the level he needed to be at. His football career was over. As he left the practice facility, the sense of failure stung him. It was the first time he had failed.

But soon he had other worries, like academics.

The science- and math-heavy curriculum gave him fits. He was always in danger of getting thrown out. The constant pressure helped him learn to operate under the gun. He learned how to speed-read. He learned how to push through pain—physical and mental.

During his first year, he found the Special Forces branch representative right away.

"What's the quickest and best way to become a Green Beret?" he asked.

"There is no abbreviated path to the top. Start by learning a language," the Special Forces officer told him.

He figured the Middle East was where he would likely find himself and so he settled on Arabic. By his second year, he figured out that he had a knack for it. He joined the Foreign Academy Exchange Program and went to Egypt, traveling to Cairo in the spring of 1999. Before his senior year, he went to Tunisia.

Walton graduated the United States Military Academy in June of 2001 and selected the infantry branch. Fort Bragg was his first duty station. During the infantry officer's basic course and Ranger school at Fort Benning, he heard that the twin towers had been hit. He was about to start a live fire exercise when his instructors came out and told them they were at war.

"If anybody has any family in New York—at the Trade Center—get on this truck. The rest, keep training."

They kept training for the next five days. Walton could feel the increased intensity.

At West Point, he fully expected he was going to war. He remembered Somalia and Desert Storm. Now he was going. At Fort Bragg, he was assigned to Bravo Company, First Battalion, 505th Parachute Infantry Regiment. It was the exact unit that his father had served in twenty years earlier. Shortly after he arrived, his unit deployed to Afghanistan. Soon after returning from eight months of missions near the Pakistan border, Walton was in Fallujah, Iraq. After returning from his second combat deployment, he got selected for the Special Forces. He served briefly at the Army's Special Operations Command before completing the qualification course in 2007. His life had been a list of goals to be checked off.

Football.

Check.

West Point.

Check.

Special Forces.

Check.

On and on and on, he met every one. And the mission in the Shok Valley was no different. He still wanted to accomplish it, but not like this. He wanted a better plan.

The recon bird's flight seemed to take a lifetime. Sitting on the back of the Chinook, Walton could hear the pilots reporting back after they had reached certain checkpoints on the map. Most of the transmissions were pilot talk, but he could tell from their tone that they were anxious. Flying by instruments with almost no visibility, they were uncomfortable. Just listening to them made him more anxious. Then one of the pilots made the hairs on his neck perk up again.

"I've found a way through the clouds."

10

Staff Sergeant Seth Howard

By the time he settled into the front of the helicopter, Staff Sergeant Seth Howard was tired. Most of the team hadn't finished all their preparations until after midnight. Then they were up at 4 a.m. While they waited for the green light, they ran the commandos through a few dry runs to make sure they could get off the helicopters efficiently.

Howard was on the same Chinook as Carter and Walton, who was sitting on the ramp listening to the radio traffic. There were only a few radio jacks and Howard didn't have one. So all he could do was wait.

Howard was a veteran of the team, and this was his third deployment in just a short period. He was senior in that sense, but only a staff sergeant with two and a half years in the Army. An expert marksman, Howard was one of the few holdovers on the team. But when Ford took over, he seemed to pick on him. Maybe it was because Howard was the antithesis of Ford. He had an easygoing, almost lethargic demeanor. In Ford's view, Howard was lazy—and told him so. He called Howard a sloth and used to rag on him for being the son of a doctor.

Raised in Keene, New Hampshire, Howard came from an upper-middle-class family. His father was a general surgeon and his mother worked in communications, but she basically raised him and his two brothers.

The team leader might be in charge, but the team sergeant really creates the synergy. He shapes the team and is responsible for the culture. And no team is ever good enough. Howard knew that every team sergeant would say he had the best group in the world. But he had a feeling that every team sergeant also secretly wished his team was ten times better than they were.

So, Howard was used to Ford's tirades and cajoling. He knew at the heart of it, Ford wanted the best team. And no matter what Ford said to his fellow soldiers, they all tried hard to win him over, especially Howard, who was a weapons sergeant. He knew Ford had just come from a sniper team and knew how to shoot and run a range better than most of the guys on the team.

With Howard's background, no one had expected him to join Special Forces.

He went to Catholic school and then boarding school at Northfield Mount Hermon in Massachusetts. He wrestled all four years and graduated from high school in 2002, before attending Franklin and Marshall College in Lancaster, Pennsylvania, to wrestle. As a freshman, he got tossed around in the gym and in the classroom. He was at the school only one semester. He signed up for four classes, dropped one, failed two, and got a C in the one for which he showed up to the final exam.

He was having a good time in college, but had no direction. He was only there because that's what you do after high school. He dropped out because he didn't want to waste his parents' money. (Tuition, including room and board, ran more than fifty thousand dollars a year.) He got a job at a syringe and cardboard-box partition factory while he handled paperwork for the Army.

It was 2003 and the Iraq war had just started. While he met with his recruiter, the play-by-play of 3rd ID's thunder run into Iraq played on the radio. He went to the recruiter wanting to be an "18X," or a Special Forces recruit. They tried to talk him into doing something with satellites, but it was a six-year commitment and he didn't want to stare at a computer screen all day.

He wanted to be part of the action. The wars in Iraq and Afghanistan were big motivators. He didn't want to miss one of the biggest events of his generation.

And he believed in the mission. He believed the United States had an obligation to act and he couldn't live with himself if he wasn't a part of it. He heard the criticism of the wars. But to him, it was hypocritical. The exact same people who were arguing against the invasion of Iraq would be yelling about all the atrocities being committed by Saddam Hussein and Osama bin Laden, and demanding that someone do something about it.

Howard was ready. His mother tried to talk him into going in the Navy, even when he was getting on the bus to head to basic training. His father had joined the Navy in order to pay for medical school. But Howard didn't want to be trapped on a ship.

Before loading the commandos onto the bird a final time, he checked them to make sure they had water and ammunition. On previous missions, they would have guys with seventeen magazines and five knives. *What in the hell are you going to do with all of that?* Howard thought. But as the commandos jumped on board, he saw they were ready to go, including a small group of ammunition bearers carrying rounds for the Carl Gustav 84mm recoilless rifle. The Carl G looked like a giant shoulder-fired cannon. It shot shells that could punch holes in the thick mud walls of the Afghan villages.

Howard had eight commandos in his group. Every patrol was broken up into three groups: assault, support, and security. Howard was in charge of the support group. As the two assault teams, one led by Walding and Staff Sergeant Dave Sanders and the other by Walton, moved toward the village, Howard would cover them. When they got a foothold, Howard and his men would move up and try to provide support by fire and start clearing houses, too. In a way, he was like a third assault team since most of the cover fire would come from the circling Apache gunships.

They had originally talked about taking a mortar. But in order to shoot it, they would have to clear every shot with the jets and attack helicopters in the airspace above since the rounds are fired in a high arc at a target.

But bringing the Carl G was tough because the weapon was heavy.

Howard remembered watching the wild promotional videos of guys running through the woods with the weapon. The gunner with the actual tube and his assistant carried the rounds in a suitcase. When they reached the target, the gunner sat down and the assistant loaded it up. Howard didn't see it going down that way. He had never carried the ammunition around like a suitcase.

Most times, guys took the rounds out of the plastic cases and threw them in the back of their assault packs. But the rounds can get damaged. Instead, Howard had taken the rounds, which came in a case of two, and ran half-inch nylon through the loops on the sides of the plastic cases. Grabbing his Afghans, he threaded the nylon through loops on the back of their body armor. When he was done, the men had what looked like little jet packs.

With everybody on board, he settled in near the front and closed his eyes. He recalled a passage from Eric Haney's book, *Inside Delta Force*, a lesson he took to heart. Don't stand if you can sit down. Don't sit down if you can lie down. Don't lie down if you can be asleep.

He knew Walton and the crew chief on the bird would wake him up with the one-minute warning when they reached the Shok Valley. So, as the engines whined and the bird picked up off the flight line, Howard dozed off.

11

Morales

The ride in the Chinook was a little bumpy, but Morales hardly noticed. Flying in helicopters had become second nature. And in Afghanistan, it was the most efficient way to travel. Humvees were fine for transporting troops a short distance—but you couldn't use them on most Afghanistan roads, which were too narrow, pockmarked, muddy in the spring, and snow-covered in the winter, especially heading toward mountain passes.

Helicopters were the main mode of transportation for troops, and Chinooks were the workhorses. With iconic twin rotors, the CH-47 could hold up to fifty soldiers and fly up to 196 miles per hour. But they also were big targets, and that's why it was always dangerous for them to land in valleys. Insurgents on high ground could use them for target practice, firing RPGs and mortars and machines guns. When that happened, it was difficult for aircraft gunners to effectively return fire. They had to be careful of hitting the rotors.

Morales tried not to think about it. He had to exude confidence because he knew the Afghan commandos took their cue from the team. If he and the other Special Forces soldiers appeared calm and in control—like this operation was another routine day in the field—the commandos would relax and stay focused. This was critical for this mission.

In a planning meeting days earlier with Walton and Ford, Morales had told them the team should expect to meet "moderate to heavy resistance because the people of the Shok Valley have not given in to anybody. Anything that has come into that province, they have resisted," Morales warned. And he made a dire prediction: "If we're spotted, they will be coming after us."

As an intelligence specialist, Morales knew all about Afghanistan's long, complicated, and troubled history.

For centuries, Afghanistan had been incorporated into a series of empires, and a succession of invading armies had passed through it. But as many empires discovered—including the British and later the Soviets—Afghans were fiercely independent people willing to fight foreign invaders.

In a way, the land that is now Afghanistan was a victim of location. It was a major crossroads in trade routes linking East and West. European and Mediterranean countries craved many of the exotic Eastern wares—silk, spices, ivory, gold—and the quickest overland routes for centuries crossed Afghanistan.

Archaeologists have traced the human history of Afghanistan back thousands of years, with the first inhabitants settling in the remote northeastern part of the country, including what is present day Nuristan—the site of the Shok Valley. But the beginning of the recorded culture began in about 550 BC when much of Afghanistan was part of the Achaemenid Empire or Persia. The empire built roads and cities in provinces known as satrapies. But the empire was plagued by constant bitter and bloody tribal revolts from Afghans living in Kandahar and other areas.

After Persia fell to Alexander the Great in 330 BC, the conqueror turned his attention to Afghanistan. While he conquered Afghanistan—and used Afghanistan as a gateway to India—he failed to subjugate its people. Like Persian rulers before him, Alexander was plagued by bitter Afghan revolts. When Alexander died in 323 BC, much of the fragile empire he created quickly broke up and was divided among his generals.

The Arabs introduced Islam to Afghanistan in 652—and forced

conversions—but the Islamic era began in earnest with the Ghaznavid dynasty in 962. That's when a Turkish slave named Alp Tigin marched his armies on Ghazni and set up an Islamic state. His successors annexed Kabul, Bost, Balkh, Herat, and parts of western Persia. Within a short period, Ghazni established itself as one of the nerve centers of the Islamic world. But that ended in 1219, when Mongol leader Genghis Khan, a brilliant military commander, swept through Asia, conquering Afghanistan along the way. His army was particularly brutal in Afghanistan, massacring many Afghans and destroying cities, including Kabul, temples, and irrigation systems, which turned fertile soil back into deserts.

Over the next five hundred years, descendants of earlier tribal rulers and empires wrestled to reassert control over Afghanistan. But every time a foreign regime gained a foothold, the Afghans pushed back. There were centuries of instability and bloodshed, especially with the neighboring Persians, who, under Safavid dynasty, captured large swaths of Afghanistan in the 1500s. Through it all, there were times when Afghan tribal leaders rose up and united the masses with promises of unifying the country, creating an independent Afghanistan.

Dost Muhammad Khan was such a leader. In the early nineteenth century, he tried to bring the country together and was even proclaimed as Amir al-Mu'minin—commander of the faithful. But in 1836, the British invaded. It was the first of three bitter wars between the two nations over the next eighty years.

It wasn't until 1919—after British forces again tried to bring the country under its sphere of influence by assassinating Afghan king Emir Habibullah Khan—that the nation was finally united. Habibullah's son—Amir Amanulla Khan—won independence for his people, and pushed pro-Western reforms in education and gender equality.

It was the beginning of the modern struggle between religious and secular leaders—a schism that continues to this day.

Afghanistan was in a state of chaos until Zahir Shah became the king in 1933. A year later, the United States formally recognized Afghanistan, which remained a monarchy for the next four decades.

But in 1973, while Zahir Shah was on vacation, his government was overthrown in a military coup, and General Daoud Khan abolished the monarchy and declared himself president and Afghanistan a republic.

That crisis triggered a series of events that led to the Soviet occupation, the rise of the Taliban and Al Qaeda, and the American presence in Afghanistan.

When Daoud Khan assumed power, he started to oust suspected opponents from his government until he was killed in 1978 in a bloody Communist coup by the leftish People's Democratic Party. (Afghanistan's Communist Party was formed in 1965.)

While the party instituted social changes, there was little love lost between the party's ruling factions. Meanwhile, the conservative Islamic and ethnic leaders who objected to the social changes began armed revolt in the countryside.

A power struggle ensued between leftist leaders Hafizullah Amin and Nur Muhammad Taraki. In 1979, Amin won, but the revolts in the countryside continued, and the Afghan army faced total collapse.

This was at the height of the cold war—and the Soviets, like other nations in Afghanistan's bleak history, wanted to maintain its influence in a strategic part of the world.

Looking to prop up a weak pro-Communist government, the Soviets sent in troops to help remove Amin, who was executed. In 1980, Babrak Karmal was installed as ruler, backed by Soviet troops.

But antiregime resistance intensified with various mujahedeen groups fighting Soviet forces. (They would later include Osama bin Laden and Gulbuddin Hekmatyar.) A strange coalition—the United States, Pakistan, China, the Islamic Republic of Iran, and Saudi Arabia—began supplying money and arms.

The United States began supplying the mujahedeen with stinger missiles to shoot down Soviet helicopters, and Karmal was replaced by Muhammad Najibullah as head of the Soviet-backed regime. In 1988, the Soviets signed peace accords and agreed to withdraw, and a year later the last Soviet troops retreated. But as with most Afghanistan conflicts, the war continued as the mujahedeen pushed to overthrow Najibullah.

By 1992, the resistance closed in on Kabul and Najibullah fell from power. Four years later, the Taliban seized control of Kabul, and instituted a hard-line version of Islam, banning women from work and introducing Islamic punishments, which include death by stoning and amputations for violating Islamic law. Meanwhile, the Taliban leadership began to allow former mujahedeen leaders, like Osama bin Laden, to set up terrorist training camps.

And those leaders began exporting a new brand of terrorism, one based on extremist Islamic views.

Osama bin Laden in 1998 was accused of masterminding the bombing of U.S. embassies in Africa. In 2001, the Taliban ordered religious minorities to wear tags identifying themselves as non-Muslims.

Then on September 11, 2001, the Islamic extremists struck in the heart of the United States.

The outrage and call for justice was swift. Within a month, the United States and Great Britain launched air strikes against the Taliban, and that December, Afghan political groups gathered in Germany to form an interim government. Hamid Karzai was chosen as chairman. And in late 2002, Special Forces—working with the CIA—persuaded tribal leaders to side with them to oust the Taliban. They did, and in a short time, the Taliban ws driven from power.

And once again, Afghanistan was an independent country.

But the more things changed, the more they stayed the same. Even after the Taliban was removed from power, the fighting continued between the insurgents—mostly Al Qaeda supporters, including the Taliban—and U.S.-led United Nations Coalition forces. Most of the battles took place in remote areas of the country, although there were terrorist attacks in the major cities, including Kabul and Kandahar.

Morales only hoped that one day Afghanistan would be at peace. Maybe the U.S. presence would help. That's why U.S. troops were there: to help defeat the HIG, Taliban, and Al Qaeda, and help restore order to a nation long plagued by chaos.

He knew Afghans could be warm and friendly. During his two deployments, he had met some wonderful Afghans, including CK, the team's lead interpreter, who was standing near the tailgate with Walding and Sanders.

CK's real name was Edris Khan. But everyone called him CK, a nickname that he said stood for "Combat Killer." During the course of the deployment, CK had become extremely close with many team members, but perhaps with no one more than Morales. CK had become his little brother, and Morales was extremely protective of him. CK followed Morales everywhere, and was by his side on most missions. But on this operation, CK was assigned to the command and control element. CK was upset, and had made one last appeal to Morales.

"Luis, we're always together, man," CK said.

"Yeah, man, but you're such an asset. You're going to be part of the main effort when you go up there. We need you up there. You're that important," Morales told him.

And it was no bullshit.

CK had become invaluable to the team.

At only five feet five inches tall, CK was a skinny but muscular guy who spent hours in the gym. Outgoing, he always seemed to have a smile on his face, and believed that women liked him because he had "handsome dark features"—short black hair and dark brown eyes. Morales thought CK looked Latino and could pass as an American. And CK wanted nothing more than to be a member of Special Forces. He spoke four languages—English, Pashto, Dari, and Nuristani—and had learned how to read grid coordinates. He even had a 9mm Beretta copied to look like an American weapon.

CK, who became an interpreter to help his single mother in Kabul, began chewing Copenhagen and picked up American catchphrases from hanging out with the ODAs and watching TV shows. It wasn't unusual to hear him ask soldiers, "How you doin'?" just like Joey Tribbiani from the TV show *Friends,* or reciting lyrics from rapper Eminem's songs. Unknown to CK, members of the team had talked about getting him a special immigration visa so he could settle in the United States. They knew CK, with his love of American culture—especially TV sitcoms and rap music—would fit right in.

The team's relationship with CK helped illustrate the special bond between U.S. fighting units and interpreters in Afghanistan and Iraq. Afghans and Iraqis risk their lives taking jobs as interpreters. Being an interpreter paid more than most positions in their impoverished nations—if they could even find work. But the dangers were extreme, and in many cases, they had to hide their identities or had to live apart from their families, because if Al Qaeda or the Taliban knew who they were, they would be marked for death. So would their families. Hundreds of interpreters, known as "terps," had been killed in Afghanistan and Iraq.

In a way, with all the high-tech equipment—smart bombs, unmanned drones, advanced weapons systems, satellite communications—U.S. troops in Afghanistan had become dependent in part on terps.

Soldiers—especially Special Forces—had to go into villages and deal with the local leaders to restore services to shattered communities. They had to understand the intricacies of tribal culture and politics as well as identifying enemy from friendly groups. They had to spend time training the Afghan police force and commandos. All were major keys to success, and in most cases, translators were critical to carrying out the missions.

Over time, many interpreters developed a great rapport with the U.S. soldiers, and many in the military believed that interpreters should be recognized with U.S. citizenship.

The bond between ODA 3336 and all their interpreters was strong. But CK was clearly their favorite. With his playful smile and dark reflecting sunglasses—the kind worn by state highway troopers in the United States—CK was an adopted member of Special Forces.

He was loyal and always wanted to hang out with the team when they were sitting around bullshitting in Jalalabad. The team had built a special movie room at the base, and he would spend hours sitting there, watching *Rome, Prison Break,* and other TV shows, and, of course, action movies. He wanted to be cool, so whatever the team had, he wanted to get one, too. And he acted like them. Not only did he start chewing tobacco, but he began smoking cigarettes because almost everyone on the team did.

He claimed to be twenty-five, but the team knew he was probably much younger. To Morales, he looked like a teenager. He was constantly asking Morales to recommend cool movies to watch. The team had a box full of them and let him borrow a few at a time.

In June 2007, CK was sent with a team of Afghan commandos to Jordan for training. It was there that he learned how to read maps and to shoot a sniper rifle. He was taught land navigation skills. CK wanted to learn as much about the military as possible. If he understood the concepts, it would help when he explained them to the Afghan commandos. Like most of the people in the country, CK didn't have an education. But he was naturally bright and street-smart.

Once when they were discussing a mission, CK began explaining the grid coordinates. Morales turned to him and said, "I didn't know you knew how to read a map." Then he stopped and thought about it. CK had to translate Morales's instructions to the commandos. So all along, CK was learning with the commandos. He was being trained at the same time.

While CK tried to spend most of his time with the team, he did hang out with fellow interpreters. A terp named Blade was his best friend, and he would often go over to his apartment to relax. They were the same age and had grown up with each other. CK told Morales that Blade was a "player," that he had a bunch of girlfriends. Morales just laughed. They tried so hard to act American.

A few times, CK told Morales that he was going to raise some money, give half to his mother, and take the rest to buy a ticket to the United States, where he would enlist in the Army with plans of joining Special Forces. Morales advised him how to reach his goals. He encouraged CK to become a language teacher for Special Forces. It was a typical big-brother moment between the men. They had spent so many nights together, just hanging out and bullshitting. But they didn't just hang out in the barracks. They would go to dances sponsored by the Army's Morale, Welfare and Recreation services, MWR, and listen to rhythm and blues, hip-hop, and salsa.

One night when Morales didn't feel like going, a few of his buddies took

CK to a dance. CK didn't like to dance, he just wanted to hang out with Special Forces and feel like he was part of the team. And he fit right in. He had been working for U.S. troops so long that he was "Americanized."

Most terps will give soldiers and their families gifts. CK followed the tradition. During the deployment, he wanted to buy Morales's wife a present. He told Morales that he thought about buying her a dress. But Morales, knowing his wife probably wouldn't wear it, suggested a jewelry box. So CK purchased two, and when she opened them in the United States, she discovered two handmade bracelets inside. The Moraleses were touched. There were times when Morales would be on the phone with Katherine and she would ask to talk to CK. She always asked about him. He was family.

Morales trusted CK because he knew the Afghan always had his back. CK would be there not only as an interpreter, but as a fellow soldier. His loyalty was critical during missions like the one they had a few weeks before Shok Valley. That's when Morales's team and another ODA landed in an area that resembled the Shok Valley: a village with possible insurgents tucked away in a canyon.

The other ODA had planned an operation to hunt for a Taliban leader whose followers were planting IEDs and hitting U.S. firebases. Morales's team was drafted because the other ODA didn't have Afghan commandos, and in Afghanistan you always had to put the Afghan face on every operation.

With CK at his side, Morales helped prep the commandos for the mission. They rehearsed over and over. Repetition was the key. Everyone had to know their role. At one point, Morales would scribble the plans on a piece of paper, or he would draw it in the dirt—like a schoolyard football play—and say, "Here's the village. This is where the river flows around it, and we're going to land just south of it on another hilltop. Then we're going to run down and take the eastern blocking position, where we won't allow anyone to come in or out. That's our mission."

That's how he planned it, and that's how they executed it when they jumped off the birds. As the other teams headed to their positions, Morales's team began running down the hill to their spot. But as Morales was moving, he glimpsed a man running in the distance who resembled the target they were looking for. He was a "big dude" and had a long red beard that was unmistakable from a hundred meters away.

Morales began chasing the suspect, and CK was right behind him. When Morales reached the bottom of the hill, he shouted at the man: *"Bast,"* which means "stop" in Pashto. But he had already started on his way up another hill, headed to a village across the river. Morales stopped in his tracks, lifted his M4, and peered through the scope. He could see the man had a weapon in his hands.

Shit, take him down, Morales thought.

He knew he had to stop him, so he squeezed the trigger and fired three shots.

Bam.

Bam.

Bam.

As soon as he did, CK opened up. So did the commandos who were right behind them. But by then, the man with the red beard had disappeared, and Morales was unsure whether they had even hit him.

He ordered his team of commandos—about forty men—to stay at the apex of the river by a building that looked like a mill. Morales had no idea whether the mill was even functional, but it didn't matter. He told his men that they knew the mission: They were in a blocking position. Make sure no one comes in or out of the area. Then Morales headed to the village with CK and three commandos.

As they rounded a corner near the village, they spotted the man with the red beard on a ledge. His hands were in the air and he was yelling something unintelligible. Morales shouted for him to come down, but the man stayed in position. *Why is he just standing there?* Morales thought. *Did he run to get reinforcements? Is this a trap?*

Morales told CK to order the commandos to bring the man down. A moment later, eleven men and some women rounded the corner. They must have been leaving the village, Morales thought. Barking orders, CK told the women to leave and for the men to put their hands in the air and move toward them slowly. At first, they all looked puzzled, but when they looked at the man with the red beard, they knew the commandos were serious; he had been shot and was bleeding from the arm and stomach.

Morales and CK began to zip-tie the eleven men while the Afghan medic treated the man with the red beard. As the medic began patching the man up, he told Morales that he wasn't the person they were looking for. Morales was skeptical and said he fit the description.

"I'm his brother," the man said.

Morales smiled. "Okay. But you're on my list, too. You're already a vetted target."

Morales cut the plastic zip ties off some of the prisoners and made them carry the man with the red beard on a makeshift stretcher to where the commandos had set up the blocking position. Morales was trudging back to the commandos with the prisoners when he did a double take. The commandos had captured eleven men who also were trying to leave the village. Now Morales had twenty-three prisoners, including the man with the red beard. They began frantically using zip ties to handcuff the new prisoners. Morales told Rhyner to get Ford on the radio. At that moment he heard his satellite phone in his pocket ring.

What the fuck? Morales thought. He answered the phone and the voice on the other end was Katherine's.

"Hi, what are you doing?" she asked casually.

"I'm kind of in the middle of something."

Then Morales started screaming at the commandos: "Don't let those guys talk to each other." He turned his attention back to his wife. "Honey, I can't talk right now. I have to go," he said, before hanging up.

As part of the PACE plan—Primary Alternate Contingency Emergency—the team all carried cell phones. Morales had given his wife the number to use in case of an emergency. But that was the first time she had called on it—and it was a little surreal. Here he was on a mission ten thousand miles from home, he had just captured twenty-three men in the middle of nowhere, and she called like he was back at Fort Bragg and she wanted him to pick up a loaf of bread on the way home from the office.

A moment later, Ford's voice crackled over the radio:

"Luis, what do you got?"

"Hey, I have twenty-three PUCs [persons under control]."

"What? You have two or three PUCs?"

"No I got twenty-three PUCs."

"Holy shit," Ford said. "All right. Send them up."

So Morales marched them to the first village and waited for helicopters to arrive to pick up the prisoners and the teams. But when the first helicopters took off, insurgents opened fire, and an RPG barely missed hitting one. *Shit, come on. Just hurry up and pick us up,* Morales thought. *Get us out of here as quickly as you can.*

Back at the base, the prisoners were separated and soldiers began interrogating them, including the man with the red beard. They asked him if he had been leading attacks against U.S. firebases in the area. He said no, and claimed that Americans had set his house on fire, and that he wasn't a member of any group. No one was sure if he was telling the truth. Was he a member of the Taliban? Al Qaeda?

Now, sitting in a Chinook headed to the Shok Valley, Morales wondered what had happened to all the prisoners. Of the twenty-three, he knew more than a dozen had been released. Maybe they were innocent and were just leaving the village to escape. In this war, sometimes it was hard to tell the good guys from the bad guys. That's why it was so important to have an interpreter you could trust. The best interpreters had a sixth sense about who was bullshitting. He recalled how he laughed with CK about the mission when they got back to Jalalabad. They captured twenty-three men, including a suspected terrorist leader. Overall, the operation was a success.

Morales smiled, and wished CK was with his team in the Shok Valley. They worked so well together. They didn't have to say a word; they just instinctively knew each other's moves.

Instead, Morales was assigned Bouya, a tall, crazy, Italian-looking Afghan who liked to wear a Cincinnati Reds baseball cap. It was like Bouya had a gigantic red target on his head, Morales thought. Someone had given him that cap and he refused to take it off because he thought it looked cool. He saw the rest of the Special Forces soldiers wearing baseball caps and wanted to be just like them. It was typical. The terps loved to imitate everything Special Forces did and wore—from kits and body armor to clothes.

As the helicopters broke through the clouds, Morales stared past the pilots out the front window and glanced at the objective. The compound was on a finger of land on top of a cliff. Concretelike structures were built on the cliff and into the side of the mountain.

For a moment he forgot where he was, and was impressed by the work. Someone had taken a lot of time to fortify the enclave. Then reality hit: This was no sightseeing tour. His team would have to scale the rocks to get to the village, and the heavily guarded structures protected one of Afghanistan's most feared terrorists.

12

Ford

Ford knew there wasn't much he could do now except knuckle up and get ready to execute. As the commandos and his team filed into the helicopter, he began pounding on his chest. As they passed, he knocked knuckles with the Afghans, Shurer, Wurzbach, Staff Sergeant Ryan Wallen, a twenty-two-year-old communications sergeant from Palm Springs, California, and Sergeant Matthew Williams, of Texas, who'd arrived with Walding, another Texan, a few weeks before the team deployed. The twenty-seven-year-old was a weapons sergeant and Texas A&M Aggies fan. Ford used to tease the Texans since Walding was a burnt-orange-bleeding Texas fan—the Aggies chief rival.

"Listen up. You need to show the commandos we are ready to get this thing done. We're going to do our jobs," he shouted over the din of the whirling blades.

Ford and Wurzbach sat near the back so they could see off the back ramp. All doubts and concerns were gone as soon as Ford heard the engines start to power up.

Go time. Let's get it done.

The wheels lifted off the ground, the nose of the Chinook dipped forward, and the aircraft seemed to leap into the air.

Ford understood how to lead foreign special operations troops. He was with the team that started the Iraqi Counter-Terrorism Force team. His team selected the first ICTF troops, trained them in Jordan, and prepared them to combat Al Qaeda in Iraq.

In 2004, he led a team to the Shiite holy city of Najaf after Shia cleric Muqtada al-Sadr's revolt. After the fall of the Saddam government in 2003, Muqtada al-Sadr organized thousands of his supporters into a political movement, which included a military wing known as the Jaysh al-Mahdi. In April 2004, fighting broke out in Najaf, Sadr City, and Basra. Sadr's Mahdi Army took over several points and attacked Coalition soldiers.

Ford worked with the snipers. Soon after arriving, he and his Iraqi team were sent into the most dangerous parts of the town to conduct sniper missions. Moving into a valley controlled by the HIG would be even more dangerous.

The HIG was one of the three strongest terror groups in Afghanistan. Led by Hekmatyar, the HIG was one of the biggest insurgent factions against Soviet and Afghan Communist forces.

Hekmateyr's group was focused on northeastern Afghanistan, with bases in the tribal areas of Pakistan. Attacks on security forces increased in 2005.

The "Nuristan-Kunar Corridor" is the gateway to Kabul, and Al Qaeda was making a major push to secure it. In response, the sector had become home to more than 3,500 members of the 173rd Airborne Brigade. The paratroopers were spread out over at least twenty-two posts, many of which were built just months before by the 10th Mountain Division.

In Nuristan in August 2006, the United States set up FOB Kamdesh—now called Combat Outpost Keating—and several other outposts in towns like Urmul and Kamu; towns along the winding narrow road that runs next to the Kunar River toward Kunar Province, then Pakistan. It was this road—nicknamed "Ambush Alley"—that the United States wanted to control.

The flight took about an hour. The whole time, Ford kept his eyes fixed on the clouds until the armada made its turn into the valley. Then he was able to start seeing the mountains. The peaks towered above the helicopter. Each one was still covered in snow.

Ford hadn't worn a T-shirt under his desert uniform top. He knew that in a little while he would be climbing a cliff and figured that with all the kit he would be hot. But glancing at the snow, he almost broke out his spare shirt rolled up in his three-day bag near his feet. *Damn, I might have to use my bag today,* he thought.

Each member of the team had one strapped to the floor. It contained extra clothes, food, and other gear that the team might need, but was too heavy to carry on the assault. The crew chiefs on the birds knew to be ready to kick the bags off if the team called for them.

As the helicopter dipped and turned around the peaks, Ford could hear the pilots on his headset calling off the checkpoints on the map. The helicopters flared out and started to settle near the wadi.

"Ice. Ice."

"Ice" meant it was a cold landing zone. No enemy fire.

As the helicopter settled into a hover, Ford peeked out of the portal on the side of the Chinook. Streaked as it was with dirt and grime, it was difficult to see anything, but he could glimpse the steep hills surrounding him.

We have to get off of this thing. We're in a huge bullet trap.

The helicopter was at a lower elevation than the village, which meant that Afghan fighters could easily look over the lip of the cliff and shoot down at the hovering Chinooks and Black Hawks.

"Thirty seconds," the pilot said.

The Special Forces soldiers got the commandos up. Ford stood near the ramp and started to beat his chest. It was his war cry. With each thump, he sent a simple message: It was time to jump off this bird and kick some ass.

"Go! Go!" the crew chief yelled.

Ford looked over the ramp. The bird was still eight to ten feet off the ground. And the soldiers were jumping out with at least sixty extra pounds of equipment.

"Put it down. Put it down," Ford yelled back.

"GO!"

Wurzbach and Ford looked at each other. They knew there was nothing they could do.

"It is go time," Ford said.

He jumped off first. Holding the ramp with one arm, he still didn't touch the ground. So he let go and landed with a *thud,* sliding off the basketball-size rocks covered in ice. Scrambling to his feet, he tried to set up security as the others made the same fall. He figured 10 percent of the force was going to be out with knee or ankle injuries. But as the last commando hit the rocks and the helicopter climbed into the air, Ford checked for injuries and only got thumbs-up and smiles. No casualties.

All that working out at Fort Bragg had paid off.

13

Carter

Carter was blown away by the scenery. Jumping off a Chinook hovering ten feet above the ground, he landed hard on the rocks just like the other soldiers. But he bounded up and grabbed his Nikon and began snapping frames. Snowcapped mountains wrapping the valley. A river snaking through the rugged terrain. A layer of ice-slicked rocks covering the landscape. Very cool, he thought. *Click. Click. Click. Click. Click.* He was snapping away like a photographer on a fashion shoot.

This was Carter's last mission before he headed home and he wanted to document the entire adventure. So on the helicopter ride to the Shok Valley, he pulled out his Sony PD170 to videotape the flight. Men's faces. Stern. Grim. Hardened. It was a documentary for a mission that had an entirely different feel from the others he had been on. Special Forces. Afghan commandos. Chinooks and Black Hawks flying in under a low, thick white shroud of clouds. This was World War II–esque.

He could tell this was serious before the helicopters deployed to the Shok Valley. Before they boarded, some soldiers were cracking jokes, but underneath he could sense that they were anxious. He really didn't know any of the Special

Forces soldiers. He had met most of them the night before the mission. But several told him that the mission might be called off because of bad weather.

When they were waved on board, the mood changed to deadly serious. It was tense.

When the helicopter arrived in the valley, the pilot couldn't land because of the terrain. So everyone jumped off the back of the Chinooks. They flowed out and hit the ground and quickly regrouped. That's when Carter began snapping away.

The Shok Valley was geographically amazing. The wadi was like a narrow, rock-filled road completely surrounded by high mountains. Think of a punch bowl. The team was at the bottom of the bowl in the wadi. Like the sides of the bowl, the mountains curved and rose to the clouds. And those mountains had high cliffs that overlooked the valley floor. But sitting on top of the cliffs were buildings—part of a village—that looked more like a fort. The structures were impressive—built on top of one another like an apartment complex. He glimpsed one that looked like it was four or five stories high.

He kept his camera out. He was still clicking as his team of Walton, Morales, Behr, and Rhymer moved toward the objective. They were looking up at the mountains like tourists visiting the big city for the first time.

One of the first obstacles they faced was the fast-moving river that ran across the wadi. A plank spanned the crossing, but it wasn't strong enough to support the men and some of the soldiers fell into the river. In a hurry, others walked straight through the water. In some spots it was ankle- to midchest-deep. *All made for the camera,* Carter thought. He panned the landscape from ground level to compound. A veneer of thin ice covered everything. It was cold, probably in the forties. He wasn't expecting that. He knew the mountain passes were closed during the winter because of snow. But for some reason, he was expecting it to be warmer. But he knew everyone would warm up once they started their ascent.

The climb was going to be brutal—especially with his all camera equipment. Thank God the guys had stripped his bag and forced him to leave some of his equipment back at the base.

Good move, he thought.

14.

Staff Sergeant David Sanders

He was new to the team, but this is where Staff Sergeant David Sanders had wanted to be all along. Even if that meant being in a remote valley far from home.

It had been a long journey for Sanders from Hunstville, Alabama, to the Shok Valley. An only child, Sanders grew up in a community nicknamed "The Rocket City" for its close history with U.S. space missions. Located in the Tennessee River Valley, it's an area nestled in the foothills of the Appalachian Mountains with rivers, natural springs, and caves. As a child, Sanders loved to explore the outdoors, but had no interest in joining the military. That all changed with the terrorist attacks on September 11, 2001.

At the time, he was in high school. But watching the images of the death and destruction on U.S. soil made him want to get involved. So when, during his senior year, the United States invaded Iraq, he decided he was going to enlist. Caught up in the patriotic fervor, he knew he wanted to serve his country. Something inside told him it was the right thing to do.

It was 2004 when he joined the Army Reserves as an intelligence analyst. He had completed one semester at the University of Alabama in Huntsville.

But he decided to drop out. He wanted to go to war but was in a quandary. The unit he joined had already deployed a few years before and wasn't slated to go again anytime soon. He discovered that reserve duty was pretty much meeting up and going to lunch on the weekends. So he went back to school for another semester and decided to go to Special Forces Selection.

He came in on an 18X contract, which essentially guarantees a new recruit the opportunity to "try out" for Special Forces. After being selected, he was trained as an engineer and signed on with 3rd Special Forces Group well after they left for Afghanistan. The clerk, when he arrived at the headquarters on Fort Bragg, asked him if he wanted to deploy.

"You ready to deploy now?"

Sanders didn't hesitate. "Yes."

"Okay. In ten days we'll have you on a flight."

He was finally on the cusp of making it to a war zone to fight the terrorists who promised more attacks on the United States. It had taken him from July 2004 to November 2007 to get to the point where he could deploy. And he was relieved to finally answer the call.

When he arrived in Afghanistan, he just wanted to fit in with the team. As the new guy in the unit, he kept his mouth shut and listened.

He went on his first live mission in early January 2008. It was nothing exciting—a routine reconnaissance patrol. For three days, they drove in the desert. At one point, a truck broke down and they had to wait for a part to be dropped off. After they resumed the trip, they ended up in a village where they talked to some locals for a few hours. Then they turned around and headed back to the base. That was it. Most of his time was spent in a Humvee.

The next mission was a little more exciting—and Special Forces–like, he thought. In the middle of the night, his team and commandos dropped into a village and busted an opium-processing facility. He knew that in Afghanistan terrorists helped finance their operations by selling drugs. The hills were some of the most fertile in the world for growing opium poppies, whose seeds were extracted to make the most addictive drugs on the black market. Opium is the source of many opiates, including morphine, codeine, and heroin. After the mission, when he had time to reflect, he thought: *This is why I joined.*

But he knew that was just a warm-up for the Shok Valley. And now, as he was walking the trail to the enemy compound, he wanted to make sure he did everything right. It didn't matter that he had only been there a short time. There was no room for error.

15

Walding

Walding leaped off the helicopter and tried to take a knee in the rock-strewn wadi. As the rest of his element scrambled to join him, he scanned the high mountains that seemed to box in the valley floor.

Well, this is going to suck, he thought.

The valley cut a sharp V in the direction of the villages of Shok and Kendal. The mountains rose high into the sky, almost cutting off the sun, and the sheer rock faces offered no cover.

The massive green Chinook helicopters and their smaller, faster Black Hawk cousins dropped off their "chalks" of Special Forces soldiers and commandos and soared back into the safety of the sky. Walding looked at the ground trying to cover his face as the dirt swirled around him. Once the echoes of the beating rotors faded, a silence fell like a blanket over the valley. It was almost spooky, Walding thought. He could hear murmurs from the others. The quiet was unnerving. But it was soon replaced by the command to move out.

"Let's go," Walding yelled to his commandos.

Walding, Morales, and Sanders led assault one forward. Behind them were Walton, Behr, Carter, Rhyner, and CK. They were the command and control element, essentially the brain, and Ford, Howard, Williams, and the others were in the last group.

For the next several minutes, groups of American soldiers and their Afghan counterparts formed up into groups and began looking for a path up the mountain and into the villages. Overhead, Apache helicopters and F-15 jets were talking to the soldiers, trying to find them the best route up the mountain. As they crisscrossed the sky, the pilots searched for enemy fighters, waiting to pounce at the first sign of trouble.

The walk from the landing zone to the path leading to the village took about thirty minutes. They moved forward in a line—commandos in their green uniforms were separated every few men by a tan-clad Special Forces soldier. ODA 3336 was in the lead. Farther down was ODA 3312, led by Lodyga. Their mission was to cover ODA 3336 as they scaled the mountain into the village where Ghafour was supposed to be hiding.

The wadi looked more like a rock quarry than a place where people lived. If that wasn't bad enough, Walding and his group ran up on a river of icy white water. Moving down the bank, they found a narrow two-by-four that offered the only dry way across. Walding stepped on it, testing to make sure it could hold him. But halfway across, he realized he wasn't going to make it, and fell in the river. The water engulfed him all the way up to his chest, soaking his uniform and equipment and sending a chill through his entire body.

Slapping the water in anger, he scrambled up the other side and waited for the others. Like ants marching, the other soldiers and commandos crossed one by one. Many were already wet and cold, and they didn't want to risk hypothermia. But all knew that one well-placed machine gun would wipe them out. So they hurried across. Walding felt uneasy when they passed a building—more like a big goat barn—near the base of the hill under the village. It was empty.

They took a few more steps and the blocking positions broke off, with Wurzbach leading one and Staff Sergeant Sean Mason the other.

Sanders, Walding, and Morales stood at the base of the cliff, staring up. On top of towering cliffs overlooking the valley stood stout buildings made of rock, mud, and logs. More like castles than houses, some of the buildings were built straight into the cliff face.

Morales glimpsed some people running with guns at the lip of the cliff. They wore the long shirt and baggy pants of the region and soon disappeared behind some rocks. Sanders and Walding pressed their scopes to their faces and scanned, in vain, hoping to spot the gunmen.

"I can't see anybody," Walding said. Neither could Sanders.

Not wanting to be stuck in the wadi, Walding led the first group up the trail. Sanders was at the rear as they started up the path—a switchback—that zigzagged up the mountain. This was their second attempt. The first route had been too steep. The second wasn't much better. It was more like erosion levels than an actual trail. But it was the only way up to the compound. Walding's hands hurt, and he cut them on the jagged edges as he hoisted himself up with all his equipment. *Shit. If we meet any resistance, we're fucked. There's no cover,* he thought.

As he climbed, Walding used his scope to peer at the compound. He hoped to get his bearings before he reached the outskirts of the village. He wanted to see what they were facing. But from his current angle, it was impossible to see all the buildings. There were just too many of them—and some were hidden by layers of ridgelines that jutted out of the mountain.

When he finally reached the top, he spotted a rock wall at the bank of a ditch on the edge of the village. Racing over to it, he and Sanders set up behind it and tried to catch their breath. The commandos fanned out around the Americans. Everybody was tired and wet. It had taken about an hour. It was grueling. But they had made it to the top.

16

Behr

The valley floor was quiet.

Too quiet.

When the helicopters disappeared, so did the noise. Behr didn't notice it at first. He was too busy staring at the rugged terrain, trying to secure his footing on the treacherous landscape. He had to watch every step. A twisted ankle was the last thing he needed on a mission, which could happen if he wasn't careful. It seemed like rocks covered every square inch of the valley floor. There were beige-colored ones the size of baseballs and softballs and boulders, and others that looked sturdy until you stepped on them. Then the rocks would either sink in the muck by the fast-flowing river or would teeter back and forth, tossing soldiers who couldn't keep their balance.

It was just another unexpected twist to the mission. Like many of the soldiers, Behr had studied the satellite images, which made the mountains appear ordinary. There was nothing to suggest just how steep they were, or how the surrounding peaks towered over the Shok Valley. That was the first thing that struck Behr after he jumped off the Chinook. *You got to be kidding,* he thought. They almost needed climbing harnesses and climbing rope and carabiners and even climbing holds to make it to their objective. These mountains were part of the Hindu Kush, with some of the highest elevations in the world. It should have been expected.

But as daunting as the terrain was, it was more unsettling to Behr that he didn't hear noise. *Something just doesn't feel right,* he thought. There was a compound built into the mountains. It was a little after 7 a.m. From intelligence reports, he knew people lived there. He should be able to hear some clatter in the distance. Maybe the *baaaaa* of goats. Or villagers talking. Instead, the valley was still.

As he moved toward the objective, Behr noticed that Carter was snapping pictures of the mountains.

"Man, they're beautiful," said Carter, momentarily breaking the silence.

Behr nodded in agreement. They were breathtaking—if you didn't have to scale sheer rock faces with an automatic weapon and sixty pounds of equipment strapped to your back. *Stay focused,* he thought.

When they reached the base of the mountain where the targets were located, the soldiers split into teams. Behr's squad of Walton, Carter, CK, and Rhymer followed Morales, Walding, and Sanders up the terraces leading to the compound.

The climb was strenuous, and they moved slowly and steadily as they edged up the mountain. Soon Morales, Walding, and Sanders disappeared from sight. Behr's unit, though, was still struggling. And there were times when Behr didn't know if he could take another step. But he kept pushing and pushing—just like he did during Selection. He wasn't going to give up.

They had been climbing for what seemed like an hour and were about halfway up the mountain when he heard Morales's voice crackle over the radio.

[Part 2]

CONTACT

17

Morales

The valley had erupted in an unrelenting wall of fire.

A few minutes earlier, Morales had reached a position where he could see the village. Before he took another step, he glimpsed a man running between buildings with a sandbag over his shoulder—a sign he had an RPG. Seconds later, he observed three more people running—and they all had AK-47s.

Man, I just went through this thing two weeks ago when I shot the dude in the gut, Morales thought.

He knew what to do. He propped up his M4. Zeroed in on the targets. He took a second to warn his team: "I got three bad guys running with guns," he said over the radio.

Then Morales squeezed the trigger and fired several rounds, hitting two insurgents.

Now his team was in the middle of a firefight—unlike anything he had ever experienced.

"Holy shit," Morales shouted.

Bullets were flying everywhere, mostly coming from the surrounding high ground. Morales turned and saw Carter standing next to him. Instinctively, he slammed Carter against the rocks for protection. He knew they had to find cover fast because there was no protection where they were standing.

"You climb up and I'll cover you," Morales told Carter.

Morales kept firing while the team moved to a ledge above. *I hope there's cover up there,* he thought. The attack was extremely well coordinated. He could hear the sharp, nonstop *crack-crack-crack-crack-crack* of AK-47s and PKM machines guns, and the thunder of RPGs exploding below. The rounds came from all directions. The insurgents had been waiting for them.

In training, Morales was taught that in a firefight, you move forward not back. So when all the men were up on the ledge, he climbed to the next terrace. But when he made it, he glanced at Carter, who was trying to drag a soldier in a tan uniform. The soldier was facedown in the dirt. Bullets were kicking up dirt near them.

Morales's heart was racing. *What the fuck?* he thought.

18

Behr

Behr had been in firefights before but nothing like this. The attack was something out of a Hollywood war movie. The barrage was sustained, coordinated, and professional. It was coming from mud-colored buildings on ledges forty feet directly above them. It was coming from ridgelines on a mountain directly across the wadi. It was coming from every direction. Bullets whizzed by their heads and impacted within inches of their feet. His team was clearly in the enemy's crosshairs.

Shit, I have to find cover, he thought.

Behr kept firing his rifle as he looked for protection. Out of the corner of his eye, he spotted Walton and CK, who'd found shelter in a crevice along a thirty-foot-high rock face that ran the length of the ledge. But when Behr tried to fit in, he discovered there wasn't enough room for all of them. His lower body was exposed, and bullets kicked up dirt near his feet.

At that point, Behr knew he would get hit in the foot or leg if he stayed there. This isn't going to work.

So he made a quick decision: He stepped out from the wall, took a knee, and started shooting his M4 in the direction of the heaviest fire while he turned his head from side to side looking for cover. But there was no safe spot—at least as far as he could see.

"Damn it," he muttered.

Here he was, in the open—a perfect target, he thought. And that's when he felt a sharp pain in his pelvis—a sensation that sent shock waves through his entire body. It was excruciating and Behr had a high threshold for pain. In training, a sergeant had used a fifty-thousand-volt Taser on him and other recruits to show how effective it was in controlling unruly people. Behr held up better than most recruits; he didn't drop to the floor like some of the others. But this pain was different. It was the equivalent of being Tased and smashed on the hip with a baseball bat at the same time. He was prostrate on the ground while bullets continued to fly over his head.

"Oh, shit. I just got shot," he screamed.

He wasn't sure anyone heard him over the noise. But at that moment he knew he was "combat ineffective." He was useless. Unable even to lift his rifle, Behr was bleeding profusely. His whole body still reverberated from the shot, and he couldn't move his right leg at all. An hour into the mission and only minutes into the firefight, his limb was dead—and he knew the round had hit a dangerous part of the body. The pelvis contains a number of arteries, including the femoral. If the femoral had been severed, he would die within minutes. Was he bleeding out? He couldn't be sure. Shurer would know, but he was down in the wadi with Ford. And with the heavy fire, would Shurer even make it up the hill to treat him? Just then, he heard a voice.

"Hey, Dillon," Carter said. "Hang in there, man. It's going to be okay."

Carter grabbed Behr under his left shoulder and tried to move him out of the line of fire. But within seconds, Behr felt another sharp pain—this one in his right biceps. He had been shot again. Unlike the pelvic wound, though, this round went straight through without hitting bone. Still, his biceps was bleeding and would need to be treated.

A moment later, Behr heard Morales's voice. "We need to get Ron up here. Fast," he said.

19

Carter

After they dragged Behr to safety, Carter turned his head from side to side, looking for cover. But again, nothing. *Murphy's Law. What could go wrong will go wrong,* Carter thought. He had a point. This was his last mission. And while he had been in combat before, it was nothing like this. This was serious shit.

He knew he was in trouble when, after climbing up on the ledge, he couldn't find any cover. He was in the open. With bullets impacting the dirt and ricocheting off the rocks, he fired his weapon at insurgents scurrying around above him. It was all happening so fast.

When he spotted Walton and CK trying to huddle against a rock wall, he ran in their direction. But when he was a few feet away, he saw CK crumble to the ground. Blood was spilling from his neck and head. He had been hit by at least one round and wasn't moving.

"Holy fucking shit," Carter yelled.

He turned around and instinctively started firing his rifle. He didn't know if his rounds were even hitting anyone. But he was angry and continued to unload to protect their position.

Without warning, he felt a bullet rip through his rucksack. At first he thought he was shot. He felt liquid dripping down his back, and thought it was blood. "Fuckin' bitch," he shouted. But when he began frantically touching his back to feel for the wound, he discovered it was water, not blood, soaking his uniform. The round had penetrated the side of his rucksack, piercing his camera bag. It smashed his camera, batteries, and water bottles. (It felt like warm water because the bullet heated up the bottles.) But his equipment may have saved his life.

It was a brief moment of relief because seconds later, Behr collapsed. Clutching his hip, he was yelling in agony. He was hit, and while Behr was alive, he was still in the line of fire. Bullets were skipping off the dirt inches from his body. There was no way Carter could leave him out there. So, without hesitation, he ran toward the fire to rescue him.

He grabbed Behr's arm and began pulling him toward an overturned tree for protection. "Come on, dude, it's going to be all right," he said.

Carter was struggling to move Behr's body, until Morales arrived at the scene. Together, they dragged him to safety. It was clear Behr was seriously injured. Blood soaked the lower part of his uniform. He was moaning.

It looked bad.

20

Walton

Walton could feel the rush of adrenaline shoot through his body.

That's what happened when you were in the middle of an attack. At any moment, a bullet could end your life or a fellow soldier. You had to think clearly and straight because every decision involved life and death.

Just before the firefight, he had received a detailed situation report, and it seemed that everything was going as planned.

"Blocking positions set, moving into the assault."

Walton knew that Sanders and Walding were almost to the village. They had one more terrace to go. He was about halfway up with Behr, CK, Carter, and Rhymer. Bringing up the rear, Ford's element hadn't even started climbing yet.

An F-15 flew low over the mountain, its engines sending a roar that echoed through the valley. Walton was getting a little concerned that the team was getting too spread out, but they hadn't made contact with the enemy. Everything was going smoothly. Maybe they could get up to the village before Ghafour and his fighters could react.

Then a high volume of fire exploded around him. They were in an open area. As bullets hit inches from his boots, Walton and CK bounded toward a small nook in the mountain. The crevice was the size of two TuffBoxes, too small to offer much cover. The rounds were coming straight in, and one ripped into CK's skull. Walton watched as the Afghan collapsed.

The captain felt like someone had punched him in the gut. CK was an important member of the unit. He liked CK, his upbeat personality. But he had to brush aside any personal feelings. Not when rounds continued to snap overhead and smash into the rock wall.

Walton and his men were stuck in a kill zone, and he had to find protection. Scanning the ledge, he noticed an overhang about fifty feet away. It wasn't much, but it looked like it could provide a little cover. But as he retreated to the area, a round hit Behr. As Carter and Morales moved Behr's body, Walton reached to get the radio from Behr's back so that he could call for help.

Walton was wearing dual communication Peltor headphones, which allowed him to hear transmissions from the team's net and from the satellite net. From the messages going back and forth between the different elements, he knew everybody was taking heavy, accurate fire.

"Assault 2, move up. We have one casualty. We need Ron up here," Walton said.

Walton wanted to keep Shurer out of the fight. He was their only medic and he didn't want him to get hurt. But he had no choice. Behr was seriously hurt and needed medical attention. And Carter and Morales didn't know enough to save him.

Plus, he needed as many guns in the fight as he could muster. Walton quickly got on the air to the commanders back in Jalalabad and Bagram.

"Monster 33. Gremlin 36. Troops in contact."

That meant that Walton and his team were in combat and would need more help.

"We're taking effective machine-gun fire," Walton continued.

"How effective is the fire?" asked the battle captain from Bagram.

"Pretty fucking effective."

Everybody in Afghanistan heard it, and they would continue to tune in and monitor the firefight for the next several hours as Walton and his team fought for their lives.

21

Ford

Even though his team was under fire, Ford was confident that the battle would soon turn in their favor. But he was surprised at the intensity of the attack. How many men did the HIG have? It seemed like they were firing from every possible position.

Just before the firefight, Ford had heard Morales's warning over the radio, and he silently scolded his intelligence sergeant. *Don't tell me what you're seeing,* he had told the team over and over again. *I just want to hear gunfire and I'll figure out what you're seeing.*

When Morales fired his shots, Ford was at the bottom of a trail that zigzagged up the mountain. He knew Sanders and Walding were well ahead and probably close to cresting the hill. Morales was halfway up the mountain with Walton and the rest of the command section.

Soon the whole valley was alive with the snap of bullets and the roar of machine guns. It was the biggest barrage of fire he had ever seen on any trip to Afghanistan or Iraq. Rounds crashed around him, forcing him to scramble for cover.

The nearby commandos pressed themselves against the cliff face. In the dirt, Ford tried to hide behind one of the many large boulders on the floor of the wadi.

The shock of the fire quickly led to amazement as Ford realized these fighters were not your run-of-the-mill guerrillas. These insurgents had training that you didn't typically see in Afghanistan. They returned fire from a knee. And the others waited until the team was spread out and working its way up the hill before opening up. This wasn't the typical "spray and pray" style, hoping Allah wills a bullet to the target. This fire was deadly accurate, steady, and punishing.

"Get that Carl G rocking," Ford shouted at Howard, who also was hiding behind a nearby rock.

The Carl Gustav was an 84mm shoulder-fired recoilless rifle. Like a bazooka, it fired high-explosive rounds that could punch through the thick mud walls of the houses where the HIG fighters were hiding. With Howard working to get the recoilless rifle up and firing, Ford stole a look skyward.

We need to start thumping them. Where are the Apaches?

All around him the commandos and Americans were shooting back. It was impossible to see any of the fighters, so they shot at windows in the buildings, holes in the walls, and clumps of trees or piles of rocks where fighters were likely to be hiding.

Grabbing a single-shot 40mm grenade launcher he was carrying, Ford started to lob grenades into the windows of the houses. After each one, he would snap open the shotgunlike breech of the launcher and slide in another baseball-size shell that resembled an egg sitting in a cup. *Thump*. Reload. *Thump*. Over and over he shot the grenades into the windows.

Soon the *thud* of the grenade was followed by the *whoosh* of an RPG. Looking around, Ford spotted a small commando the team had nicknamed "Joe Pesci" staring at him with a shit-eating grin, his RPG loaded and ready to fire. Soon the pair were smashing windows of houses, hoping to kill or at least suppress the machine gunners on the ridge.

Ford could feel the battle turning. They had taken the first blow, but they were returning fire, and when the Apaches finally started firing, they would be in good shape. A few more minutes and maybe they would have the initiative. Then he heard Walton call him over the radio.

"You need to get up here now."

22

Behr

With bullets zipping by their heads, Morales and Carter dragged Behr twenty feet to the base of a small, uprooted tree near the edge of the cliff. All that protected them was a big clod of dirt and the tree's thick dark trunk. But it was better than being out in the open.

They were stranded, trapped on a wide-open stretch of rock—right in the enemy's line of fire. The entire ledge was about sixty feet long and ten feet wide. A thirty-foot-high rock wall ran the length of the ledge. And perched directly above that back wall were several mud-colored buildings filled with HIG fighters. They were so close the team could hear their voices. There were a few nooks and crevices along the wall, but those indentations offered little cover to the soldiers.

The only place that seemed to offer any protection—a sloping overhead rock—was on the south side of the ledge. And it was there that Walton and Rhyner were pinned. It was a space just eight feet long and ten feet wide—the size of a bedroom. But there was more danger: Part of the ledge was surrounded on three sides by cliffs with vertical drops of nearly sixty feet. One wrong move and a soldier could roll off and fall to his death.

"Calm down, dude, I got you," Morales said to Behr. "It doesn't look that bad."

Behr knew he was lying. He had to be. He'd been shot twice and could barely move. He could feel the blood seeping from his wounds. Morales was no medic, but he knew how to apply a tourniquet. That's something soldiers learn in basic training. Crouching, Behr watched his teammate pull a tourniquet from his medical pouch. Morales was about to work on Behr's arm, but Behr quickly stopped him.

"No, here," he screamed, pointing to his hip.

"Okay, dude, I got it," Morales said.

Morales stared at the wound, then turned to Behr. "It's too high up."

Behr knew what that meant: The tourniquet was useless for his pelvic wound. Tourniquets are used to help control severe blood loss, and are only used as a last resort. You have to put a tourniquet directly above an injury and tie it tight to cut off the blood flow. But tourniquets are mostly used on limbs. Direct pressure is the best way to stop pelvic wounds. And that's what Morales did. He began applying pressure on Behr's pelvis to stop the bleeding. When that failed, he removed a pair of "penny scissors" (scissors so sharp they can cut a penny in half) from his kit and sliced Behr's pants to get a better look at the injury. Morales took a deep breath and pulled out an envelope of QuikClot, a blood-clotting agent in powder form, and poured it on the wound. When the powder mixes with blood, it turns into a cauterizing liquid that helps form a clot—a mass of coagulated blood—to stop the bleeding. Morales continued to work on Behr, applying pressure and more QuikClot—anything to halt the blood flow. Anything to keep Behr alive until Shurer could reach them.

Behr watched as his friend worked feverishly to save his life, and he felt like a burden. He should be on his feet returning fire. Protecting his buddies. Instead, they were taking care of him. Behr began surveying the scene. It was total chaos.

They were trapped on this damn ledge with no way to escape—at least not with the heavy fire.

Then Behr's eyes spotted CK's body. Blood was pouring from an open wound. The interpreter was foaming at the mouth, and pieces of his skull had been splattered on the rocks. *No way he survived. Too much blood.* In fact, so much blood had spilled that the light brown dirt had turned maroon.

Behr saw that Walton was struggling to use his radio, which had fallen to the ground when he was hit. Behr wanted to show the captain how to get it going, but he couldn't move. The captain was shouting something at Morales, who was a few feet away. The gunfire was nonstop, and his pain was growing more and more unbearable. He closed his eyes.

We're never going to get out of here, he thought.

23

Walding

Just before the barrage of gunfire echoed in the valley, Walding had planned to get a quick head count. It was in preparation to storming the nearest compound and setting up a strongpoint while the others climbed the mountain.

But everything had changed.

Pressed against the brick wall on the bank of a ditch, Walding wasn't sure what to do. It was a worst-case scenario: They had been lured into a trap. But the strange part was that none of the bullets were being aimed at Walding or Sanders or their commandos. The insurgents were shooting over them—and directly into the middle of the pack at the team.

"Hey, dude, they're not shooting at us, man," Walding said to Sanders. "I don't think they see us."

Sanders agreed.

"Game on," Walding said.

Walding and Sanders sat there and, like duck hunters at dawn, began picking off insurgents one at a time. "We got them, man," Walding shouted. "They don't have a fucking clue."

The soldiers sat there patiently and waited. And when an insurgent appeared in their scopes, they would pull the trigger. It was like a game of Whac-A-Mole. Still, it was tough to just stay in one spot. They could hear the gunfire. They wanted to help their team. It was one big shitstorm.

They didn't know how long they had been perched in the spot. They just kept firing—until they heard over the radio that Behr was shot, and that they were calling in air strikes on the compound.

To help with the aerial assault, Walding and Sanders tried to mark the buildings for bomb drops. They fired rounds from their rifles into the side of the buildings to let the pilots know which ones to hit. Sanders also marked the buildings with his M203 grenade launcher.

Walding then began to spread his commandos strategically on the side of the mountain so that if one got shot, it would just be one. Not the entire group. But with all that, Walding still faced a dilemma. He recalled that Ford had told him that if the shit hit the fan, "go up and take a house. There's not an enemy out there that can freaking withstand an ODA house stronghold."

Walding considered storming and securing the building in front of him. Maybe they could turn that into a casualty collection point to move people out of harm's way. But he scrapped the idea because it was just too hard to get up the mountain. There was no way the wounded could physically do it. Not with the incessant fire.

The whole team was strung out over the mountain. He was up there with Sanders and a few commandos. Ford was somewhere. Walton was pinned down and Behr was wounded.

All they could do was hold their ground and wait.

24.

Morales

The sound of Morales's voice momentarily cut through the firefight.

"I just got fuckin' shot," he shouted "Damn."

He sounded more pissed off than scared. He needed to keep fighting to protect his fellow soldiers. He didn't want anything to slow him down. Now this? He was injured? It was just bad luck. The whole mission was surrounded by bad karma.

Moments before, Morales had been working feverishly to save Behr's life. He had tried to apply a tourniquet. Even poured QuikClot in the wound and applied pressure.

The whole time, there was no lull in the action. Bullets were kicking up around them, but Morales was in the zone. He focused on Behr like a laser beam.

"Come on, dude, man. You're going to make it. You're going to make it, man."

In the middle of working on Behr, Walton turned to Morales and began shouting something. But with all the gunfire, it was hard to make out the words. It seemed that the captain was asking Morales to fix Behr's radio. It wasn't working and Walton needed to use it.

Morales started shouting instructions to Walton. But the captain couldn't hear him because he was wearing Peltors that were connected to his radio. Morales knew there was probably heavy traffic over Walton's radio. That would have made it even more difficult for the captain to hear him.

"Luis, fix this," Walton yelled again.

Morales spotted the problem. The wire that connected the radio to the antenna was ripped out. All he had to do was reconnect it. It was simple. Just like connecting a cable wire to the back of a television. Twist and turn. He stood up to help Walton when he felt a sharp pain in his thigh. It was like a bodybuilder had just smashed his thigh with a sledgehammer. It knocked him down. He realized what happened when he looked at his bloody thigh.

"I just got shot!" Morales yelled.

"What?" Walton said.

"I just got fuckin' shot," Morales screamed. "Damn."

Morales grabbed his upper thigh around his crotch and began squeezing. He wanted to see if the round had penetrated his femoral artery. The round opened a six-inch long wound and he was losing lots of blood. If his femoral wasn't severed, it was pretty close.

Morales was on the ground near the edge of the cliff. His only cover was that small tree. That was it. And he would have to share the cover with Behr. There wasn't much room. Morales continued taking care of Behr—even with his own wounds—and firing his rifle. But now the pain was so great that he grimaced and shook his head. He was going to beat it. Deal with it. He was going to stay in control. *A Morales never quits,* he thought. From his grandfather to his father, they overcame obstacles to make a name for themselves in the military. That was his goal, too. He was going to carry on the family tradition.

Scanning the enemy positions, he noticed that most of the fire was coming from a mountain on the side of the ridge opposite to where the team was trapped. It was about a football field away.

"Kyle, the guys who are shooting at us are over there," he said, pointing to the mountain.

Before Walton had a chance to respond, Morales felt a knifelike pain in his ankle. No one had to tell him what had just happened. He knew right away.

"Are you fucking kidding me?" Morales shouted. A round had ripped apart his ankle. Now he was really angry. He'd been shot twice, and the pain was excruciating. It was nothing like he had ever experienced in his life. Parts of his flesh were excoriated—he could see tendons, bone. Pools of blood soaked his uniform. But Morales didn't panic. *Keep cool, keep your bearings,* he thought.

But now there were limits to what he could do. When he got shot in the thigh, he told himself it was fixable. He could still move his leg. It wasn't broken. When he was hit in the ankle, he knew he was screwed. That wasn't fixable. He was immobile. The irony wasn't lost on Morales. A strong, athletic Green Beret, he worked out all the time—push-ups, sit-ups, weights—and ran hard, not jogged. It was always faster and stronger. He pushed his body to the limit and prided himself on his endurance. Now he was helpless.

25

Master Sergeant Jim Lodyga

With gunfire erupting in the valley, Master Sergeant Jim Lodyga had to rethink his plans.

When ODA 3336 started toward their objective, Lodyga and his team, including Eric Martin, Staff Sergeant Nick McGarry, and Sergeant First Class Sergio Martinez, peeled off toward the other side of the wadi.

It was their job to scale the opposite mountain and set up a machine gun to cover ODA 3336's ascent.

From the wadi, the team could see a massive two-story mud-walled building and six other buildings clustered nearby. That was their target. The plan called for them to climb the mountain and clear that village while they also set up a machine gun to cover ODA 3336's assault across the wadi.

Lodyga had broken his ODA and commandos into fire teams. McGarry, the team's senior weapons sergeant, was leading one group, and Martin, the team's communications sergeant, was leading the other. With McGarry's Alpha team concealed and covering the mountain, Lodyga sent a half-dozen commandos forward to the cliff. It was a fifty-meter sprint over the rocks. When the Afghans got to the base, they started to climb.

The imagery of the mountain hadn't done it justice. It was massive, and even the Afghans, accustomed to living and fighting in the terrain, were having problems. They had made it about a quarter of the way up, clawing for every inch, when the first shots echoed across the valley.

Lodyga knew immediately that ODA 3336 was in a fight. The fire started with a few pops and then it quickly built into a roar. Lodyga and his teammates knew the sound well.

A few months earlier, ODA 3312 had been in a similar ambush. They were on a reconnaissance patrol near Gowardesh in the mountains. Their mission was to clear the valley of insurgents who had been attacking Coalition forces. But while on patrol, in January 2008, they were attacked. It was a brutal firefight, and one of the Green Berets, Staff Sergeant Robert Miller, was killed while providing fire for his teammates to escape. (Miller was posthumously awarded the Medal of Honor in 2010.) To Lodyga, the Shok Valley's landscape—and mission—reminded them of the earlier operation.

They weren't surprised by the Shok Valley ambush and knew all the insurgents' tactics.

"Squat hold right here. We need to see what is developing," Lodyga told his team. "It sounds like these guys are getting hammered."

As the machine-gun and rifle fire built to a crescendo, Martinez, the team's medic, could see children running down a trail away from the fighting. Lodyga could hear the radio calls from ODA 3336 as they tried to call in air strikes.

Lodyga knew he had to wait on his objective in order to figure out what was going on with ODA 3336. After talking to McGarry, he decided to put his mission on hold because he didn't want to get strung out climbing the mountain and not be able to help if ODA 3336 called.

Finally, Lodyga heard Ford calling over the radio. He told them that ODA 3336 was getting hammered and they needed Lodyga's team to start moving to help.

"Things are bad," Ford said. "You might want to come over here."

If we are not going to make it to my target, we have to go up and help Ford, Lodyga reasoned. He made the call to abandon his objective and started moving to help his brothers across the valley.

26

Wurzbach

From the beginning, Wurzbach didn't like the mission. Too many obstacles. Fighting uphill. Landing in a valley. It felt all wrong, and had the potential to be a "really bad day."

Now, pinned down as he was by heavy enemy fire on a hill, his dire feeling was looking like a prophecy. *We're never going to get out of here,* he thought. He hoped he was wrong. But with everything that had already gone awry from the time they jumped off the helicopter, he wasn't sure.

First, when the Chinook pitched forward, Wurzbach fell out of the bird and almost landed on his head. After scanning the landscape, he saw that the intelligence was all wrong. They said the weather was "quite pleasant" in the valley. It was icy and cold. They said the wadi was dry. But they ran into a river and Wurzbach had to wade through the water to get to the other side. And when they got to their positions, the satellite imagery was inaccurate. *All bullshit,* he thought.

His team had to find a new route to get to their blocking position. That was critical. A blocking position denies the enemy access to a given area or prevents the enemy's advance in a given direction. Essentially, Wurzbach's team would have to seal off the valley and protect the rest of the unit. But first, they had to find a way to get in position.

When a pilot reported that he had glimpsed a path that led up into the northeastern part of the canyon, they took it. They humped up that route until Wurzbach could no longer see the assault team. At that point, he began moving his team, which included his interpreter, Noodles, and several commandos, into position.

His goal was to get his team to higher ground, where they would be midline or above the village. That way they would have a clear vantage point. So if something happened—a firefight erupted—his men would be shooting on a more even plane, rather than shooting up. It would enable them to see better in general—a critical factor for a blocking team.

Wurzbach pushed forward about three hundred meters and found a patch of rocky ground. It wasn't perfect, but at least his team would be able to cover the assault team and help close off the valley during the operation. Just as he was ready to radio the assault team to tell them he was in position, dirt kicked up around him.

"Did anybody see that?" he asked his men.

They all looked at Wurzbach like he was crazy. Nothing.

Wurzbach grew uncomfortable with the location. He glanced up and tried to decide whether to move up to even higher ground. Before he had a chance to make up his mind, he noticed more dirt flying up—and he realized what was happening.

"They're fucking shooting at us," he shouted.

"I know. I've only been saying that for ten minutes," Noodles said to him

"Why didn't you say it to me?" Wurzbach asked.

"The commandos thought I was being a girl."

He was stunned. *What the fuck?* he thought. "I don't care what they think. I'm the fuckin' one you have to talk to."

Wurzbach ordered everyone to take cover behind a shoulder-high rock wall. It wasn't great, but it was better than being out in the open. Wurzbach crouched and scanned the terrain. He could see people up in the village about six hundred meters away. But they quickly disappeared in a building. One man was carrying a backpack with part of a warhead sticking out—a telltale sign he was carrying an RPG. Wurzbach pulled the trigger of his M4. He was unsure whether he hit him. Without warning, other men began running between buildings. He opened fire on them. Again, he wasn't sure if he hit anyone.

Wurzbach turned and stared at his team: Noodles and three commandos. Another member of his team, Staff Sergeant Dan Plants, was set up about two hundred meters down the canyon by a big tree. His job was to cover Wurzbach's team, to make sure nobody could sneak up on them.

Sitting behind the rock wall, Wurzbach radioed the assault team. He told them what happened and that the HIG fighters had disappeared in the buildings and rocks.

But then more rounds began impacting the dirt surrounding his position. At one point, the bullets landed inches in front of him, and the dirt and rocks kicked up in his face. Wurzbach was irritated. *I have to move to a better position where I can scan and try to find them, see where they are shooting from.* He didn't see any muzzle flashes. Wurzbach pushed forward to a spot where the canyon dropped down, and found a broken-down goat shed. He crawled into it and used it for cover. His eyes scanned the compound, trying to figure out from where they were shooting. "Where the fuck are they?" he asked. He stayed there for several minutes. When he crawled out, he heard gunfire reverberating in the valley.

Wurzbach sprinted to a small tree at the apex of the rock wall that he had been using for cover, and then turned his attention back to the compound. That's when he discovered what appeared to be a bunker complex—with at least three different openings for firing ports. He kept his eyes on the target, trying to identify muzzle flashes coming from the openings. Wurzbach also was scanning the village itself, staring into the dark windows and doors to see if he could see something. But whoever was there, they were on their game.

He could tell from the radio traffic that his friends were in trouble. Behr and Morales were wounded. He heard Walton's voice frantically telling commanders they were stuck. They had nowhere to maneuver. Wurzbach was pinned, too. Plus, he couldn't just abandon his position. With no way to reach his teammates, the only thing he could do was wait.

27

Howard

Like some great hunter on an African safari, Howard waited for his elephant gun.

He was going hunting with the only weapon the team had that could possibly penetrate the mud-walled compounds protecting the enemy fighters: the Carl G.

He didn't know how long he and his commandos had been trapped at the base of the mountain, trying to make their way up to help their wounded comrades. They were held back by hellish fire, but that only made Howard more determined. Maybe it was his New England stubbornness, Yankee roots dating back to the American Revolution, but Howard was going to find a way to get the job done.

Before the first rounds were even fired, Howard and his commandos had moved to the far side of the wadi hoping to set up so that they could get a clear shot at the houses above. Peering up at the edge of the cliff, he could see men running along the ledge. But he couldn't see any guns through the ten-power scope mounted on his SR-25 sniper rifle. People always move when you show up in helicopters at a village. People are going to walk around and tell the others something is going on. That is to be expected. As long as they don't have a gun, you can't shoot them.

But when one of his commandos started yelling and pointing, he knew something was wrong. Howard strained to see what the Afghan was pointing at, slowly scanning each man through the scope. Without an interpreter, though, he had no idea what the Afghan was saying.

Howard called into his radio: "Hey, I need a terp over here."

His eyes continued to slowly scan the ridge for any men carrying guns. Frustrated, Howard turned to a commando. "I can't see what you're pointing to. I can't see it."

Without warning, he was caught in a maelstrom of fire. Pressing himself against the boulders in the wadi, Howard tried to find cover. Any cover. Jamming as much of himself as he could behind a basketball-size rock, he got behind his sniper rifle and searched for a target.

No one was visible.

The fighters who were up in the ridge moments before were now behind cover and concealed. He started to methodically scan the buildings, looking into windows and at holes and creases in the wall for muzzle flashes or smoke. Anything that would give away their position. All around him the others were shooting at the buildings and the windows, even bushes where they thought someone might hide. Anything to suppress the fighters.

A few minutes into the fight, Howard saw Ford start calling for a cease-fire by waving his hand up and down in front of his face. Sometimes you have to stop shooting to make sure you're actually getting shot at and to figure out where the enemy fire is coming from.

During the previous rotation, Howard remembered how they had hit a target with the Afghan National Police. As the police got out of the vehicles, one of the Afghan officers accidently fired his gun into the dirt. No one shot at them, but everybody on the back side of the house started shooting. It took a few minutes to figure out that no one was under attack.

Soon all the commandos had stopped firing—except one. Howard stopped scanning and turned to him: "Cease fire. Cease fire."

Howard knew the commando understood him. It was one of the first commands they taught their Afghan counterparts. But the man kept shooting.

"Cease fire. Cease fire," Howard said again.

Finally, he grabbed the Afghan, punching him in the shoulder. The Afghan turned and looked at him in amazement.

"Cease fire!"

Howard had barely gotten the words out when two rounds hit a rock in front of them. Both men dove behind the rock.

"Never mind," Howard said. "I don't know where you are shooting at, but keep doing it."

That's when he called for the commando carrying the Carl Gustav.

"Bring me my rocket."

He called the gun a rocket because the commandos knew that word. In seconds, the commando ran up to Howard and handed him the green tube. It was heavy and the Afghan was happy to get rid of it.

Fired from a pistol grip and trigger, it is aimed with a massive black optical sight. It can be fired standing, sitting, kneeling, or prone.

"Ammo. Ammo," Howard called next.

Sanders and Walding had identified a two-story building that overlooked the whole wadi. Walton and Rhyner had called over and over again trying to get the pilots to drop bombs on it. The bombs would drop to the left or right of it, but never on it. From inside, the fighters could keep up a steady barrage.

Calling down to Howard, Ford wanted him to use the Carl G to mark the building. The Hellfire air-to-surface missiles from the attack helicopters were bringing buildings down, and Rhyner and Sergeant Robert Gutierrez of ODA 3312 were trying to talk the Apaches onto the other buildings where the fighters were hiding. But the Air Force JTACs had no way of identifying the target. The Carl G was big enough that the rounds could be seen from the air, making it perfect for marking targets.

"I'm going to shoot and try and mark this building that we're trying to blow up," Howard called up to Rhyner. "So tell me when they are looking."

In the distance, he glimpsed two Afghan commandos with heavy rounds attached to their backs running toward him. When they reached him, he removed the rounds he had tied to their body armor with nylon webbing. He broke open the breech and slid the round into the tube. The gun can fire a number of different rounds from high explosive to antitank and even smoke. He was shooting high explosive. With his sights on the building, Howard checked to make sure no one was in the back-blast area and then fired.

The round slashed across the valley, smashing into the building.

Howard fired three rounds from the wadi, but the building was so solid it was like he had fired a pebble. But the pilots from the Apaches spotted the rounds and launched Hellfires that would soon level the building. Finished, he called the commandos back.

"Okay, take my gun," Howard said, handing the tube to the Afghan and grabbing his sniper rifle again.

Taking up position behind the rocks again, he started to fire through the windows of the remaining houses. He had a feeling it was going to be a long day.

28

Walton

Walton knew their survival probably depended on getting air cover. He glanced at Rhyner, who was huddled behind a small tree at the edge of the cliff. Then he yelled at the JTAC: Start bringing in close air support.

Sanders had identified a large mud-walled building close to where he and Walding had set up, and told Walton he needed CAS—close air support—in a hurry.

"Bomb that shit," Walton yelled.

Rhyner started to put together a nine-line, a script used by pilots and spotters with all the information needed to target an air strike. It included the type of target, the location of friendly and enemy forces, and other information. The idea is that both sides, the pilots and the spotters, have a common script that can be used during a stressful combat situation.

Rhyner turned to Walton. "Hey I need your initials. This is danger close," he said.

The building was close to where Sanders and Walding were positioned. In order to hit targets so close to friendly units, a commander must approve the request with his initials.

"Dave, are you sure, man?" Walton said. "You're danger close, man."

"Fuck it," Sanders told Walton. "Hit it."

"All right," Walton said, giving Rhyner his initials to carry out the attack.

Sanders, using his M203 grenade launcher, marked the building with a round as two Apache gunships flew in side by side and unloaded their rockets and missiles into the building. The explosion was massive and Walton was sure his men were dead.

"DAVE, DAVE, DAVE, YOU OKAY?" Walton shouted into the radio.

"Keep it coming," Sanders radioed back.

"Fuck it. Hit it again," Walton furiously barked at Rhyner.

This time, a fighter thundered out of the sky and strafed the building with guns, followed by a bomb strike. It was so close, Walton had to open his mouth to let the concussion clear through his body.

"Keep putting fires all along that mountain," Walton said after the last blast. "Bring every bomb in danger close and use my initials."

"This is danger close. I am going to need your initials," the pilot said.

"KMW, motherfucker," Walton said, referring to the initials of his name. "Don't ask me again. Everything is danger close."

If they were going to survive, they needed those fighters to give them some breathing room.

29

Carter

Carter was no medic.

Yet here he was, trapped on a cliff and pressed into medical duty. Behr was seriously wounded. So was Morales. And Shurer was nowhere in sight. Unknown to Carter, Walton was a paramedic. But the captain was so tied up on the radio helping Rhyner with the air strikes he didn't have time to take care of the wounded.

The wounds were horrific. Morales's thigh and ankle were ripped open. Behr's uniform was bathed in blood. Carter had been administering first aid to the two wounded soldiers. It was a less than ideal scenario. Although Carter had some first-aid training, he was rusty, and this wasn't the time or place for on-the-job training. Plus, he had never administered first aid to a seriously wounded soldier. And it was important for a medic to treat a wounded soldier right away and get him to a hospital as quickly as possible. Studies showed that the quicker a medic can treat and stabilize a seriously wounded soldier on the battlefield—and get him to the hospital—the more likely the soldier was to survive.

In this case, the clock had been ticking.

Carter had no idea how long they had been trapped. The fire was continuous. Under these conditions, you lost all concept of time. How long had they been under attack? One hour? Maybe. Carter wasn't sure and he was worried. They had to get help for the wounded soldiers. And the only way to do that was to find a way off the mountain before everyone was killed.

He knew Walton was trying to find a solution. He'd overheard him on the radio with Bagram. From what he could tell, they were trying to set up more air strikes. Bombs kept falling, but they hadn't stopped the insurgents. From the helicopter traffic, he heard that almost every building had fifteen to twenty HIG fighters on rooftops with guns bristling out of windows. The buildings were built with flat roofs and made of rocks and mud. Many of the buildings in the compound sat on the edge of the cliffs overlooking the valley. The enemy had the vantage points. *We're fucked,* he thought.

Carter knew they were in a precarious situation. They were cut off from the other ODAs and most of the commandos. They were alone, and the insurgents probably sensed that they were close to inflicting major damage on an elite Army unit. If that happened, HIG commanders could use it as a recruiting tool.

The pilots needed to be precise. One wrong coordinate and a bomb could explode on their position. They had to be careful.

But without air support, they were doomed.

30

Shurer

Shurer had to reach Walton's team. He knew his teammates had life-threatening wounds. But he was pinned down by fire. To get up there, he had to run at least seventy meters and then climb the mountain to their position.

Since the first bursts of gunfire, the medic had been tied up treating wounded soldiers at the bottom of the trail leading up the mountain. His first call for help came a few minutes into the battle when a commando told him someone in his squad had been hit. So Shurer bolted about thirty meters in front of him and spotted a commando frantically trying to take off his pants.

"What's going on here?" he asked.

The soldier was muttering and Shurer couldn't understand a word he was saying. He turned his head from side to side, looking for an interpreter, and couldn't find one. By the time he looked back, the commando had pulled his pants down to his ankles and Shurer discovered the problem. The bullet had grazed the commando's skin just inside his left thigh and burned his testicle. He was incredibly lucky. While the round didn't penetrate the commando's body, it was close enough that it burned. Shurer examined the commando closely and determined there was no serious damage or bleeding.

He stared into the commando's face: "You're okay," he shouted over the noise. "Pull your pants up and get back in the fight."

The soldier just nodded his head yes. But Shurer could see the sheer terror in his eyes. It almost looked like the commando was going to cry.

With the soldier back in action, AJ, an interpreter, reached Shurer and they quickly turned their attention back to the commandos. They began resetting the squad, making sure the commandos acted as a cohesive fighting unit. At that point, they weren't doing this. Some were trying to hide behind big rocks and not firing their weapons at all. Then, through all the clutter, Shurer heard the high-pitched whistling of an incoming RPG. When he looked up, he saw it explode about seventy-five meters in front of him.

The next thing he heard was a chorus of "Ron, Ron, Ron, Ron, Ron" echoing down the valley. At that moment Shurer knew that Staff Sergeant Ryan Wallen had been injured. When they were training the Afghans, Wallen would bring each commando on his team to Shurer and would jokingly instruct them that if he was hurt in combat, they were to "find Ron. This is what he looks like." Wallen said it was a joke, but Shurer knew there was a method to his madness. No soldier wants to be wounded in the field without a medic. Timely care could mean the difference between life and death.

But the training paid off because Shurer knew who the injured soldier was in advance. So he packed up his kit and ran until he reached Wallen, who was clearly pissed off that he was hit and couldn't return fire.

"Fuck, look at this," Wallen said, pointing to his neck.

Shurer analyzed the wound: Wallen was bleeding from his neck. So he pulled out gauze and started examining the wound to assess the damage. Wallen's airways looked fine. There was no vascular damage. The medic could tell that the wound wasn't life threatening, but the blood was still flowing.

"You're going to be okay," he said, wrapping gauze on the wound. He began exerting pressure to stop the bleeding.

"Are you sure?" Wallen asked.

"Yes. I'm sure."

The fire was nonstop. Shurer didn't think it could get much worse. Until he heard a frantic call from Walton on the radio: Behr, Morales, and CK had been hit and they needed Shurer up there fast.

"Did you hear that?" Wallen asked.

"Yeah. I heard it."

Shurer glanced at Wallen. His bleeding was minimal.

"I'm good," Wallen said. "Go get them."

Getting to Walton's team, though, posed a great risk. A medic is taught not to put himself in any unnecessary danger. He has to stay alive so other soldiers can live. But it had reached a point in the battle where he had to go. So Shurer grabbed his bag and headed into the fire.

31

Walton

Walton recognized the sound: a sharp scream. Another soldier had been shot.

When he turned his head, he saw Rhyner clutching his leg and blood on his pants. There was no one else to take care of him, so Walton tore open the airman's pants to expose the wound. He feared the round hit an artery. But luckily, he had only been grazed.

"You're okay. You're okay, man. Just keep going."

Rhyner was shaken. But Walton needed him to be alert. His job was too critical. He was the pilot's eyes on the ground. He was responsible for coordinating air strikes. Find a target and lead the pilots to the right positions. But Rhymer seemed a little shaky. He was young and this was his first major battle. So Walton had to keep tabs on him. In fact, Walton was bogged down. As the commander, he had to coordinate the mission. But having to help with the air strikes was an added responsibility.

After treating Rhyner's wound, the medic in Walton urged him to check on CK.

He had been putting it off as he frantically radioed commanders about the battle, trying to get reinforcements. In this mind, he knew CK was dead. His body was pinned up against the mountain in an open area near the crevice. But what if he was really alive and just wounded? Walton had to find out.

Firing some rounds hoping to suppress the enemy fighters, he raced from the ledge to CK's body. Rounds skipped off the rocks as he weaved his way to the Afghan. One bullet struck his rifle, smashing the flash suppressor, a cigar-size tube on the end of his barrel.

Grabbing CK's body armor, he turned him over. Walton could see that the terp's eyes had rolled back in his head. Blood was coming out of his mouth, ears, and nose. There was no pulse. CK was dead. Rolling the Afghan's body for cover, Walton started barking at the commandos nearby. Only a few were firing. The rest were pressed against the rock face. "Just don't stand there. Fire," he screamed.

Walton knew they were in trouble. Accurate fire was hitting all around them. There was little cover. He knew Behr was bleeding out. Morales was seriously wounded, too. But scanning the ledge, he knew there was a bigger problem. Behr and Morales were still too much in the open. While the overturned tree had provided some protection, it wasn't enough—and with the enemy snipers, it was just a matter of time before they picked them off. One wrong move and they would be dead.

Walton bolted back to his original position and grabbed Carter.

"Here's what we're going to do," he told Carter. "I am going to go right and you're going to go left. We're going to get up and grab these guys and drag them back."

"Okay," Carter said.

"ONE. TWO. THREE."

Both men bolted to the wounded soldiers and dragged them to the position underneath the sloping rock. The spot wasn't that much better than the tree, but it offered some cover. Huddled near the rock wall, Walton grabbed Carter's hand.

"Make a fist," he ordered, putting Carter's hand near the wound on Behr's pelvis. "Press it here as hard as you can."

Walton then rushed back to CK's body and dragged it to their position in order to shield Morales and Behr from some of the fire. Before leaving the Afghan, he checked for vital signs again.

Nothing.

Walton just didn't want to believe that CK was dead. He took a deep breath and finally called over the radio that the Afghan had been killed. And for a moment the radio, which had been so busy with traffic, fell silent.

32

Ford

Ford found Shurer and together they bounded up the hill.

All of the team's firepower was at the bottom of the hill. There was no point in going up the hill. He urged Walton to move the wounded down, but to no avail. The switchbacks leading to the ledge where the team was trapped were so narrow that the two were having difficulty navigating them quickly. They were weighed down by body armor and gear, but there was no time to waste. They had to get up there fast. It was almost like a game of leapfrog. They would run and climb, stopping only to help the other up the steep terraces. It was grueling and dangerous. Bullets were hitting the rocks.

Meeting Williams on the way up, they spotted a group of insurgents moving to get in firing position. Shouldering their rifles, Williams and Ford opened fire, cutting down the fighters and buying a little more time or their teammates trapped above.

Climbing over the last ridge, Ford finally reached the ledge where the team was trapped. Carter was trying to treat Morales and Behr. The rocks around them were soaked in blood. Behr was pale white. Carter was exerting pressure on Morales's leg trying to keep it from bleeding. Morales appeared composed.

Ford stared at CK, then turned to Walton, who was pressed against the rock wall talking on the radio. With no medics on the ledge, Ford figured Walton, a trained EMT, would be working on the wounded.

CK's body was set up front.

But the captain, almost sensing Ford's reaction, spoke first: "He is fucking dead, dude."

"Are you sure?" Ford snapped. He knew never to assume that someone is dead.

"Yeah. I'm sure. I just checked."

Ford could tell Walton was pissed that he was questioning him, but CK was his friend, and he wanted visual confirmation that he was dead. CK's body was still out in the open and nobody had even checked him. Ford just wanted to ensure that they didn't need to treat him.

Ford and Walton could be stubborn. They wanted things done *their* way. But to make Ford happy, Walton put a knee down on CK's body and pulled off his glove to check him again; some blood in his mouth began bubbling.

"Look, it's bubbles," Ford said.

"It's me," Walton said. "It's my knee on his chest. I'm pushing out the last bit of air in his chest."

He was dead.

Fuck, Ford thought. It was true. He turned his head away from CK's body and noticed that the terps were up against the wall doing nothing. There was almost no cover.

Staying close to the wall, Ford started to think about how to improve their position. He noticed Rhyner sitting by a tree near the ledge facing away from the village. It was Rhyner's job to get the Apaches and F-15s above to drop bombs and fire rockets at the bunkerlike buildings above them.

But the young airman looked stunned. To Ford, who was unaware of Rhyner's having been grazed by a bullet, he appeared to be in shock.

"You okay?" he asked.

"I'm doing all right," Rhyner replied.

Ford knew the other ODA was calling in air strikes, but Rhyner wasn't. And the helicopters weren't doing anything. Their ordnance just hit the side of the buildings and wasn't leaving a dent.

"You need to get CAS going. Get some fast movers in here. Get the helicopters out of here. They're worthless."

Rhyner still seemed kind of dazed. He looked at Ford, then back to a map and then the radio, then looked back at Ford.

It was the biggest firefight Ford had been in, and this was his eighth deployment. It was Rhyner's first. He could only imagine what Rhyner was thinking or feeling.

"Hey, if you're calling for fire, you need to face the objective," Ford said. "I need you to turn around."

Moving back toward Shurer, he wanted an assessment on Morales and Behr.

"Urgent," Shurer said, by now covered in blood as he tried to stop the flow from the massive wound in Behr's pelvis.

That meant they had no more than thirty minutes before Behr was likely to die. He was as white as ghost and Ford didn't think he was going to make it. He had to start getting these guys off the ledge. Looking around, he realized that he had lost all situational awareness. It was total chaos. He didn't see Sanders or Walding on the ledge and had no idea where they were.

"Hey, where are they at? Sanders? Walding?"

"Up there," said Walton, pointing higher up the mountain toward the village.

Ford immediately signaled them on the radio. He was afraid they would get cut off since they were right by the village. And if they were cut off or got pinned down, he knew there was no way they could get down.

"Come down to us," he told Walding before turning his attention back to the ledge.

Walton looked at Ford. "Are we still going to continue the assault?"

Ford knew ODA 3312 was pinned down in the wadi and they still weren't getting enough close air support. He had no idea what ODA 3325 was doing, but their objective was in another part of the valley.

"No. The assault is done. We need to get these guys packaged and headed toward an LZ. Until we get CAS rolling and get the casualties out of here the assault is done."

"Okay, Scott," Walton said. "Get these fucking casualties out of here."

"I'll take care of it," Ford said.

Ford figured Ghafour was already gone. And if he wasn't, they would get him with air strikes—as soon as the fighters got going. Heading back to Rhyner near the tree, Ford hadn't gotten his point across to the man the first time. And getting air cover to relieve some of the pressure was quickly becoming the difference between surviving and dying on the cliff.

Ford was pissed off.

"I am going to throw you off the mountain," he barked, getting in Rhyner's face. "We need to get it rolling."

The Ledge
(April 6, 2008)

After hours of fighting, the team eventually got trapped on a small ledge over-looking the valley 60 feet below. Three of the Special Forces soldiers were gravely wounded.

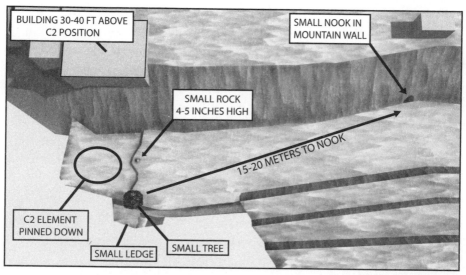

Top View of C2 Position

Detail View of C2 Position

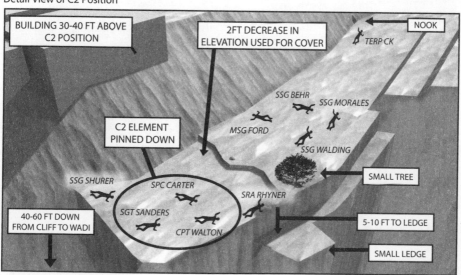

[Part 3]

THE LEDGE

33

Behr

Behr knew he was in deep shit. Shurer had finally arrived, but Behr was struggling to maintain consciousness. *Helpless,* he thought. *I'm fucking helpless.*

And he was feeling guilty.

Not only was he unable to contribute to the ongoing firefight, he was drawing somebody else to his aid. Fellow soldiers were trying to protect him at great risk to their own safety. He knew Morales had probably been shot because of him. He felt like a burden. You're not supposed to get shot. You're just dragging other people down.

Now Behr's memory was becoming cloudy. He couldn't even recall the soldiers who'd moved him to the new spot on the ridge. He opened his eyes, but everything seemed blurry. He noticed his only protection was a nearby rock wall. That was it. But it didn't seem to be providing much cover at all. Not with the bullets impacting near his body.

Lying in the rock-hard dirt with half his uniform cut off, Behr was too weak to do anything. While his arm hurt, it was his pelvis that worried him. It was throbbing, and when the pain welled up, he would bite down hard on his lip. Someone on the team had removed his body armor to make it easier to exert pressure on his pelvis to stop the bleeding. The reality was that Behr was slipping into shock. If that happened, his body would start shutting down.

In the minutes after Behr was shot, his adrenaline had kicked in, and this helped keep him alert. But now he was drowsy. He blamed this, in part, on the morphine. Each Special Forces soldier carried a morphine-filled needle he could inject if he was wounded in combat. Someone on the team had injected Behr. While the drug relieved some of his excruciating pain, it left him disoriented. He had lost all concept of time. He was unsure how long he had been in this spot, or how long the battle had been raging.

He only knew that Shurer was there beside him. He noticed the serious look on the medic's face. *Not a good sign,* Behr thought.

Shurer was on top of Behr, pulling gauze and other material out of his kit, starting an IV, and then putting pressure on the wound. While he worked, Behr glimpsed a building on the other side of the valley. He spotted flashes of muzzle fire coming from it.

We need to eliminate that building, he thought.

He gathered all his strength and pointed at the building. But no one saw him. He wanted to reach for his radio and call in air strikes. But Walton had his radio, and the captain was busy using it. Even over the deafening noise, Behr could hear planes streaking toward the area. At least it sounded like planes. He couldn't be sure of anything.

34

Lodyga

Things weren't going well in the wadi either.

Since the insurgents held the high ground all around them, it was hard for Lodyga's team to move without drawing fire from the houses in the village. Now the team would again have to cross the river, but this time under fire, and move up the valley to rescue ODA 3336.

Every step was met by the crack of a bullet or the explosion of an RPG.

Since ODA 3312 had left Patriot 2, it had taken them a long time to get close to Walton's team. That's because as soon as Lodyga's team returned to the river that bisected the valley and headed toward ODA 3336, they started taking accurate fire. And it was coming from both sides of the valley.

Pressed up against the western wall, Lodyga scanned the cliffs above. Bullets snapped around him, striking the rocks. The fire was coming from both sides and bullets plunged down on them from above.

He and McGarry paused to get their bearings. They knew that in order to make it to ODA 3336, they would have to fight through this kill zone. Their only chance was to start dropping bombs on the houses around them.

Gutierrez was already in contact with the jet fighters and Apaches overhead and soon had them vectored in on the buildings covering their approach.

He and Lodyga decided to focus on the east side of the wadi. That way they would be covered by an overhang as they moved forward into the valley. Plus they had seen HIG fighters moving around on trails between fighting positions. Soon Apaches were raking the trails with gunfire and slamming Hellfire missiles into the houses that dotted the ridge of the wadi.

Martin received a call from Walton on the satellite radio saying that a suspected sniper was hiding in a cistern in the village. Peeking out from his perch near the cliff wall, Lodyga unslung an AT4, an antitank rocket, and started to aim at the cistern. It was one of the few weapons, like the Carl G, that had enough firepower to at least rattle the fighters in the buildings above.

Clearing his back-blast area, he prepared to step out and fire. His interpreter, standing nearby, waited for the signal to cover him. Shouldering the rocket, Lodyga stepped out and immediately bullets started to crash around him. Nearby, McGarry watched as Lodyga flinched when he tried to fire. Nothing happened.

"Hey, take the safety pin out, asshole," McGarry called to him.

"Fuck you. I did take it out," Lodyga said as he checked the rocket, shouldered it, and blasted the cistern.

While the Apaches hammered the east side of the wadi, Lodyga got his guys ready to move forward. The only way through the kill zone was to send one team forward while the other covered. McGarry's team would cover while Martin pushed forward. Martinez and his machine-gun team had already pushed forward and set up farther up the valley.

The team could feel the bullets whipping past their faces.

On their first push, Martin and his team were caught in the open. Lodyga watched as Martin emptied a magazine right along the ridge on the east side and then scanned the west side as he reloaded. All of the windows were open and looking down on the team's position.

Lodyga started to yell at Martin to get back, but no one could hear over the roar of the fire. A bullet struck a commando near Lodyga. The Afghan was trying to climb up over a rock. Almost in slow motion, Lodyga watched as the little dust clouds sprang up as the rounds impacted around him. One round struck the side of the commando's body armor and Lodyga watched the Afghan crumble.

Racing back to cover, Martin and the commandos waited for a lull in the fire so that they could make another push. Martin looked down at his leg and saw a growing bloodstain. His lower pant leg was soaked.

"Hey, man, you're bleeding," McGarry said.

"I think I got shot," Martin said.

"Yup, looks like it."

McGarry cut open Martin's pants to see the wound. It was probably some shrapnel from an RPG or bullet fragments. There was a chunk of skin gouged out of his thigh, but it wasn't serious.

"You're going to be okay," McGarry said.

"I ain't got time to bleed," Martin joked, stealing a line from the movie *Predator*.

Despite the heavy fire, Lodyga and his men were calm. They had been in much worse shape when their teammate Staff Sergeant Miller was killed. They knew the importance of keeping their heads. It meant life or death during that ambush and it meant the same thing in the Shok Valley. But they also knew the pain of losing a teammate, and despite the stiff resistance, they kept fighting to get to their brothers trapped on the ledge.

By this time, the air reaction team, a small team of reinforcements, had landed and took up position with ODA 3312. They waited in the wadi while Lodyga led his team forward.

It took three tries, but ODA 3312 finally pushed deep enough into the valley to see where ODA 3336 was trapped. Setting up their machine guns in the wadi, they started to rake the village with fire, hoping to give Walton's team some relief.

35

Shurer

If there was ever a time the team needed another medic, this was it.

As Shurer was running up the hill to reach the wounded, he had no idea what he would be facing. He could tell by Ford's tone, though, that it was bad.

Now he knew.

First, he glimpsed CK's body, which was shocking enough. Then his eyes were drawn to Morales and Behr. It was worse than he thought. And he would have to check Rhyner, too, just to be sure he was okay.

With all the injured soldiers, there was a danger that only one medic could be overwhelmed and might run out of supplies. That was a real concern. So here Shurer was, in the middle of a battle, with two down. Another slightly wounded. CK dead.

And he was the lone medic.

As he scanned the area, he knew it would be difficult to move the wounded to a spot where they could be rescued. What happened if someone else was injured? It would be a logistical nightmare. He couldn't think about that now.

During their training, medics are taught to be on autopilot with trauma victims. You had to stay detached and look at every wound in a "totally objective way: This person needs that. And that one needs this." Above all, stay focused. Like with the commando who was burned on his thigh and testicle. The soldier was upset, but it was something he was going to have to live with. Get your pants on and get back to work.

Shurer knew a medic had to be cold. That's because he had to divide the wounded into two groups: those who were going to live with their injuries, and those who were going to die without help. These were the only two categories in battle. And Shurer only had time to focus on those whose wounds were life threatening.

Kneeling by Behr, he noticed there wasn't a lot of cover. They were protected by a rock wall, but the rest of the area was wide open. He was trying to stay as close to the rock wall as he could, but he could still feel dirt kicking up in his face from rounds hitting close by, and the shock waves of exploding RPGs.

Shurer began examining Behr and assessed that he had been hit twice. The injury to his arm wasn't serious. It was a glancing wound and trickled blood. He had blood flow to his fingers. A good sign. So he turned his attention to Behr's pelvis, and that was a different story. It was bleeding profusely. At that point, Shurer began methodically thinking about all the possible scenarios with the wound. Ideally, a human has from five and a half to six liters of blood. The pelvic area is vascular. You would expect that a person was going to lose one or one and half liters right there. Doing the math in his head, Shurer surmised that Behr was already in borderline shock. He wasn't at the point of total shock.

Not yet.

But he was headed in that direction—and it would be potentially deadly. Shock is a life-threatening medical condition that occurs when the body suffers from insufficient blood flow. It is a medical emergency and can lead to other conditions such as lack of oxygen in the body's tissues (hypoxia), heart attack, or organ damage. It requires immediate treatment.

With a pelvic wound, there was really no good way of applying adequate pressure on the injury. Shurer knew Behr needed serious attention. So he took off his helmet and set it down to the side. He wanted to examine underneath

Behr's body without moving him too much. He rolled him gently and determined that the downside wound was about the size of a quarter. It wasn't bleeding much. But the interior wound—the entry point of the bullet—was different. While it was smaller in diameter—the size of a pinkie—it was oozing blood. That was the problem spot.

"My leg doesn't feel straight," Behr told him.

"Look, man, you're going to be okay. Let me take care of this wound first."

Shurer removed gauze from his kit and began packing it into the topside wound. Then he turned to Carter. "Just keep pressure on this as hard as you can." Carter nodded and took over while Shurer searched for his morphine. He found the syrette and injected ten milligrams of morphine in Behr to help ease the pain. He knew he had to turn his attention to Morales. But he was worried. They had to get Behr off the mountain or he would die. Shurer turned to Behr. "You're going to be fine. It's no big deal."

But then he lifted his head and screamed at Walton, "We need to get him out of here now!"

Behr reached up and grabbed Shurer's arm. "So you're telling him I'm going to die and you're telling me I'm okay, right?"

Shurer was momentarily caught off guard. Behr was correct: He was in danger of dying. But Shurer had to stay upbeat with his diagnosis. He couldn't tell Behr the truth, or he might give up. "You're fine," the medic said.

But inside he knew it would take a miracle to keep him alive.

36

Carter

Just as Carter began focusing his attention on firing his rifle at insurgents, Shurer drafted him again.

The medic had his hands full. Behr and Morales had life-threatening injuries. It wasn't enough to just patch them up. Shurer needed Carter to exert pressure on wounds, hand him gauze, and watch the flow on the IV the medic had set up for Behr. All this while they were dangerously close to the edge of a cliff with a sixty-foot drop.

"I haven't done this before," Carter said. "But I'll do whatever you need me to do."

"I'll give you directions. Don't worry," Shurer told him.

The laid-back Texas combat cameraman wasn't worried about that. He was more concerned that they could be overrun. The HIG had at least a hundred fighters. Hell, probably more. It sounded like a company. And sooner or later, Carter figured they would probably launch an assault. If that happened, his team would fight to the end. They would never surrender. But the reality was that there were only a handful of Special Forces soldiers on the mountain to counter such an assault—and two of them were seriously wounded. The commandos weren't doing much at all.

As Carter tended to the wounded, Ford, who had been looking for a path down the hill, appeared from a corner on the ridge. He moved calmly toward Walton, firing his rifle while his eyes scanned the action.

"Get the fuck down," Walton shouted.

What the fuck? This dude is a hard-ass. We're pinned down here and he comes strutting up. That guy is a tough. If that doesn't give you motivation, nothing will, Carter thought.

Carter noticed that Ford and Walton were animated as they talked to each other. Over the battle noise, he heard bits and pieces of the conversation. They argued about how they were going to get off the mountain and air strikes. Helicopters and planes had been pounding the compound, but the enemy fire was still steady—and still focused on the team.

37

Behr

Everything began to fade to black.

In the background, Behr could still hear the noise. And where it had once been loud, it was now muffled. Just like he was wearing earplugs.

Behr tried to fight the drowsiness, but it was easier to close his eyes. And when he did, he thought about family and friends back in the Quad Cities. Growing up in a Christian home, he was taught to have faith. And as a teenager, he did. He never questioned God or His ways. His faith was still strong.

But this was grim, and he was pessimistic about the chances of getting off the mountain alive. Bullets were everywhere. There was no letup in the battle. They were trapped. Not that he was giving up. He was just being realistic. Behr wanted to make peace with God, so he whispered a prayer.

"God, I know that I haven't always been the greatest person and I can't promise that if I live I will be the best person or change everything. But if You want me to live and carry on, make it so. If not, then I guess I'm ready to go."

Behr had just put his faith in God, and after the prayer he felt a sense of calm envelop his soul. No matter what happened to him on this day—whether he lived or died—things were going to be fine. He was at peace—until he felt a sharp smack across his face. Stunned, he opened his eyes and Shurer was standing over him.

"Wake up, Dillon," he shouted.

"Holy shit."

Behr was awake and alert, and he took that as a sign from God that he wasn't supposed to die—at least not yet.

38

Walding

Walding had made it to the top of the mountain. But that was easy compared to his next task: trying to sneak back down to rescue his trapped unit. The team was depending on him and Sanders. Ford had just told him over the radio that they were needed to provide cover. Behr and Morales were wounded, and Carter and Shurer were treating them. It was hectic for Walton and Rhyner, who were trying to call in air strikes. And Ford was coordinating security and trying to find a way off the mountain. The commandos? They weren't doing much. They returned fire now and then. But for the most part, they hugged the rocks, trying to stay out of the line of fire. Things were not going as planned.

But Walding was about to face his own set of problems. This was the most sustained regular fire he had ever encountered during a deployment. He was surprised at just how much ammunition the insurgents had at their disposal. It was just like the movies. And now the HIG fighters were firing in their direction. At first, Walding and Sanders and their commandos had been unnoticed. But not anymore.

Now they were being asked to edge down the rocks to reach their fellow soldiers who were trapped halfway up to the compound. Not an easy task. But Walding had never turned away from a challenge. In high school, he wasn't the tallest or strongest player on his football team. But he sure as hell hit the hardest. Knock him down and he jumped back up to this feet.

So as difficult as it was, Walding began carefully descending the mountain, followed by Sanders and some of the commandos. He didn't want to slip. If he fell, he would be of no use to anybody. He didn't want anyone to have to scale the mountain to rescue him. *Come on, you can do this. Keep going,* he thought.

Climbing down was no easier than going up—and there was more pressure. He had to move faster. His hands hurt as he lowered himself from terrace to terrace. The jagged rocks on the cliff face poked into his body. But by now, like always, he was oblivious to the pain. Mind over matter.

After about a half hour, Walding reached the area where the men were clustered. From the distance, he saw Shurer working on Behr and Morales. Carter was helping them, too, and Walton and Rhymer were on the radio. He immediately provided cover for the casualties, firing his M4 at the direction of the compound across the wadi.

Moments later, Ford joined him and the two of them fired in unison. "Damn, they're right on top of us," Ford shouted.

Walding knew that. It was an ambush and it seemed like the insurgents' weapons—and snipers—were fixed on this tiny patch of scrubland. It was a miracle anyone was still alive.

39

Ford

Ford knew they would eventually achieve fire superiority, but they couldn't overcome the fatal flaw of the whole mission: HIG fighters had the key terrain above them. The operation had quickly turned into a nightmare scenario, and there was no fast way off the mountain to a medevac bird. There were few options. They could fight uphill—something no one wants to do—or pull back, get the wounded to safety, and regroup.

"Everybody stay where you're at," Ford yelled at the commandos nearby. "Lay down a base of fire."

Between orders, Ford leaned over the edge and fired a few shots at a window or clump of trees in the distance. Overhead, more and more Apaches and fighters were delivering bomb and rocket strikes. Ford's plan was to let the air strikes level the village so that they could move the wounded to safety.

And for the moment, at least, the strikes seemed to be working.

But Ford had another problem.

Some of the team's other terps had glimpsed CK's lifeless body, which was now being used to shield Morales and Behr, and angrily shook their heads from side to side. In particular, AJ was stunned and insulted that they would use their friend's body for cover. But his anger quickly turned to despair and he began sobbing. The other terps followed. With the interpreters inconsolable, Ford and the others couldn't coordinate fire with the commandos. The Americans were left mute.

Ford had enough. They needed the terps to stay in control. They had to shape up. So he grabbed AJ by the shoulders and forcibly shook him.

"We've got to have you because you're our link to the commandos," he yelled into the distraught Afghan's face. "You have to focus or more people are going to end up like CK. You're my lead terp now. You've got to get it done."

Over the radio, Staff Sergeant Robert Gutierrez Jr., a combat controller from ODA 3312, warned them that a two-thousand-pound bomb was on the way. The target was the large, multistory building on a ridgeline across the wadi. Inside, HIG fighters could zero in on the ledge. It was impossible to move without one of the HIG fighters in the building getting a bead on them. But while the building was across the wadi, the straight line distance to the ledge was only three hundred meters.

"One minute out!" Ford said, keying the radio to warn Howard at the bottom of the wadi.

But the radio failed. Unable to call Howard, Ford crept to the edge and started to yell down, signaling with his arm.

"Incoming. Get down. Everybody get down."

He doubted that anyone downhill could hear his warning, but from the corner of his eye he saw Shurer throw his body over Behr to shield him from the blast. From his previous deployments, Ford knew the kind of damage a two-thousand-pound bomb could inflict on enemy positions. If it landed right, it could smash a structure to pieces. Hunkered down against the base of the rock wall, he watched the bomb sail down toward the house.

At the last second, he buried his head in the crook of his arm. The blast pushed Ford against the wall followed by a shock wave that hit him deep in the chest. The impact of the explosion spewed a cloud of debris and dust that swirled in the valley. It blocked out the sun, and made it impossible for Ford and the others to even see a few inches in front of their faces. Baseball-size rocks and pebbles flew in their direction, and a small one hit Behr in the gut with the force of a fastball.

As the dust slowly dissipated, an eerie silence again fell over the valley. But then the shooting erupted again. *Shit, these guys are fucking relentless,* Ford thought. "We're going to move a casualty every time a bomb is dropped," he told Walton. Then he turned to Shurer: "Ron, get those guys packaged up and ready to move."

Ford had taken over. He was in control and decisive. Through sheer force of will, he was going to make damn sure they moved to safety. He quickly huddled with Sanders and Williams. They had to get off the ledge or the wounded were going to die, and likely so would the rest of the team.

"You need to grab five or six commandos apiece and set up on those ledges," he told them.

The idea was to establish security on the ledges leading down the mountain to the wadi. Then Sanders and Williams could help carry Behr and Morales while the commandos provided cover fire. Moving them was imperative. After the massive bomb, the fighters had started to really zero in on the ledge.

Suddenly an insurgent came rushing toward them from the same path Sanders and Walding had taken to join the team. Dressed in a gray top and a military-style hat, the fighter apparently hadn't seen the Americans, and seemed to be focused on ODA 3312 in the wadi.

Williams and Walton saw him first and shouted a warning. Ford heard them and, in a smooth motion, wheeled around and snapped off a shot.

The burst knifed into the fighter's chest and he crumbled to the ground, his AK-47 rifle crashing into the dust before him. Ford figured he likely hit the fighter in the spine because 5.56 rounds don't have that kind of stopping power.

Everybody was stunned. With the fighter lying in a heap, Ford scanned the hill waiting for another fighter. Anyone coming down now was going to get shot.

Ford knew they had to move or get overrun. The fighters were starting to probe for an attack. Even for Ford, a veteran of many battles, the level of fighting was overwhelming. It was time to get off the ledge. Gathering up the team, he refined the escape with Walton.

Ford decided he and Walding would stay on the ledge with the team while Williams and Sanders set up on the ledges below. Down in the wadi, he wanted Howard to pull back to the small building that looked like a goat shed that they had passed earlier in the day. There, they could collect the wounded and regroup.

When the hastily convened meeting broke up, Ford and Walding returned to shooting at muzzle flashes. Ford was fixed on a window in a house overlooking the ledge, a perfect vantage point to shoot down on the team as they tried to get off the mountain. He kept firing burst after burst, hoping to suppress the fighters in the house, even pointing to Walding to shoot at it.

"What?" Walding said over the gunfire.

"Windows. Shoot windows," Ford yelled. "We're going to suppress windows."

There were so many houses around them and Walton and Rhyner were dropping bombs right above the team's ledge, showering them with dust, pebbles, and baseball-size stones. Ford could feel the grit and dust on his neck. The fighter planes overhead seemed to be coming and coming at a steady clip. One fighter after another released its payload of bombs before roaring up and out of the valley. Each time the bombs were hitting closer to their ledge.

Glancing back over his shoulder, Ford could see his guys rounding up the commandos.

He and Walding continued to fire into the nearby windows. In order to get off a clear shot, they both had to quickly step out from the base of the cliff and shoot, exposing them to fire for a split second. It was a risk, but without the cover fire, Ford knew there was no way they would be able to get the wounded down to the house in the wadi.

40

Walding

Always looking to protect fellow soldiers, Walding noticed an area near the wounded that needed to be covered. He took one step toward the location then felt something slice through his leg. The force knocked him off his feet; he flew a few feet in the air and landed near that overturned tree. The pain was excruciating. It felt like someone had smashed his lower leg with a sledge-hammer.

"What the fuck?" Walding screamed.

When he glanced down, he saw blood, ligaments, tissue, and bone. A round had filleted the lower part of his right leg. It was barely attached to his knee. Trying to keep his wits, Walding knew he had to find cover before he could take care of his wound. He crawled to the shrub. It wasn't much protection, but without it, he would be completely in the open and an easy target for a sniper.

He turned over and sat on his ass and stared at his leg. At that moment he knew his leg was gone. There was no way to save it.

Shit, there goes my SF career, he thought.

Sanders bolted over to him. "Damn," he said.

Walding pulled a tourniquet out of his pocket and turned to Sanders. "Man, I need you to help me with this."

"Sure," Sanders said breathlessly. Walding knew his teammate was jacked up. *He has every right to be. He just saw my leg hanging off,* Walding thought.

Sanders slipped the tourniquet above the wound and tightened it. But Walding saw spurts of blood continuing to flow from the injury.

"You may want to tighten this tourniquet a little more," Walding told Sanders. Sanders complied and the blood stopped—for the moment.

Walding was seriously injured but he promised himself he was going to keep fighting. The lyrics of one of his favorite songs popped into his head: *I'll have you know, I've become indestructible.* So he lifted his rifle and resumed firing. But every time he moved, his leg hurt so much he would growl. *Damn leg.*

He needed the pain to stop. He needed to function—to be combat effective. So Walding did the unthinkable. He turned the lower part of his injured leg—the area below the knee—toward his groin and removed his bootlace. Then he tied the lower leg to his thigh so it wouldn't flap around. It was a drastic measure, but one he had to take to stay in the fight.

41

Ford

Out of the corner of his eye, Ford saw Walding almost jump into the air.

Focusing on the enemy, he continued to fire rounds from his M4, before turning his attention to Walding, who had almost rolled off the side of the mountain. The tree near Rhyner was the only thing that kept him from rolling off the ledge.

Ford could see that Walding was hurt badly. His leg was mangled. A bullet nearly severed his lower leg—and blood was spurting like water from a garden hose. It didn't look good. Ford fired a few more bursts, but it was hard to turn away. He wanted to help Walding, but he was the only one left who could shoot and provide cover.

All the while Ford kept shooting.

Standing up and leaning out away from the wall, he took a bead on a new window when a round struck him in the chest. The blow knocked the wind out of him, forcing him to one knee. Since he had left his heavier body armor at Jalalabad, his plate carrier lacked any of the padding that absorbed the shot of the bullet.

Sliding his hand behind the shattered plate that stopped the bullet from tearing into his chest, he looked for blood. His hand came out clean. No blood. He had to shake off the jolt. Taking a few deep breaths, he slid his almost spent magazine out of his rifle and replaced it with a fresh one. He had been hit. So had his teammates and CK. At first, Ford figured that the insurgents were getting lucky by filling the air with bullets.

Then it dawned on him.

All of the wounded were wearing tan desert uniforms. The commandos wore older green camouflage uniforms. The HIG sniper was zeroing in on the Americans. He had mistaken CK, who also was wearing the tan uniform, for a Special Forces soldier.

"Stay down. Stay back," he barked at his men.

He was mad. Sliding out to shoot another burst, he was focused on buying enough time for his men to escape.

Top: American Special Forces looking through scope on weapon up at Kendal village in Shok Valley with two interpreters. *Middle*: Looking back to the helicopter landing zone in Shok Valley, guys avoiding crossing the freezing deep river. *Bottom*: Movement to Kendal village in Shok Valley. *U.S. Army photo/Sgt. Michael Carter*

CK (interpreter) and Afghan commandos crossing a freezing river in Shok Valley.
U.S. Army photo/Sgt. Michael Carter

Afghan commando giving a child some candy in Uzbin Valley.
U.S. Army photo/ SFC Morales Luis

ODA 3336 on the border of Nangrahar and Pakistan, reinforcing a combat outpost from possible attack. *U.S. Army photo/ SFC Morales Luis*

Staff Sergeant Morales and CK (center) explaining how to hold on to rope when fast-roping, Jalalabad. We're on the roof of a four-car-garage motor pool that was transformed into a hockey rink. *U.S. Army photo/ SFC Morales Luis*

Staff Sergeants Walding, Shurer, and Morales prepping demo on hood, Tagab Valley, Kapisa. *U.S. Army photo/ SFC Morales Luis*

SSGT Rhyner (left), Staff Sergeant Morales (center), CK (right) with squad of Afghan commandos in Nangrahar Province waiting at helicopter landing zone to get picked up in Nangahar. *U.S. Army photo/ SFC Morales Luis*

CK (interpreter) pulling security on mission in Nangrahar Province.
U.S. Army photo/ SFC Morales Luis

Air Force Combat Controller SSGT Zach Rhyner and CK (interpreter) on way to mission in Nangrahar Province. *U.S. Army photo/ SFC Morales Luis*

CK, our interpreter (center), with two Afghan commandos posing for a picture in middle of fire fight in Tagab Valley. *U.S. Army photo/ SFC Morales Luis*

Master Sergeant Ford rehearsing exiting an aircraft quickly with Afghan commandos, Bagram Airfield. *U.S. Army photo/ SFC Morales Luis*

Afghan commandos in Chinook on way to Shok Valley.
U.S. Army photo/Sgt. Michael Carter

Staff Sergeant Morales and Sergeant First Class Mason react quickly to a threat outside the gate on Jalalabad Airfield. *U.S. Army photo/ SFC Morales Luis*

ODA 3336 with Afghan commandos and interpreters at Torkham Gate.
U.S. Army photo/ SFC Morales Luis

201st Afghan commandos and ODA 3336 on top of hill. Puli-Charki, Kabul. *U.S. Army photo/ SFC Morales Luis*

Afghan commandos MODDEMO (Modular Demonstration). They lay out the equipment and explain how they use it to their higher command. Puli-Charki, Kabul.
U.S. Army photo/ SFC Morales Luis

Captain Walton and another American Special Forces in helicopter rehearsals for Kandahar mission. *U.S. Army photo/ SFC Morales Luis*

ODA 3336 in Kandahar prepping for mission with Afghan commandos. *U.S. Army photo/ SFC Morales Luis*

Staff Sergeant Shurer and Staff Sergeant Morales prepping demo charges on the hood of our vehicle in Tagab Valley. *U.S. Army photo/ SFC Morales Luis*

Afghan commandos and American Special Forces (front) after training for mission. Staff Sergeant Walding, Staff Sergeant Marquez, Staff Sergeant Howard, Staff Sergeant Williams. Puli-Charki, Kabul. *U.S. Army photo/ SFC Morales Luis*

Staff Sergeant Walding reenlisting (left), Master Sergeant Ford (holding flag), and Captain Walton (right) giving the oath of enlistment to Walding at Torkham Gate.
U.S. Army photo/ SFC Morales Luis

ODA 3336 at a KTC range, Kabul. Beginning of deployment.
U.S. Army photo/ SFC Morales Luis

Afghans and Americans prepping for a mission. *U.S. Army photo/Sgt. Michael Carter*

Staff Sergeant Howard training the Afghan commandos in how to secure someone on the battlefield. *U.S. Army photo/Sgt. Michael Carter*

Afghan commandos loading a helicopter. *U.S. Army photo/Sgt. Michael Carter*

American Special Forces and an interpreter get the Afghan commandos loaded.
U.S. Army photo/Sgt. Michael Carter

Sergeant First Class Terry and CK (interpreter) rehearsing how to load a helicopter with the Afghan commandos. *U.S. Army photo/Sgt. Michael Carter*

Afghan commando company commander (also a Mula) in knit cap speaking to villagers in Uzbin Valley. CK is sitting front center interpreting for Captain Walton, sitting front right. *U.S. Army photo/ SFC Morales Luis*

42

Shurer

Shurer had turned the mountain into a makeshift emergency room. The conditions were less than ideal, and he braced himself for the possibility that insurgents above would toss grenades down to their position, or fire an RPG in their direction. *It's just a matter of time,* he thought. It was tough even to think straight with all the chaos. Shurer had trained for this. He knew this day might come when he enlisted and pushed to be a medic. But reality was different from training, and this was his first real battlefield test. He had to stay in control.

Like Behr, Morales was in poor shape. Not as bad as Behr, but close. Morales had highly visible wounds in his right thigh and ankle. Shurer administered a morphine shot and began closely examining his teammate's injuries. It wasn't pretty. His right leg was badly damaged. Shurer could put his hand straight through Morales's thigh. It was just flayed open. But Morales had been lucky; there was no femoral damage, or injury to the femur.

Shurer knew the key would be to apply enough pressure on the thigh to keep it from swelling. With that much tissue damage, the thigh would normally swell up and, left untreated, would keep swelling. If that happened, the bleeding would continue. But the blood loss wouldn't necessarily be visible. It would be hidden under the swelling. A real danger.

So Shurer packed the wound with Celox—a hemorrhage-control medication that quickly stops bleeding. (Pouring Celox into a wound prevents blood loss by forming a gel-like clot as the medicine binds to the surface of red blood cells.) Shurer then wrapped the area as tightly as he could to keep pressure on the thigh.

He then turned his attention to Morales's ankle. He cut off Morales's boot—and tossed it so far it tumbled off the mountain. But after examining the wound, he realized the only thing he could do was to try to stop the bleeding. He didn't have time to do anything else. He used a bandage and, after the bleeding was under control, gave Morales a "fentanyl lollipop." (Fentanyl is more powerful than morphine.) The lollipop helped ease the pain.

After that, Shurer bounded to CK, whose body had been moved by the soldiers near the rock wall. Shurer, who didn't know that Walton had already examined CK, wanted to perform a more thorough examination of his friend. Maybe there was a chance—albeit a slim one—that he was still alive. People can be nearly dead and you might not see it with a quick glance. So this time, Shurer checked the terp's pulse. Checked his breathing closely. Nothing. CK was dead, and Shurer had to regroup and focus his attention on the living.

When he returned to Behr, he heard Ford's voice.

"Where's the Skedco?" Ford asked. Made from a special plastic formula, a Skedco is a portable stretcher that unfolds like a Fruit Roll-Up. (Skedco is the name of the company that manufactures the stretcher and other military equipment.)

"I didn't bring it," Shurer said. *Shit, it figures,* he thought. It would have been stupid to bring the Skedco, which weighs about twenty-five pounds. Ford had encouraged his team to pack light for the mission. Keep the rucksacks lean, he said, because they would be climbing a steep hill. If every pound was going to be important, it was better to leave the Skedco behind, Shurer figured. He did pack a poleless litter—an ultralight polypropylene stretcher. It rolled up to the size of a towel and weighed only a few pounds. But it wasn't as sturdy as a Skedco.

Shurer knew Ford was coordinating the evacuation plan and was trying to assess what equipment they had to move the injured soldiers. Sanders and Wald-ing's element had a pole-less litter—and they needed it now. But both men were on a ledge above them, firing at enemy positions. It could take some time.

While Shurer worked on Behr he could hear Walton and Rhyner on the radios, frantically calling in air strikes and trying to get medevacs in the area to rescue them. They also were talking to the other ODAs that had been cut off from their position. Neither could reach them because of the heavy fire.

Shurer glanced at Behr's pelvic wound and it wasn't getting better. So he turned to Celox—the same medicine he had just used on Morales. With Behr, it was a more complicated process. The bleeding was intense. He poured the Celox on top of the wound and then, with his fingers, shoved what he could inside. Then he poured a little bit more and repeated the process until he thought he had used enough. But with each step he had to apply pressure for at least five minutes or the Celox wouldn't hold.

It was when he was applying Celox to Behr that the medic heard Walding scream and saw that he had been shot. Shurer wanted to run and help him, but at the moment he couldn't. He had to keep his hands inside Behr's wound so the Celox would hold.

Walding was just twenty-five feet from Shurer. But it might as well have been a mile. Walding couldn't move, and Shurer couldn't leave his position. For Shurer, it was a tough decision. If he left Behr in order to help Walding, who knew if the Celox would hold? If it didn't, this would create another set of prob-lems. If you release the pressure even just a little, you could break the newly forming clot. If that happened, the bleeding would be buried underneath all the junk you just put on top of the wound and you would never gain access to it.

Again, Shurer had to quickly evaluate the situation. Walding had suffered a traumatic amputation. The wound was below the knee and the bottom part of his leg was nearly severed. *Get a tourniquet on it and it will be fine,* Shurer thought.

Of the three injuries, Walding's was visually the most shocking and most upsetting. But in the medic's view, it was the easiest one to deal with: Put a quick tourniquet on the thigh. Squeeze the tourniquet around the femur. Squeeze it around the femoral artery. And that should stop the bleeding.

But nothing on this mountain was easy.

43

Walding

Walding was in severe pain.

After his leg was hit, his adrenaline kicked in and kept him going. He believed if he kept shooting or told the others where to aim, he would forget about the pain. And it had worked for a while. Not anymore. The pain was overwhelming. He needed morphine.

He pulled a morphine injector needle from his rucksack but was unsure how to use it correctly. He couldn't remember which side of the injector to place against his thigh. With the pain and chaos, it was confusing, and Walding wanted to make sure he did it right. Shurer was busy taking care of Behr and Morales. He hadn't made it to Walding, who was about twenty-five feet away.

Walding placed the purple side of the injector on his thigh and exerted pressure on the device. But to his surprise, it was upside down and the needle jabbed into his thumb.

"Aw shit," he shouted, loud enough for everyone to hear.

The soldiers all looked at Walding, and when they realized what had happened—that Walding had injected the morphine into his thumb—they broke out laughing. It was a funny, almost surreal moment in the middle of disaster. While Walding didn't laugh, he understood why the others were cracking up. It was a dumb mistake. Shurer screamed something about turning the needle around and trying again. But Walding knew it was too late. And he was upset. He needed something to relieve the agony.

Even after the morphine mix-up, Walding kept returning fire. *Keep it up,* he told himself over and over. *I can't give up.* But he was at the breaking point and becoming light-headed. Was he going into shock? He didn't know. But things were getting bleak.

Walding began thinking about his wife and children. He wasn't giving up. That would be out of character. Growing up on his grandfather's Texas farm, Walding had experienced pain. Once, he fell out of a second-floor window in his house and broke his arm. He didn't cry or even say anything. He just walked around with a broken arm for days. As a linebacker on his high school team, he loved to hit people. Running backs catching screens out of the backfield. Or fullbacks trying to run up the middle. He never gave up. But now his mind was playing tricks on him. He hated thinking that his children might not have a daddy. He was a family man, and they were his life. And what about his wife? What would she do without him? Who would tell her? *Damn, stop it,* he thought. If he continued to fight hard, at least he'd be able to hold his head high and know that he'd never given up. At least if he kept shooting and directed his team where to shoot, he would stop thinking about his family and the physical pain.

But as the battle wore on, the physical suffering nearly crushed him. Sometimes he would just lie back, put his head down, and say, "This freaking hurts." Worse, he hadn't been examined by Shurer. He knew the medic had his hands full, but this was ridiculous. *I'm just an old country boy from Texas and I don't know shit about medical stuff. My tourniquet is tied real tight, but come on, man. I need help,* he thought. As much as he hated to do it, he shouted to Shurer, "Ron, you want to check me out, man?"

The medic just poked his head up from working on Behr and Morales and gave Walding a thumbs-up. "You're good," he told him, too busy with Behr's injuries to minister to Walding.

"Are you kidding me?" Walding replied angrily. "That's bullshit. Don't tell me I'm good. Fuck you, I'm good. I have no fucking leg!"

44

Behr

Behr was losing hope.

As much as Shurer worked on him, he was still bleeding and in severe pain. He knew that if he wasn't treated by a doctor soon, he would die. He had no idea how long the team had been trapped. They started the mission at dawn. It was early morning when they landed and it had taken at least an hour to get into position before they were hit. Looking at the sky, he figured it had to be the afternoon. If they stayed there too long, night would fall. Medevac birds couldn't fly in at night. It would be too dangerous. And the temperature would drop, too. It was in the forties when they landed, and hadn't gotten much warmer.

It was getting harder and harder to think that they were going to make it out of there. When people are still shooting at you and helicopters can't land and you're up on a mountain and there's no way they can evacuate you, it's hard to be positive.

Behr knew there was usually a ratio of how many people you want alive to people you need to medevac. The proportions were starting to tip. They still had Afghan commandos, but Behr didn't think of them as saving the team members' lives. The SF soldiers would have to do it themselves.

Walding screamed for Shurer to help, but the medic continued to focus on Behr. He didn't leave Behr's side. That was another sign that Behr's wound was serious.

And Behr could tell that Shurer was tense. It was overwhelming for the medic. Shurer pulled back from Behr's face for a moment and put his helmet back on. Seconds later, a bullet pinged off the helmet. Shurer was only a foot away from Behr, and Behr knew he was lucky that the round didn't ricochet off the helmet and hit him in the face. Stunned by the impact, Shurer lifted his hands and looked like he was going to remove his helmet. As he did so, a scene from the movie *Saving Private Ryan* flashed into Behr's head. In the movie, a bullet bounced off a U.S. soldier's helmet during a battle, and when the soldier took it off to see if he was wounded, another bullet ripped into his skull. Behr mustered all the energy he could, screamed at the top of his lungs, *"Noooooo,"* and stopped Shurer from making the same mistake.

But the force of the bullet had disoriented the medic. He was woozy and discombobulated. A few minutes earlier, Walton had also been hit in the helmet by two rounds, smashing the captain's face into the ground and causing him to gag on some dirt.

"I just got shot," Shurer screamed.

Ford yelled at him: "Check yourself. But I don't see anything."

But Behr could tell it would take some time for Shurer to regain his composure.

45

Morales

It wasn't getting any easier. The fire continued to rain from the high ground. They were pinned on the ledge against the rock wall. An Afghan commando on another part of the ledge had just been hit in the head with a round and wasn't moving. With blood gushing from his skull, he was probably dead. And at this point, it was unclear how they would even attempt to get off the mountain.

This was no time for reflection, but Morales couldn't help but think about his wife and his family. He wanted to survive so he could hug her. Tell her and his family how much he cared about them. The battle was a disaster, but he wasn't giving up hope—that wasn't in his DNA. He would keep fighting. But the reality was, if things didn't improve soon, there was a chance that the insurgents would overrun their position.

In all the confusion, he didn't have time to think about CK. When he saw the Afghan's lifeless body, he was startled. Then angry. CK was his little brother. They had spent so much time together during the deployment. They watched endless episodes of *Friends* and spent countless hours talking about their lives. Morales knew everything about CK. How he wanted so badly to be an American. How he dreamed of joining Special Forces. And like a big brother, Morales was always giving CK advice. He told CK that Special Forces really needed interpreters and he should focus on that. He remembered the days when they went to bazaars and how CK had looked out for his friend. He would barter with the merchants every time Morales picked up a trinket for Katherine. He would make sure he didn't get ripped off, and the two of them would laugh about it later.

Morales truly cared about CK. Now he was dead.

When Shurer arrived, Morales waved him off and told him to work on Behr first. No question Behr was in worse shape than he was, Morales told the medic. He'd been shot first and needed immediate help. Behr was only a few feet from Morales, who had been watching the events unfold. He tried to help, firing his weapon, pointing out enemy positions. But it reached a point where the pain was just too great to do anything.

Morales didn't know how many insurgents were above them, but he estimated that there had to be at least a hundred, probably more. They had been entrenched in that village for who knows how long. This was their turf. They knew every cave and every hiding spot for snipers. They had the weapons. He could tell. The only hope was to bomb the shit out of their positions. But his team was so close they might be injured in any bombing run. It was a conundrum for sure. Bomb the enemy and run the risk of taking friendly fire. Or do nothing and run the risk of an entire Special Forces team being massacred in a remote valley. Not much of a choice. And something must have happened to the other ODAs and those commandos. Were they pinned down, too? *Why aren't they here?* Morales thought.

When Walding was shot, it was like Morales was hit again. Being wounded was one thing. Morales could handle that. But watching his friends—especially Walding—in agony was another. Walding was his best friend in the unit. There was nothing physical that Walding couldn't do, and they pushed each other in the gym, or when they ran on the airfield. And when it was time to unwind, they would download TV shows and movies on their iPhones and stream them on the big screen TV in the recreation room. *Big Brother* was their favorite. They loved the intrigue and backstabbing and strategy as contestants brokered deals in order to last to the end of the show and possibly win $250,000. It was like real life. So many hours in the last few months were spent laughing their asses off watching back-to-back-to-back episodes of *Big Brother*. They even joked about trying out for the show when they returned home.

Morales smiled for a moment when he recalled how Walding had reenlisted just a few weeks earlier during a routine border patrol mission. The goal of that operation was to protect a remote outpost, which had been attacked a few times at night. The Army had information that it was going to be hit again, and they needed soldiers to help reinforce the outpost. So Morales's team and the commandos, along with an Army National Guard unit, rolled out of Jalalabad and headed east to the outpost in the desert.

It was a huge convoy. His team drove to a small wadi and parked. They waited there all night while the National Guard trekked two more miles to the outpost with supplies. Morales's team had to stay in position and wait just in case of an attack. They couldn't leave their vehicles. Morales didn't mind. The night before the trip, he had been promoted to staff sergeant, which meant he had his own vehicle and driver. For the longest time, he had been chauffeuring Wurzbach.

And on the trip, they rolled past amazing scenery—like they were in some kind of travelogue.

In one spot, they saw a tent with two hundred camels standing outside with one leg tied to another. That was the way to prevent the camels from walking off. Or as Morales put it, they had on their parking brakes. During the trip, they traveled on a mountain pass that doubled as a superhighway for donkeys and camels headed back and forth from Pakistan to Afghanistan. He knew the Pashtun people don't recognize that Pakistan-Afghanistan border. To them, it didn't make sense. They were all Pashtun people on both sides anyway.

The next morning, the team had to go to a base near the Torkham Gate on the famed Khyber Pass. As they were driving down an asphalt road close to Pakistan, they reached a checkpoint near the base that looked like a tollbooth on the New Jersey Turnpike. When the U.S. troops peeked inside Walding and Ford's vehicle, they asked, "Hey, what unit are you guys in?"

Walding, who was Ford's driver, looked over at him. Without blinking, Ford responded, "We're in the 201st [Afghan] Commandos." They all started laughing, and when they neared the Pakistan border, Morales heard Walton ask Walding if he wanted to reenlist. Right there. In the middle of traffic. "Fuck yeah. I want to do it," Walding said.

So Walding exited the vehicle and Walton left his Humvee. Someone held up an American flag as a backdrop and Walton read him the enlistment oath. *It* was *cool as shit,* Morales thought.

But now Walding was in the dirt, and there was nothing Morales could do to help him. He would do anything to just summon the strength to run over to his friend and help him put on the tourniquet, or sprinkle QuikClot or something on his wound. Just tell him he would be okay. But at this point, all he could do was watch.

And pray.

46

Ford

Tucked behind the butt of his M4 rifle, Ford kept shooting.

Then he heard a snap, and the rifle fell from his left hand and dangled in front of him, clipped to his body armor by a carabiner. His left arm, his dominant hand, started to sting. The pain wasn't tremendous. Kind of like that numb feeling when you hit metal with a sledgehammer. Ford looked down and tried to lift his arm up and couldn't. His triceps was hanging off his arm. He had been shot.

That sucks, he thought. It was probably that damn sniper.

Sliding down against the wall, he pressed his helmet against the rock face in pain. Blood was starting to squirt onto the wall. *I am going to bleed out and die if I don't find the artery.*

Grabbing at the wound, he tried to put pressure on it. The left side of his uniform was soaked in blood.

"Break your artery," Shurer yelled from the other side of the ledge.

Sliding his thumb under his arm, he found the slippery, blood-soaked artery and pressed it against his body. The bleeding stopped immediately.

Stunned by the wound, he stayed against the wall for a few minutes to collect himself.

"Fuck," he said.

Sanders, shooting nearby, saw the wound.

"Hey, man. You're going to be okay," he screamed.

Ford looked down at his torn triceps. The muscle looked like a piece of rare steak.

"Bullshit, I'm fucked," he said.

"We need to get the fuck off this mountain," Walding shouted.

Ford was demoralized. Tired. The bullet had knocked some of the fight out of him. Pressed against the side of the cliff, he thought about life. For the first time in a long while, he thought of his family. His daughter and his girlfriend. Thoughts that had never crossed his mind during a fight in the past. For a few minutes, he felt mortal. He didn't think he would die. But he knew he was hurt badly.

Stealing a glance back at the ledge, he saw that the team wasn't doing well. There were four guys down. Ford knew they had to get off the ledge or die there. Forcing the emotions down, he took a few deep breaths before standing up.

"Hey, we need to get the fuck down there. We need to start getting this shit set up," he said.

Ford knew they had been in the same spot a long time. Too long, and with every minute the insurgents were getting closer. Shurer was taking too long packaging the wounded to move, and Walton was consumed by working on air strikes. At this point, all Ford was concerned about was survivability.

But first, he needed to stop the bleeding. His team's standard operating procedure was to centerline their tourniquet by rubber-banding it to the front of their body armor instead of in a pack on the side of their kit. That way, they could use it with either arm. But Ford couldn't get to his because if he let go of the artery, he would bleed out.

"Ron, I need a tourniquet!"

Shurer, working on Behr, looked up at Ford. The medic was covered in blood and seemed overwhelmed by the carnage around him. Ford had watched him try and patch up his teammates for the past several hours, but the constant crack of rounds nearby and now more and more wounded stacking up had finally taken a toll.

"I need to regain my composure," Shurer said.

Ford immediately forgot about the burning pain in his arm. He forgot about his family. He forgot about everything. Regain his composure? All Ford was seeing was red.

"I will throw you off this fucking mountain."

But Shurer had been hit by the same bullet that passed through Ford's arm. It ricocheted, striking Shurer in the helmet. Shaking it off, he finally scrambled out and slid the black tourniquet over Ford's shoulder, cinching it tight with the Velcro band. Spinning the windlass rod, Ford could feel the pressure as the tourniquet slowed and then stopped the blood flow.

But the pressure quickly built up and Ford's arm started to hurt. The tourniquet's band was also crushing nerves in his shoulder. Getting shot was nothing compared to how his arm hurt with the tourniquet. It sent pain shooting throughout his body.

Struggling to the edge of the rocks, Ford was going to lead the evacuation. First, he had to climb down and help secure the shed in the wadi to use as a casualty collection point. Then he would give the orders to bring the men down. He was taking Williams with him. Ford had told him to grab a couple squads of commandos and set up along the two ledges to help move the casualties down.

Ford sat down at the edge and pushed off with his good arm, sliding down the rocks toward the wadi. The descent was grueling. It was hard enough for someone in top physical shape to scale down the steep rocks. But Ford only had one good arm—and he knew the insurgents would have him in their crosshairs.

He had to take it slow. One step at a time. And when the space between the ledges was too wide, he would drop down and hope he didn't tumble off the mountain. As Ford moved, several rounds hit nearby. Soon several enemy fighters above him started taking shots at him as he slid down the mountain. He had to stop on several of the ledges and hug the rock face to avoid being hit again.

As he crawled down, Ford tried to keep his arm close to his body and out of the dirt, but after a few minutes he just let it hang. His torn triceps, exposed and hanging from his arm, dragged in the dirt and rocks. Each time he slid down the mountain, soil packed into the meat of his triceps. He didn't care. He figured the arm was gone anyway. The only thing that mattered was making it to the bottom.

47

Howard

Howard's radio didn't work. Unknown to him, he had hit the radio on a rock and broke the connection between it and the battery pack. So he wasn't sure what was happening on top of the mountain. But from the gunfire he was hearing, it didn't sound good.

In the wadi, Howard had been looking up at the ledge where his team was pinned down. And that's when he spotted Ford on the ledge signaling him to come up. Rounds were impacting in the dirt and rocks near him. Enemy fighters were shooting from the cliff above, so Howard figured they would be safe at the base of the cliff because of the angle.

He signaled all of his commandos and they raced to the base of the cliff. On the way, he passed Wallen, who was trying to get a commando to move forward. Howard, safely at the cliff, looked back and saw Wallen still struggling with the man. He had the Afghan soldier by the shirt and was trying to lift him up to get him to move forward. But the Afghan was just not moving.

All around them, bullets were smacking the rocks. Howard was yelling to Wallen at the top of his lungs, "RYAN! RYAN! Get over here. Now!"

It was one of those decisions that had to be made in a split second. Did Howard want to run out and grab Wallen, and risk getting shot? No. That wouldn't help anybody, especially if they both went down.

"RYAN! You are being shot at!"

Wallen finally turned to look at Howard, then at the rounds impacting around him.

"OH!" he said.

Getting up, he sprinted to the cliff face. The commando, seeing him run, jumped up and headed toward Howard and the others.

With everybody together, they started up the cliff toward Ford's ledge.

About halfway up the mountain, Howard could see Ford and Williams picking their way down the path. As they approached, Howard was shocked. Ford, the inspirational leader of the team, looked like shit. Howard could see the muscle and tissue from his arm hanging out of his shirt. He was caked with blood and dirt.

"I've lost my arm. CK is dead. John lost his leg. Dillon has been hit," Ford said as the groups met on the path.

Stopping onto a ledge, Howard examined the arm and began inspecting the tourniquet.

"Okay, calm down," he said, pulling Ford's injured arm closer so that he could bandage it.

Ford jerked it away.

"I need to get down," he said, trying to move forward. Ford was convinced that he was going to bleed out and didn't want Howard and the others to have to carry him down.

But Howard refused to let him go.

"Hey," he screamed. "You need a field dressing on that!"

Cutting open the shirt, Howard discovered a stream of blood oozing from the arm. Grabbing the tourniquet, he began to tighten it down. Digging in his kit, he fished out some Kerlix gauze and an ACE bandage. Covering the wound with the gauze, Howard tried to wrap the entire wound in the bandage to keep everything in place.

But Ford was clearly annoyed. Between pushing Howard's hands away and trying to stand up, the bandage was barely secured as they climbed the rest of the way down to the wadi.

Howard could tell Ford was fighting a losing battle against the pain.

"What do you need me to do?" he asked.

"I need morphine," Ford said.

Howard took out his syrette and handed it to his team sergeant. It would be the first of about five as Ford asked everyone he encountered for morphine. Since his radio was broken, Howard got on Ford's and called Walton.

"Hey, Kyle, what do you need?"

Howard could tell that his team sergeant was hurt badly and out of it. That's because Ford wasn't yelling at him and telling him that he was doing stuff all wrong. Instead he was just standing there, letting Howard talk on his radio.

"I need you to shoot that building with the Carl Gustav," Walton said.

"What building?"

Peering up to the top of the mountain, he could see several mud-walled houses still standing.

"Okay, do you see the power lines?" Walton asked.

"Yeah."

"Right on the other side of the power lines, do you see that building?" Walton said.

Scanning the ridge, Howard thought he knew which building Walton wanted destroyed.

"Stay with Scott," Howard told Wallen as he rounded up his commandos.

"I'm good, man," Wallen said, preparing to go with Howard. "You said I was fine."

While not as badly hurt as Ford, Wallen was still injured, and Howard didn't want to keep putting him in harm's way.

"I know I said you're fine," he said. "But I really need you to stay here because I was lying to you."

I'm a weapons sergeant, not a medic, he thought. *Don't listen to me. I don't know what the fuck I'm talking about. I'm just making shit up to keep you calm.*

48

Walding

Mind games. That's what they are, Walding thought.

He was getting tired because he was going into shock. He knew it. He tried to keep firing his rifle. It was the only way to stay alive. Sooner or later, they were going to be rescued. They were going to get off the mountain. That's what he told himself. Walding was trying to stay positive. But he knew his leg was in bad shape. Being a country boy, he had blown his fair share of animals in half. So it wasn't a shock seeing the effects that a bullet actually had on flesh. This helped him cope with the disturbing visuals.

From working on a farm, he had inherited his grandfather's grit and steel. How many times when he was baling hay did he feel like giving up? How many times during football practices—two-a-days in the brutal August sun—did he cramp up but stay on the field? How many obstacles had he overcome in his life? His parents' arrest? Moving in with his grandparents in a new town with a new set of rules. Walding was digging deep to deal with the misery. He had no morphine. Nothing to kill the pain. He had been lying on the ground for at least an hour with his lower leg tied to his thigh with a bootlace. And he was still functioning.

But when shock sets in, the waves consume the mind like a tsunami to the soul. He closed his eyes and whispered prayers: "Our Father, take care of my family if anything happens to me."

It was his moment of clarity. He wasn't thinking about himself—what would happen if he bled out. If he died on the mountain. He was thinking about his wife and children. Who would take care of them?

Then his mind drifted to his grandfather—the most important figure in his life. He'd learned so much from the old man. How to live a good moral life. How to treat people with respect. He'd learned to be mentally tough and face adversity like a man.

I'm going to come home, Papa. I promise.

49

Walton

Walton knew he couldn't keep coordinating the entire operation, so he asked the other team leader in the wadi to take over.

"Hey, get your TOC [tactical operations center] set up and start talking to Monster 33," Walton told the other captain.

He didn't know how much longer they would be alive. Rhyner was directing the bombs in closer and closer. Fire was coming from three sides and fighters were right above them in a house. He could hear them speaking Arabic, but couldn't make out what they were saying. Walton was sure he and the others were about to get overrun.

One of the last intelligence reports he'd read before the mission was that the fighters protecting Ghafour had obtained a lot of grenades. He knew all they had to do was reach out of one of the windows and start tossing grenades.

Walton rolled over and felt for one of his own grenades. For a second he considered cooking it off and tossing it into the window above. But missing would just mean the grenade would land on them. Only the air strikes could save them now. Walton decided that if Rhyner was killed or they lost their radios, he was going to order the team to roll the wounded off the cliff and jump behind them.

It was a hard decision, but it was the battlefield calculus that he was trained to perform. He had already stopped the medevacs from coming in until they were off the mountain. He knew Ford and Wallen were down there bleeding. There were several commandos wounded and at least one dead. But he knew they might only have one chance to bring in the helicopters and he couldn't risk it. It was a hard decision because Behr, Morales, and Walding were lying in the rocks in front of him bleeding to death.

Bullets and fragments bounced off Walton's helmet again. He turned to the Afghan terps hiding behind them.

"For Christ sake, just shoot in that direction," he begged them.

Walton could feel things spinning out of control. The longer they had been pinned down, the more desperate the situation had become. He had been on a quick reaction force for a unit in the 82nd Airborne. Some paratroopers got in trouble in Fallujah, but the force had been able to rescue them. He had always imagined that once all the planes showed up here in the mountains, they would bomb the shit out of the insurgents, and his team would be saved. That's because the American government has the ability to save you.

But it was very clear now that the team was on its own. Nobody could save them. It seemed that every U.S. fighting unit in Afghanistan was stopping and moving toward them. Walton could hear the traffic on the satellite radio.

But it still wasn't enough. They wouldn't get here in time. Shurer was running out of medical supplies. Soon he wasn't going to be able to treat any of them.

"We've got to get the fuck out of here," Shurer yelled at Walton. "They're bleeding out."

Walton turned to Sanders and Carter.

"Listen, you guys have to find a way to get down that mountain."

"Down that fucking cliff?" Sanders said.

"Find a way down that cliff. I don't care how bad it is."

On the radio again, Walton called back to Bagram.

"Listen, we're combat ineffective," he said. "We have an SF element about to be overrun. We need immediate CAS. We need a B-52 or B-1 because this CAS is not having its desired effect."

50

Carter

Carter knew it was an incredibly difficult task. But if the wounded were going to survive—if anyone was going to live through this day—he had to help Sanders find a way down the mountain. In addition, the path had to be hidden from insurgents. If it wasn't, HIG snipers would be able to easily pick off the wounded soldiers. But Carter wondered how they were going to find it. Their position on the ledge was surrounded on three sides by cliffs with sixty-foot drops. With the insurgents' buildings thirty to forty feet directly above them and more across the way, it was suicide.

He knew the path they had used to climb up the mountain at the beginning of the mission was the only safe way down to the wadi—as far as terrain was concerned. But that route was now too dangerous. Enemy snipers were lurking everywhere. He knew that Ford and Williams had just used that path and were lucky to make it to the bottom. Ford's plan had called for positioning commandos at various points along that trail to provide cover for the wounded. But with Ford out of the picture, this option had become unfeasible. Besides, the Afghan commandos—the fighters hyped by U.S. and

Afghan commanders as the Wolves—were too unreliable. While some commandos had provided fire, too many had cowered behind rocks.

The team had run out of options. For Carter, the reality began to set it: If they stayed on the mountain, they would either be killed by insurgents or by friendly fire. The bombs were danger close—and they were having little effect on the insurgents. The HIG fighters were just too entrenched in the rocks and caves and underground passageways in the compound. They were like cockroaches in a tenement apartment embedded deep in rotting wood—they just wouldn't go away. The only chance he and his team had was to find another way down the mountain while the aerial assault slowed down enemy fire.

And that was the plan.

So here was Carter, ready to take on another assignment. He had gone from combat cameraman—someone who observes and documents missions—to active participant, firing at insurgents. He spent most of the mission as a medical assistant, tending to wounded soldiers. Now he was ready to find an escape route. Of all the assignments he'd undertaken on this miserable day, this one might be the most important.

51

Wurzbach

Wurzbach was looking for guidance. He wanted to help the assault team but knew he couldn't leave his position without permission. So he called for Ford over the radio. He knew Ford was injured, but was still actively involved in the battle.

"Do I abandon my position?" he asked.

No response, but Wurzbach heard ODA 3312 over the radio saying they couldn't get through to help Ford's team because of the heavy fire. So he came to the startling conclusion: If another ODA with a platoon of commandos couldn't get through, neither could his team.

So Wurzbach decided to stay in position. If nothing else, he could keep the bad guys from maneuvering around the back side of the village. That was his goal.

At that point, Wurzbach was pretty much resigned to the fact that no one was getting out of there. The fighters and attack helicopters were either going to kill everybody with bombs or he and his team were going to be killed by insurgents. Not good thoughts.

Hugging the rock wall with his back, Wurzbach recognized Staff Sergeant Plants heading in his direction. Plants dove behind the wall.

"Why didn't you call me up?" he asked

"This is it, dude. There's nothing here, as you can see." Wurzbach replied. "I figured you were in a safe place, rocking."

Plants glanced at the cover. "I was, and you're right. We can't all fit here."

The explosions were loud and continuous. The Apaches and fighters were trying to level the village. When there was a brief lull in the bombing, Wurzbach decided to see what was going on closer to the action. To do that, though, he had to move across an open field to try to get a clear view of the assault team's position. There was no cover. He needed his interpreter in case they ran into Afghan commandos. He told Noodles his plan.

"You ready to do it?"

Noodles agreed, but Wurzbach could see the terror in his eyes.

So Wurzbach turned and began running. He bolted across the field—it was about 150 feet long. All he had to do was reach a thicket of tree and rocks. If he got there he would be safe. He was running as fast as his legs would kick. It was all adrenaline—like he had just downed a six-pack of Red Bull. *Keep going,* he told himself.

He hit some cover and turned around. Noodles hadn't moved an inch. He was frozen in his tracks.

"Come on," Wurzbach shouted.

Noodles just stood there.

"Damn it, you can do it."

Noodles finally mustered the courage and ran. When he reached Wurzbach, Wurzbach asked what happened. "As soon as you took off, dirt was flying at your heels," said Noodles, trying to catch his breath. "They were shooting at you the whole way. It's amazing they didn't hit you."

Wurzbach had no idea. "Damn, really?"

"Yeah," the terp, said huffing and puffing. "I can't believe you didn't notice. It looked like something out of a movie." He paused for a moment. "What about me?" Noodles asked.

"When you ran I saw a few pieces of dirt kick up, but it was behind you."

Wurzbach now had a good vantage point. He could see fire still coming from the compound toward the assault team on the ledge—it seemed to be coming from three different directions. He could tell that the assault team hadn't made it far up the mountain—and that their flank was horribly exposed.

Wurzbach knew it was time to consolidate and provide cover for the assault team. Maybe then, they would have a chance.

[Part 4]

ESCAPE

52

Ford

Wallen kicked open the door.

The squat house at the base of the hill was little more than a hut. It was probably a temporary home built while the Afghan farmers constructed their larger houses in the village. Made of thick dried mud, it had been converted into a goat barn. Crawling inside, Ford collapsed against the wall in the dark room. Wallen set Ford's rifle next to him. All of a sudden the floor underneath Ford began to move. Startled, he jumped up when a baby goat shot out from under him.

Motherfucker, he thought. *What's next?*

Settling back down against the wall, Ford began placing urgent calls for morphine. He had neglected to get another syrette from Howard, and now the pain was tremendous. Calling medics from the other team, he asked for anything to stanch the pain. It came in waves. Each time, he dug the heel of his boot into the dirt, until soon he had scraped a trench into the floor.

"I need your medic," Ford called to Lodyga, who was up the valley. "We're running down on morphine."

ODA 3312 was already moving toward Ford. The team had packed up its support positions. But as the soldiers moved closer, they started to take fire from enemy fighters on the hills above.

"I will try and get up there, but we're pinned down right now," Lodyga responded over the radio.

Over and over, Ford called for morphine. Each call, he tried to stay composed. He didn't want his voice to betray the fact that the shit was bad and he was hurting.

When the morphine he had gotten from Howard finally started to work, it hit him hard. He hadn't experimented with drugs before the Army, so when the painkillers began to take effect, his speech became slurred. His voice seemed to roll out of the radio like syrup.

Between radio calls, he struggled to retain consciousness.

With his left arm in tatters, it was hard to get comfortable. Every time he tried to feel at ease, his left arm failed. It offered no support. One time, he closed his eyes and woke up after being bumped.

It was a goat again, its head pressing against his good arm. Using his right arm, Ford would shove the goat away only to have it return. The goat was determined to push him out of the building. As Ford struggled with the animal, he glanced around the room. Wallen had left, but he spotted an Afghan commando sitting nearby. He yelled and gestured for him to help. But the soldier just shrugged.

Shoot the damn thing or something, Ford thought, again fending off the goat with his good arm.

Finally, the commando got the message and grabbed the goat by its horns. Ford could see the animal struggling to stay put as the commando dragged it out the door.

Moments later, Wallen returned. He had been relaying messages or questions from Walton to the team sergeant.

Ford knew the others needed to get off that ledge. But they hadn't moved yet. In his view, the problem was simple: Nobody had a sense of urgency about getting the team down. The team was getting chewed up, and they needed to head to the wadi.

"Ryan, what the fuck are they doing?"

But Wallen didn't have an answer.

53

Carter

There was nowhere to go but straight down. Carter and Sanders had been examining possible escape routes. But they ruled out the best ones because of heavy fire from HIG fighters. So they turned their attention to the back side of the mountain.

They quickly discovered that there was no enemy fire from that location. But the landscape was daunting. To reach the bottom, they would have to find a path on the side of a cliff that dropped nearly sixty feet to the wadi. Not an easy thing to do without carrying the wounded. An impossible task while hauling soldiers with life-threatening injuries.

Still, it was the only way.

Without gunfire, at least they had a chance. If they used the switchbacks they had taken up the mountain, the wounded soldiers would be easy targets for the HIG fighters. That's why Walton had ordered them to find another way.

Now they had to use all their skills to find the best route. While Carter found some narrow ledges leading downhill, the drop-offs between some of those ridges were wide. In a few places, ten to twenty feet separated the two ledges. At those points, the soldiers would have to hang from one ledge and drop to the next. Their landings would have to be perfect or else they could roll off the mountain. If that happened, the fall could kill them— they could tumble down and their bodies would be smashed as they landed on the sharp, jagged rocks.

And there were other problems, too. They had to carry their guns and gear. More importantly, they had to haul several seriously wounded soldiers who were barely alive. Glancing at the possible escape routes, they wondered, *How could we do it? Could the wounded soldiers survive those drops?*

Carter and Sanders tried over and over to navigate their way down the mountain. Several times, they slipped on loose rocks and had to hang on to shrubs. The two had taken an Afghan commando with them to help. But he was useless. He was too afraid to move from his position, so finally Carter and Sanders had to push him out of the way.

As Carter climbed, his hands hurt. They were bleeding. Drenched in sweat, he dug his fingers deep into the dirt and the rocks cut like a knife. His muscles felt ready to explode. There were too many drop-offs, and this was freestyle rock climbing. No ropes. They just used their strength to pull up or to hold on when they were headed down. It was frustrating. You had to be Spider-Man to scale these cliffs. *This is a bad place, a fucking bad place,* Carter thought.

"Shit, I don't know," Carter said to Sanders. "This is going to be tough."

Sanders agreed.

The soldiers were exhausted. They had been fighting for hours and there was no end in sight. Covered as they were in blood and dirt, it would have been easy to give up. But they had to keep moving forward. Find a way off. Everyone was depending on them. So with the firefight raging in the background, they resumed their mission. They climbed up and down the sides of the mountain, desperately trying to find the right path. They even retraced their steps. Maybe there was something they'd missed. Finally, Sanders found a route that might work. There were still some extreme drop-offs in the beginning. But about halfway down, the drop-offs weren't as bad and the path wasn't as steep.

Sitting on the rocks about halfway down the mountain, Sanders turned to Carter. "If we go this way, we might make it."

Carter knew what he meant. This route seemed to provide enough traction. Not as many loose rocks. And there were some shrubs to hold on to just in case. Not perfect. But it was the only way. This was an emergency. They had run out of time. Even in a best-case scenario—if the firing had stopped and they could move quickly down the mountain—the wounded soldiers could die. But with the incessant fire, the battle was far from over.

Carter took a deep breath and looked at Sanders. He liked the way this Special Forces soldier handled himself. He was diligent. He didn't give up in the face of a difficult challenge. The irony of this assignment wasn't lost on Carter. They were both pressed into an unbelievable situation. They were an unlikely pair. And yet they were the ones who found the path that could save the team.

"Let's do it," Carter said to Sanders.

So Carter and Sanders bounded back to Walton.

When they reached the captain, he was still on the radio. But he quickly turned his attention to the men.

"Can we get them down? Are they going to make it?" Walton asked.

Carter paused for a moment to collect his thoughts. "Yeah, they'll live, but it's going to be a bitch getting them down."

Sanders agreed. "Well, are broken bones going to be all right?"

Walton didn't hesitate. "Fuck it. Let's go," he shouted.

It was time to pack up and leave.

54

Howard

Pressing his body against the rocks, Howard took a deep breath.

For a half hour, he had been frantically climbing up the mountain, followed closely by Williams and several Afghan commandos. It was a mad dash over unforgiving terrain to try to reach Walton. What Ford had told him was disturbing. The team was badly shot up. Just looking at Ford, he could tell that.

Howard began thinking about his friends. How they were stuck on the ledge, bleeding and desperately fighting for their lives. Walton needed help getting the wounded off the mountain. He could hear Ford's words in his head as he climbed. That was his motivation. Nothing was going to stop him. But just as he was about to scale the last switchback to reach the captain, Williams grabbed him.

"What are you doing?" Howard said.

"You can't go up that way," Williams said.

Howard pulled away. "I have no choice."

Williams hesitated. He didn't want to say the words he had been thinking. But finally he did. Howard needed to know the truth. "Everybody who has gone up that way has been shot."

It stopped Howard in his tracks. "Okay. Good point."

Now they had to find another way—and quickly. Howard had his Carl Gustav team and AJ in tow. But now rounds started cracking near them. They ricocheted off the wall and impacted the dirt near their feet.

Howard still didn't have a radio, and Williams was unable to reach Walton on his despite being less than fifty feet away. They had no idea if anyone was alive on the ledge, which was just above them. It was difficult to hear anything over the belching gunfire and the bombs exploding in the villages. It was frustrating. All they had to do was reach up, grab the ledge, pull themselves up, and they would be there. They were that close. But with the firefight, they might as well have been back in Jalalabad. It's hard to maneuver when you're inches away from death.

"We're going to wait two minutes, and if we can't get in touch with Kyle, we're going to go over there," Williams said.

Williams was always putting time lines on things.

"Okay. Good plan," Howard said.

But they never followed the time line. Less than two minutes later, Howard and Williams came up with another plan. Grabbing AJ by the shoulders, Howard explained to him what they wanted to do.

"Have all of the commandos step out and those two guys are going to shoot that way," he said, pointing toward the closed portion of the valley. "Those two are going to shoot that way. And they are going to cover us and we're going to climb around the rock face over to where Kyle is at."

Slinging their weapons, Howard and Williams prepared to move.

"One. Two. Three. Go!"

The commandos were supposed to start shooting, but all of them hugged the rocks. Finally, one of the commandos leaned out and fired off a short burst. His comrades soon followed, but Howard and Williams were long gone. They were already moving up the mountain in a different direction. They were trying to find a back way to Walton's position—a path that didn't expose them to deadly gunfire—when Williams signaled to Howard that he'd discovered one. They found a few good hand- and foot-holds and made it to an outcropping large enough to stand on and peek over the ledge directly behind Walton's position.

Williams poked his head over the ledge. Both Walton and Rhyner were huddled below a sloping rock ledge. Rhyner was lying there motionless.

"What's up? Are you guys okay?" Williams said.

Walton finally heard them and turned. His satellite radio had lost its secure link to Bagram and Jalalabad.

As Howard crawled past to start providing cover fire, Walton tossed the radio to Williams.

"Matt, the radio is fucked."

Breaking open the backpack, Williams quickly reloaded the COMSEC, the codes that allowed the radio to make a secure link to the Army's satellite communications network.

Bullets skipped off the rocks, making it nearly impossible for them to stand up or move forward. Howard was shocked at the conditions up here. The space on the ledge where the team was pinned down was small—no bigger than a typical living room. Yet they were all squeezed in there. It was claustrophobic.

"How many guys do you got?" Walton said, relieved to finally have some fresh bodies.

"We have like five or six commandos," Williams said, scrambling to where Walton was concealed.

"Um, no, we don't," Howard said.

"What?" Williams said, looking back at the ledge. Only AJ was standing there.

55

Morales

They were finally getting ready to move, and Morales would be the first to leave.

Everything was set. Carter and Sanders had found a path. Howard and Williams had rejoined the team. Walton, Rhyner, and Shurer were ready, and so, hopefully, were the handful of commandos and interpreters trapped on the ledge.

Still, it would be a difficult evacuation. HIG fighters were still firing at will—nothing seemed to slow them down. Morales could hardly move. Only one leg was functional and his entire body recoiled every time he took a step or made a move. His body was broken.

Walton devised a plan. He would help Rhyner and Williams lay down suppressive fire while Howard moved to the front of the position with his sniper rifle. The rounds should provide enough cover for Sanders, Carter, and Shurer, who would transport Morales, Walding, and Behr.

"Let's do it," Walton said.

The men let out a barrage of fire. Meanwhile, Sanders and Carter moved quickly to Morales. They tried to be gentle as they lifted him. Morales leaned on them as he hobbled to the edge of the cliff. He climbed over and slid a few feet. Then he stared at the drop. It was unreal. One wrong move and he was dead. Everyone had to be careful. But how can you be 100 percent careful when you're literally lowering a seriously injured solider from one ledge to another—with steep drop-offs. It just couldn't be done.

Morales didn't want to be a burden. So he pushed himself to act like he wasn't seriously wounded. Even though his thigh was punctured and his ankle was shattered, he still tried to walk by himself. He tried sliding down some of the way. He even tried lowering himself. But at one point in the journey, he just couldn't hang on. Crawling down, he reached a ledge and shouted to Carter, "Mike, you have to catch me, man. I have to let go."

And let go he did, falling several feet, but Carter somehow managed to catch him. It was like that almost the entire way down. With every move, Morales could feel the strength being sapped from his body. And that had never happened before.

He always had a reserve that he could tap into—whether it was training, running, or on missions. But now the well was dry. He was a proud, tough man. A team player. He didn't want anyone to help him. He was the one who should be helping others. But at the moment he had no choice. With his injuries, this was strenuous. It would have been even without the wounds. But with the injuries? Nearly impossible. He kept repeating *a Morales never quits* over and over in his head. It was his mantra. His way of dealing with a massive amount of pain that consumed his body.

But finally, he reached a slope at the bottom of the mountain that led to a clearing, and he felt relieved. It was a big step. Now there was a chance of getting out alive. At the bottom, he was surrounded by Special Forces soldiers from ODA 3312 who were anxious to help, including his buddy Nick McGarry, who, along with an Afghan commando, wrapped his arms around Morales and escorted him to the casualty collection point.

On the way, they passed Morales's boot—the one Shurer had tossed off the mountain when he began working on his ankle.

"Hey, you want it?" McGarry asked.

"Nah, fuck it. I'll buy a new one when I get home."

56

Walding

It was Walding's turn to leave—and it was just in time.

The situation was grave. Walding knew it. All you had to do was count the wounded: Behr, Morales, and Ford. Rhyner was grazed. Rounds had bounced off Shurer and Walton's helmets. CK was dead. Walding wondered who else was injured. The reality was that no one was safe. No one. And now he himself was fading fast. He could feel it. His body was shutting down.

In retrospect, Walding should have seen it coming. From jumping out of a hovering helicopter and landing hard in a rock-filled wadi to falling into an ice-cold river to scaling a steep mountain that was reminiscent of the Rangers' famed climb to take Pointe du Hoc during the D-Day invasion.

Nothing had been easy. Walding's hands were cut and bleeding from the climb. But he looked back with pride. He had reached the objective with his team. He and Sanders were so close to the village that they could almost reach out and touch the first building in the compound. But then the shooting started and everything changed.

Sanders was the one who told Walding they were leaving. He explained that he'd found a way to get everyone off the mountain. It was risky—there were steep drops along the way. But it was much riskier staying on the mountain. Sooner or later, they could get overrun. Despite heavy bombing, the insurgents hadn't gone away.

"Are we going to make it?" Walding asked.

No one had the answer.

But now, on this small patch of rock, he was optimistic. Morales had made it to the bottom, right? How dangerous could it be?

In preparation, Shurer ran to Walding and began checking his tourniquet. Although Walding was only fifteen feet away, it was the first time the medic had examined him. The tourniquet was a mess. It seemed that the wound was bleeding more now than at any point since he was shot. Shurer adjusted the tourniquet to try to stop the bleeding.

"We have to move, John," the medic said.

Walding's eyes were closing. He was fighting so hard to stay alert. He was blacking out.

"John, we have to move."

Walding nodded weakly.

It was Shurer's job to take care of Walding. One of the terps, Blade, and a commando, ran over to Shurer to help.

"We have to get you down the hill," Shurer told Walding.

"I can't. I can't do it."

"No, you have to do this. You have to get up."

The battle was raging. While planes had been bombing the compounds, insurgents were still firing a steady barrage of rounds and RPGs at the soldiers. It seemed that it was getting worse, not better, and if they stayed where they were any longer, no one would get out alive.

"I need you to listen to me," Shurer said sternly to Walding. "I need you to hold your leg and get up."

But Walding refused to move. Shurer believed that the image of his nearly severed leg was just getting into his head.

"I can't do it," Walding said.

"Focus," Shurer shouted at him. "Focus. You can do it."

Walding finally nodded his head yes. He would do it. The soldiers lifted him and began moving him toward the edge of the cliff. He was extremely weak but he tried his best.

Moving Walding was a little different from moving Morales. Morales had tried his hardest to help. He would slide and crawl. Walding, however, couldn't move at all. He was probably in shock and incredibly weak from losing so much blood. So when the soldiers reached the edge of a berm, one man would lower Walding down to another. It went on like that until they came to a drop-off that was too wide to lower him by hand. They were stuck.

But then Shurer had an idea. He removed a green nylon cord from the cargo pocket on his pants—the one Ford had forced the entire team to carry—and wrapped it underneath Walding's arms. Then the soldiers lowered Walding to the next rock. Shurer had questioned why they had to carry the chord. He didn't think they would ever need it. But if he hadn't had it now, there'd have been no way they could safely lower Walding.

It took a half hour or so, but Walding was finally at the bottom of the cliff. The soldiers waiting there moved him to the casualty collection point, where he was placed on stretcher near Morales. He heard Morales say something to him, but he couldn't answer. He was too feeble.

It was easier for him just to close his eyes.

57

Behr

They were finally ready for Behr.

"You're next, man," Carter said.

Behr tried to smile, but was too weak.

He was glad they were attempting to move him from this hellhole. And for the first time since the firefight began, he had a sense that he could get out of there alive. But he also had some concerns. How were they going to move him when he was immobile? Would the move exacerbate his wounds? His right leg was dead—he couldn't move it at all. The bullet must have dislocated bones, he thought.

Sanders and Carter lifted Behr slowly. The soldiers also helped him into his body armor. They wanted to make sure he was protected on the way down. Once on his feet, Behr felt light-headed. He had lost a lot of blood, and if he wasn't already in shock, he was close to it. The morphine had played a role, too. The narcotic makes you sleepy and slows your breathing. He knew he had to be alert, because any way off the mountain—short of a helicopter— would involve climbing, and he was in no condition to walk, let alone climb.

But they had to get off the ledge quickly. He knew his fellow soldiers were risking their lives by standing and firing at the enemy. They were doing it to draw their attention away from him. Sanders and Carter wrapped their arms under Behr's torso and began walking toward the edge of a cliff away from the gunfire.

When they reached the edge, Behr peered down—and it didn't seem like that was a good way to leave. It was steep, but it was the only way they could move off the mountain without being exposed to gunfire.

Behr took a deep breath. He was always searching for meaning in his life. From his teenage days in the Pentecostal church to Bible college to acting to the Green Berets. His search had led him here, to the edge of a cliff. If he survived this, he could face anything. No more running. But first he had to survive. Moving down the mountain was dangerous. And even that didn't go as planned.

It began with one person on a ledge lowering him to another soldier stationed on the rocks below. It was a slow, tedious process. They had to be careful. One wrong move—a slip or a fall—and it could exacerbate Behr's wounds. At first, it went smoothly. And then it happened, like everything on this mission, another glitch. As they were lowering him, his body armor snagged on a jagged rock that jutted from the cliff face.

"I can't move," he shouted. "Don't drop me, man."

Carter and Sanders tried pulling him back up. Then they tried tugging him down. But nothing seemed to work. Meanwhile, Behr was dangling and in excruciating pain. He was afraid about aggravating his injuries. At that point, the soldiers had no other option but to cut off his body armor with scissors. When they did this, he dropped more than ten feet, but landed on top of a soldier. This cushioned the impact of the fall, but Behr was in agony. *I don't know how much more I can take,* he thought. His body had been jolted with two rounds from an AK-47. A rock had smashed into his stomach after a two-thousand-pound bomb blasted a building. Now this?

But just when he was ready to stay down, his will to survive kicked in. He wanted to get out of this place alive. He didn't want to die on the side of a mountain so far from home. He wanted to see his family and friends. And he was so close to escaping. He was already halfway down the mountain. *I'm going to get out of here. I'm not throwing in the towel. Dying is not an option,* he said to himself.

The soldiers resumed moving Behr and he promised himself to drill deeper and muster enough strength to make it to the bottom. With the guns blaring in the background and Apaches buzzing overhead, the soldiers gingerly lowered him from ledge to ledge. He didn't know how long it took, but he finally reached a slope at the base of the mountain where SF soldiers and Afghan commandos were waiting. They quickly moved him to a casualty collection point. But shortly after he was placed on a Skedco, a softball-size rock rolled off the hill and bounced off his side.

"Are you fucking kidding me!"

58

Howard

Sliding behind his sniper rifle, Howard started to scan windows again for gunmen. He had to buy time for the others to get off the mountain. The soldiers on the ledge were still taking pretty regular fire.

Between bullets impacting the rocks in front of him, Howard shot into the windows of the buildings above him. He started picking spots where he would hide. A crack in the wall. A clump of bushes. He never saw anyone. It wasn't like they were fixing bayonets in preparation for a charge. He made steady work of shooting into every dark space in hopes of stemming the fire.

Howard was shooting his SR-25 inches over the top of CK and the dead Afghan commando they had dragged over for cover.

"Hey, Kyle, they're both dead, right?" he asked.

Each round skimmed inches over their bodies about ten feet away. If they weren't dead, a sudden move by one of them would change that.

"They're both dead," Walton said.

Rhyner was next to Howard, firing in between calling in air strikes. Every time he shot, shards of rock would cascade down on Howard. Howard figured Rhyner wasn't elevating his barrel enough and was burying rounds into the ledge in front of them. It happens when the shooter doesn't adjust for the sight on the rifle, which sits above the barrel. After several repetitions of this, Howard had had enough.

"Zach, what the fuck, man? You're shooting the wall. Stop shooting the fucking wall."

Rhyner turned to him. "No, I'm not."

Just as Rhyner said it, more rocks hit Howard in the face.

"Never mind. It wasn't you."

A few shots later, the sniper missed short. The bullet hit a few feet in front of Howard. When a bullet hits at a shallow angle, it will cut a line down and then ricochet up and over. The shallow shot gave Howard a line pointing directly to where this asshole was hiding.

Before the mission, the team had rolled an RG-31, a massive armored truck, on the way from Kabul to Jalalabad. The trucks are equipped with a Common Remotely Operated Weapon Station (CROWS) that allows the gunner to sit inside the truck and work the machine gun on the roof.

The remote system means gunners don't have to stick their heads outside of the armored hull. On the outside, the machine gun sits on a motorized mount with a large camera underneath it.

The gun is controlled by a joystick that resembles a helicopter pilot's controls with a target and toggle switches that allow the gunner to zoom in on targets. The camera has a laser finder to measure ranges, and night vision, which allow the gunners to pinpoint targets and zoom in close enough to see the enemy's face, even at night.

When the team crashed the truck, Howard picked through the wreckage and snagged the laser range finder with a small LCD screen. He put a button on it to activate the laser and mounted it on his sniper rifle.

Now, up on the ledge, Howard lined up the shot with the range finder, following it up to a stable built into the side of the mountain next to a massive house the team had been trying to blow up since the start of the battle. From his scope, Howard could see two tiny windows facing the wadi.

It was 217 meters away.

Adjusting his scope, he emptied half of his twenty-round magazine through each one of the windows. He couldn't go up and check to see if he had hit the sniper, but the shooting dropped off significantly.

Seeing an opening, one of the team's interpreters, Max, raced to retrieve CK's body. Walton had told the Afghan that they might have to roll CK off the side of the cliff to get him down. No one wanted to leave CK there, but it seemed to be the only option at the time.

"You have to move CK out of here. I don't care how you do it," Howard told Max. "You have to do it and you have to do it right now."

While Howard covered him, Max dragged CK under the sloping rock. It was a sad scene. Max and a few of the terps slowly removed all his equipment and left it at the edge of the cliff. They tied CK's shoes together and did the same with his hands, making it easier to carry him.

As soon as CK's body was dragged away, the commando who had been shot in the head popped up and stumbled off the cliff to escape. Howard was stunned. A few minutes ago, he was firing bullets inches above the Afghan's body. Now watching him rise was like watching a scene from *The Night of the Living Dead*.

I guess he wasn't dead after all, Howard thought.

59

Walton

Now that the wounded had been evacuated, it was time for the rest of the soldiers to leave.

Walton glanced at the ledge and saw that there were only a few team members and Afghan commandos up there.

The terps had already left to carry CK's body down the mountain. The wounded commando—the one they feared was dead—followed close behind. Walton knew there was no tactical reason to stay on that ledge. For all intents and purposes, Commando Wrath was over. At one point in the firefight, he had requested a "sizable QRF [quick reaction force]" with the "intent of reorganizing and reattacking after [they] evacuated the casualties." He knew they didn't have enough Special Forces advisers or terps to get the commandos to do what they needed them to do. In his view, the commandos—the celebrated fighting unit—were "completely ineffective in turning the tide of the situation."

Walton was angry that they didn't accomplish their goals—that Haji Ghafour, one of the top terrorists in the world, probably escaped. But Walton was pragmatic. He realized they had to get off the mountain and get out of the valley. Now it was all about saving lives.

"It's time to go," he shouted at Howard. "I need you to hold the ground."

Howard understood; he would keep firing while the others tried to escape.

One by one the remaining commandos and team members began leaving, disappearing over the edge of the cliff while Howard provided cover. Williams started his descent, followed by Rhyner and Walton.

It was treacherous.

Walton was in top physical shape. But he was having a difficult time climbing down. Maybe it was because he had watched his fellow soldiers getting blown apart. Or that CK's blood and brains were splattered on his uniform. Maybe it was because he came face-to-face with his own mortality. Whatever the reason, the battle had taken a toll. The West Point graduate who prided himself on setting and reaching lofty goals was physically and emotionally drained.

So as he climbed down, he slipped and fell twice, at least twenty feet. At one point, he was holding on to no more than a tree root. He used every last bit of strength to pull himself up. As he sat there, he realized that without that root, he would have fallen to his death. Rhyner had also slipped and tumbled and used the same tree root to save his life.

With all the slipping and sliding, rocks became loose and rolled down the mountain. Walton watched as some of the rocks hit soldiers in the wadi.

And he also noticed that the terps were having trouble carrying CK. They had been slipping, too, and near the bottom, they were forced to drop him the remaining distance. That was hard for Walton to watch. CK was a terp, but he was also brother.

He had to stop thinking about CK. Even though the captain was close to the bottom, the mission was far from over. They were still under fire. And now that they were off the ledge, he knew the insurgents would focus their full attention on the wadi.

60

Howard

The ledge was littered with equipment.

Howard was the last American on the mountain and quickly started to toss the gear over the side.

A squad automatic weapon.

CK's body armor and rifle.

Handfuls of M203 grenade rounds.

Even his own assault backpack.

The gear landed in the wadi below with a *thud,* much to the chagrin of the wounded soldiers. But there was no way Howard could carry it all down, and he didn't want to leave it for the insurgents.

With the ledge clean, he began his descent with another commando who had stayed behind. Before that, Howard had handed the SR-25 to commandos scaling down the mountain. The rifle passed from commando to commando all the way to the wadi. Howard didn't want to mess it up while he climbed down.

Armed only with a pistol, he quickly ran into trouble. He knew the route was steep, but he had trouble keeping his footing. At one point, he lost his grip in the dirt and the soil gave way. Grasping for anything, he latched onto a root that stuck out of the mountain, the same one that had saved Walton and Rhyner. It looked like something Wile E. Coyote would use to steady himself.

When Howard was about halfway down, Rhyner, unknown to Howard, had called in a two-thousand-pound bomb strike. Howard could hear the bomb whistling in and then his world went black.

The bomb hit the building directly above him—the one that he had been trying to hit with the Carl G. The structure was less than sixty feet away, but because it was up and over the ledge, there wasn't a direct line to Howard. The angle of the cliff protected him from the pressure, but not from the debris, dust, and smoke that covered the cliff face. The entire mountain shook. Pressed as he was against the cliff, huge boulders bounced over him.

He couldn't help but think how ironic it would be if, after everything he had been through this day, he died because of an American bomb—not an insurgent's bullet.

Howard finally made it to the bottom. After he checked on the conditions of the wounded soldiers, he searched for his sniper rifle. But when he found it, he noticed that the LCD screen was cracked. The range finder was broken, but he wasn't too upset. He'd stolen it, and the jerry-rigged device had served its purpose.

61

Sergeant First Class Sergio Martinez

The bottom of the hill looked like a triage ward.

Rhyner was crawling down the last steep incline of the hill, when Martinez arrived with his aid bag. As he approached, Martinez could see the interpreters rolling CK off the mountain. He watched as the terp's body fell the last few feet to the wadi below.

While Lodyga met with Walton to coordinate the medevacs, McGarry set up a security perimeter around the bottom of the hill to ward off any attacks. Positioned near the goat barn where Ford waited, Martin was on the satellite radio calling in the medevac helicopters. They had gone to refuel and it would take a few minutes for them to return.

Martinez went straight to the wounded. They were laid out at the bottom of the cliff. He asked Shurer what he could do. The medic was focusing on Behr because he appeared to be in the worst shape. Nearby, Carter was tending to Morales.

"Help John," Shurer said.

Kneeling at Walding's side, Martinez broke open his medical bag.

"You're going to be okay."

Walding was scuffed up. His teeth were covered in dirt. Martinez could see his lips were dry from being dehydrated. Walding had a little smile and he kept asking for morphine. He was complaining about the pain and that he was having problems breathing. Martinez didn't give him any because morphine depresses a patient's respiratory drive.

He started an IV on Walding and then helped Carter start one on Morales. Since Shurer was short on medical supplies, Martinez's aid bag became the only means of treating the wounded until the helicopters arrived.

We've got to get these guys out of here, he thought.

The shooting had slacked off a little, but Martinez knew they weren't safe yet. He was amazed that the wounded were still alive, but the clock was ticking. *When are the medevac helicopters going to show up?*

62

Walton

When he reached the wadi, Walton consolidated his team and rushed to the goat shed. The captain's goal was to "reestablish communications and control." He wanted to know how the other ODAs were doing, and how close the medevac birds were to the valley. More importantly, he wanted to check on Ford's condition. He was worried because the last time he saw Ford, his arm was ripped apart. Outside of Shurer briefly helping Ford tighten his tourniquet, no medic had checked on his wound. Walton was afraid that his condition had deteriorated. Shurer was busy tending to the wounded at the casualty collection point at the base of the mountain. So Walton knew he would have to use his medic skills to treat Ford.

When he entered the shed, Wallen was still in charge. Despite being wounded, he had kept control of the commandos around him and held the house. Walton was impressed. He knew Wallen had been injured early in the battle. Yet he stepped up and kept things under control.

Walton glanced at Ford, who was propped up against the wall.

"Kyle, you got to help me, man," Ford said. "The pain. I need morphine."

Kneeling down, Walton checked the tourniquet and Ford's vital signs. He was stable, but had lost a lot of blood. He had already had three hits of morphine, and Walton was about to give him another, but stopped. He was afraid that another shot would decrease his respiratory drive. But Ford was still in pain.

Looking around, he noticed commandos on the other side of the stable.

"Get the fuck out there," he furiously shouted, kicking them out the door. "Quit pussying out. Get back in the fight. This is where the casualties go. Not where you go."

Walton turned his attention back to Ford, who looked tired. Ford was the backbone of the unit. He'd helped shape it. If they performed well under fire, he deserved much of the credit. He worked their asses off. Walton wanted Ford to stay in the shed—he didn't want him moving around. That would only make things worse.

"You're going to be okay," Walton said.

"Are you sure?"

"Yes. The medevac birds will be here in two minutes and we're going to get everyone out of here."

Walton walked outside the building and found Mateen, the commando company commander.

"We're going to bound back," Walton told him. "Your next priority is getting accountability of your men."

And he warned him: If Mateen didn't have everybody accounted for, the commandos would go back up the mountain.

Walton hurried to the radio and reestablished communication with the other ODAs. He discovered that Mason's unit was still holding its ground and fighting off the insurgents from its blocking position to the northwest of the casualty collection point. Wurzbach was also holding his ground to the southwest, and his unit was fighting a battle of its own against snipers and HIG fighters armed with AK-47s and RPGs on the western side of the objective area.

Up on the mountain, Walton had been so focused on finding a way off that he didn't know the full extent of the enemy attack in the valley. Now he did, and he realized that this was a well-coordinated attack—and not just a defensive reaction to the American soldiers' presence in the valley. The insurgents were too well prepared.

63

Wurzbach

Wurzbach was anxious to rejoin Walton's team.

He knew the helicopters were headed to the valley to evacuate the soldiers. Besides, it was too dangerous at his team's position. The enemy had a bead on them. His team had been dodging rounds and RPGs. But he also was worried about friendly fire. Helicopters and planes were flying over them, dropping bombs and strafing HIG positions. Every time one of the big bombs exploded, debris rained down on his men. It was just a matter of time before a bomb missed its target and hit too close to them.

Wurzbach called Plants on the radio and told him to bring everybody back to his position. After running across the open field with Noodles, Wurzbach had been sitting there scanning the objective area, trying to catch a glimpse of the assault team.

"We're consolidating our location. If nothing else, it's for friendly force identification. I don't need the air crews dropping bombs on us, or strafing at us. We have enough shit going on. I don't need them shooting at us," he shouted.

When the commandos joined him, Wurzbach told them the plan. Through his interpreter, he said they were going to take a different path from the one they had climbed to get to the blocking position. Maybe that would catch the HIG fighters off guard. He wasn't sure. He only knew that they had to leave—and sneak away.

Wurzbach and his men headed northeast toward the wadi. They moved slowly and carefully, and surprisingly, they received little fire. They managed to make it down from their position unscathed.

As his team neared the wadi, they reached members of the B team. They had been the air reaction force, dropped off by a helicopter earlier in the battle to help. Wurzbach began pumping one of the soldiers for information, trying to find out as much as he could about the assault force. What did they know? What was going on?

He was told that Walding was seriously injured—his leg was nearly severed by a bullet. Morales had been shot twice trying to help Behr, who took a round in the hip. It didn't look good for Behr. He also said that Ford had been hit in the arm and that CK was dead. Other soldiers and commandos were wounded, too.

Wurzbach just shook his head in disbelief.

"It's been fucked up, man," the soldier said. "A lot of bad shit."

It was a fucked-up mission from the start. Every suggestion had been rejected. At that moment Wurzbach felt very disillusioned. But he had to stay in control.

"Did you know there were people up above you?" the soldier asked Wurzbach.

"I suspected, but I didn't have proof. I couldn't see anything," Wurzbach said.

"Yeah, dude, that's why they dropped on top of you like that," he said. "I'm pretty glad you decided to consolidate because we didn't know where you were. We had been trying to call fire on that area for a while."

64

Walton

It had become increasingly difficult for Walton to report the team's situation to Monster 33 because of the heavy volume of satellite radio traffic. But he could discern chopper traffic on the radio. And that was encouraging. With helicopters on the way, Walton had to restore order amid the chaos.

His main priority was getting Afghan commandos in position to establish security for the medevacs. But before he had a chance to do this, Lodyga's voice crackled over the radio asking Walton if he had any more pole litters. Walton didn't. There were so many wounded, they had run out of stretchers.

As part of his plan, Walton wanted to hit the HIG fighters hard before the helicopters arrived. Maybe that would provide a little cover. Because he knew that once the birds arrived, the HIG fighters would focus on shooting them down. He remembered reading in one of the intelligence reports that Ghafour had obtained SAMs. Whether they were functional was the question. If they were, it could spell trouble. But he knew the HIG fighters had RPGs. And, with the right strike, an RPG could bring down a helicopter.

Walton told Williams to grab the commandos and start firing at a suspected enemy fighting position. Then he instructed Rhyner to order as many air strikes as possible just before the medevacs approached in the hope of suppressing the enemy and giving the birds a chance to land.

The captain jumped back on the radio and told the pilots that they were "flying into a hot HLZ." Then ODA 3312 took control of guiding the aircraft in, using smoke and identifying power lines as they came inbound. The power lines were forty feet off the ground.

The entire wadi seemed to explode with CAS strikes and strategically placed fire at the insurgents.

In the distance, Walton could hear the helicopters approaching the valley. But he was worried. Enemy fire continued. Even with all the CAS strikes, with all the American firepower, there was no letup.

Walton knew the wounded couldn't stay at the base of the hill. Helicopters couldn't land there. And even if they could, the birds would be right in the line of fire. It was too dangerous for everyone. So he ordered the casualties carried to the middle of the wadi in front of the river. Maybe that would be far enough away to load the men safely on the medevacs.

65

Shurer

The casualty collection point had quickly filled up with soldiers. The wounded were on pole litters and Skedcos or sitting on the ground. All waiting for the dust-off. It kept Shurer busy. The medic was doing rechecks on the men when Martinez from ODA 3312 showed up carrying supplies. It was a blessing because Shurer had run out of just about everything. At that point, he knew that Walding and Behr were in shock. Maybe Morales. He had all the wounded drink water to pump up their fluids.

As he waited for the helicopter to land, Shurer moved from soldier to soldier saying the same thing: "You're good. Don't die."

Everything was moving in fast motion. They were down the hill, but they were far from safe. They needed to load the men on helicopters. They needed to get them to a hospital fast. But while they were waiting they were told they had to move the soldiers to a new position in the wadi. There was no time to waste. So some of the commandos immediately picked up the stretchers and began carrying the men to the river's edge.

As they moved, Shurer could hear the helicopters over the din of bullets. Maybe everyone would be okay. Maybe they would all get out alive. It was the first time in hours that he'd felt this way. But then he noticed that his arm was hurting. At first, he shook it off. But when he looked, he discovered a one-and-a-half-inch burn on the inside of his right arm with blood and bruising around the elbow.

What the hell happened? he thought.

He examined his uniform and saw a bullet hole in his sleeve. Then he lined up the sleeve with the wound. It was a perfect match. He shook his head in disbelief. He had been shot and hadn't even known it. He wasn't sure when it happened. It didn't matter. The only thing that was important was that he worked hard to save lives.

And now all he wanted to do now was get out the valley.

66

Ford

Ford could still hear gunfire as he staggered toward the landing zone. He was at the front of the line because he could walk. In the distance, he could just discern the green Black Hawk, with small painted red crosses, dip down into the valley. The helicopter flew in and started to hover.

Blasted by the rotor wash, Ford got one hand on the floor of the helicopter as it started to come down. The flight medic leaped off and headed toward the other wounded soldiers. Suddenly Ford heard a scraping noise overhead.

This thing is coming down on top of me, he thought.

It sounded to him like the rotor was hitting the mountain. Before he could duck for cover, the helicopter's engines screamed and the aircraft leaped back into the sky.

It had taken hours to get a helicopter this close, and now the medevac bird was gone.

Ford had heard over the radio that if they didn't get out of the valley soon, they would have to stay overnight.

Not good. Not good, he thought.

Spreading out, everybody took cover as another bird slid down the valley with plans to land in the wadi. But they would have to cross the fast-moving river of melted snow to reach the chopper. Slogging through the crotch-deep, frigid water, Ford had made it halfway over when he started to lose his balance. Afraid that he would fall and drown, he grabbed at another soldier, who was helping Morales across the wadi.

Holding on to the back of the soldier's shirt, Ford waded across. Cold, he reached the Black Hawk and climbed on board. He crawled to the front so there would be room for Walding and Morales in the back.

67

Carter

Watching the birds try to land in the valley, Carter knew there could be trouble. The volume of enemy fire had increased, and one of the helicopters took off after receiving multiple hits.

Before the helicopters arrived, Carter had pulled security at the casualty collection point and helped the medics. It was strange, but the on-the-job training he had received while they were trapped on the ledge really helped. He handed them gauze and bandages. It was like being in an inner-city emergency room on a busy weekend night. They had set up a makeshift trauma center.

But what good was all that if the helicopters couldn't land?

Carter watched another bird come in, trying to find a landing zone. It found one—but across the river.

That presented another set of problems. The only way to get across was to wade through the cold water with the stretchers. He was worried that the commandos would drop the wounded, which could aggravate their conditions. And he was concerned about the enemy fire. They were still shooting at the birds.

With Walding on a stretcher, Carter helped provide cover as they moved toward the helicopters. When they approached the river, he heard Walding's voice.

"Please don't drop me [in the water]," Walding said.

Inside, Carter was relieved. It was the first time Walding had said anything in a long time. He had gone into shock and was sleepy—not a good sign. Carter was worried that Walding would die before dust-off. Now he had hope. If, at this stage, Walding could remember that the river was cold, his mind was still working. He was trying to fight to stay alive.

68

Morales

They had to cross the river again. Morales couldn't believe it. After everything they had been through, they had one more obstacle. But at least the birds had landed.

Dave Kagle, a medic from the B team, and several commandos helped carry Morales's stretcher to the medevac. He peered up and spotted some of the commandos shooting at the village on top of the mountain to provide cover. They pounded the enemy position while the soldiers ran through the water carrying Morales to the helicopter. The water splashed on him. It was cold, but at this point, he didn't care. It was all about getting on the helicopters. Anything to get on those birds.

As they drew closer, Morales lifted his head. Maybe it was the adrenaline. Maybe it was the thought of seeing his wife and family again. Maybe it was because he was so close to leaving the valley. Whatever the reason, he managed to summon the strength to jump off the stretcher and hobble toward the aircraft without any assistance. He had two brutal wounds—to the ankle and thigh. The pain was excruciating—even with the fentanyl. It didn't matter. He was going to make it.

But when he was a few feet away, he stopped. He had been through hell in his past—in order to get to the Ranger battalion, he'd gone through RIP (Ranger Indoctrination Program). He had made it through Selection and Green Beret training. He had been through some really hard times, but he never quit anything. When his wife wanted to quit something because it was too hard, he would turn to her and say, "What's your last name? It's Morales. You don't quit." But right at that aircraft—when he was only an arm's distance away—he faded. He had lost so much blood and his bandages were coming undone and he was physically and emotionally drained. Finally, Lodyga helped him into the aircraft.

When he was inside, on a stretcher, one of the crew came over to help. Before he had a chance to speak, Morales looked up at him: "Man, you guys don't know how good it felt to hear you guys flying overhead and shooting back at that village because I was shot twice. Just to have you guys cover us is awesome."

For Morales, the *whoosh* of the rotors preparing to leave was therapeutic. For the first time that day, he took a deep breath and tried to relax. He knew it would be a long, hard journey to recovery. In fact, he wasn't sure if he would even survive at all. But just knowing that he was heading to a military hospital, he felt like he had a fighting chance.

69

Walding

Shock had taken over. Walding had tried to stay awake, but it was difficult. He was drowsy. He could hear the bullets and explosions and the rotors of the helicopters. But all the sounds blended together.

How long had he been at the casualty collection point? He didn't know. At least a medic had looked at his wounds. Bandaged him. Given him water, and morphine for the pain.

Still, he wasn't sure what would happen next. Would he live? He was fighting hard. He thought about his wife and children again. His grandparents. He was trying everything to just stay focused, to just stay awake. He was afraid that if he fell asleep he would never wake up.

He knew his fellow soldiers were doing everything they could to keep him alive. He wanted to live—even though he knew if he survived, his leg was gone. No way a surgeon could reattach it. Collapsed on the stretcher, he didn't want to think that far ahead. He *couldn't* think far ahead. He didn't know if he would even survive.

He opened his eyes and glimpsed the helicopters. Moments later, the commandos began carrying his stretcher. They had to cross a river—the same one that he had fallen into at the beginning of the mission. And in their haste, they dragged him through the water again. He was drenched. The water, though, momentarily shocked his senses. *Shit, I lived through the firefight, but the hypothermia is going to kill me,* he thought.

As the commandos carried him to the medevac, the enemy gunfire increased in intensity. They were aiming at the helicopter, which, despite being hit, continued to hold its position. They had to wait before loading him. The soldiers laid down a line of suppressive fire. And when the firing subsided, they moved Walding on board.

Once inside, he heard voices and glanced up at a face hovering over him. Then he passed out.

70

Behr

It was the first time Behr had felt safe since the battle erupted.

He was no longer trapped on a mountain. He was wrapped up in a Skedco in a clearing surrounded by Green Berets and a few Afghan commandos. But by no means was he out of the woods. He could still hear the gunfire and explosions. At least the medevacs had arrived. It was just a matter of time before they loaded his ass on a bird and whisked him and the others to safety.

Behr noticed all the activity around him. The Special Forces soldiers were talking to one another, shaking their heads, running back and forth. Some were on radios, talking to the helicopter pilots. And he noticed that one of the helicopters flew past him and landed in a clearing where Walding was being treated. The bird became an instant target. Immediately the insurgents began shooting at it.

"What the hell?" Behr asked.

At first he was concerned that the chopper pilots didn't see him. But then it dawned on him: Walding was probably in worse shape than he was. He probably had to be evacuated first.

Shurer returned and told Behr he would be on the next bird.

"Just hang in there a little bit longer," Shurer told him.

What choice did he have? He had waited this long—and he was still alive. That in itself was a miracle. Soon another helicopter swooped into the valley and landed nearby. Shurer ran over and told four commandos to help load Behr onto the helicopter.

But there was a hitch. They had to cross the river again to get to the helicopter, which had to land a safe distance from the attack.

As they were about to cross the river, Behr warned them to be careful. He didn't want to get wet again. But this time, the soldiers didn't dance from rock to rock trying to avoid plunging into the river. Instead, they plowed right through the water. When one of the commandos dropped his end of the litter for a moment, Behr got a little wet.

He was cold, but it was better to get wet at the end of a mission than at the beginning. When they finally reached the bird, a doctor and a medic from another ODA greeted him. They loaded him inside and strapped his stretcher near a window. Rushing to treat his wounds, they placed a mask on his face to sedate him.

As the helicopter lifted out of the valley, Behr glanced out the window and stared down at the mountains. He was grateful to be leaving, but overwhelmed by a sense of sadness. His team was still there. The firefight was still going on. *What's going to happen to these guys?* he thought. He felt even more helpless. Not only was he wounded and unable to help while he'd been in the field, now he was leaving his friends behind.

But as he stared out the window, he had a better sense of what had just happened and the difficulty of the mission. He saw how steep the mountains really were. On the way in, he didn't get a full picture of what was ahead because he had been staring out the back of a Chinook. But on the way out, he got to see the valley for all that it was.

"Holy crap, we were there. Crazy. Just crazy," he whispered before passing out.

71

Ford

As the others climbed aboard, Ford could hear rounds pinging off the helicopter. Peering into the cockpit, he watched the pilots sit and wait as the bullets rained down on them. They never flinched. With the last wounded soldiers inside, the pilots hit the throttles and the helicopter quickly climbed out of the valley. For the first time, he relaxed. It was finally over. He was safe, but hurt badly.

"We're going to make an emergency landing," the crew chief yelled at him as the helicopter strained to climb out of the valley. "We're going to put it down and transport you to another helicopter."

Ford could see Walding, Morales, and several wounded commandos spread out on the floor in the back of the helicopter. The brain of one of the commandos was exposed and he was frothing at the mouth.

When they landed at the Kala Gush firebase, Ford hustled to the other bird while the medics grabbed the wounded. But before he climbed in, he watched one of the flight medics grab a frazzled colleague. Ford thought the frazzled medic was acting like someone who'd drunk twenty energy drinks.

"I will throw you off this bird if you don't calm down," the flight medic said. "Sit down and shut up."

Ford again found a seat in the front of the bird. As soon as the nose of the helicopter dipped down and started toward Jalalabad, the frazzled medic started trying to undo Ford's tourniquet. Ford was afraid that if he loosened it too much, the artery would suck up into his chest and there would be no way to stop the bleeding.

"Don't touch it," he yelled at the man.

But the medic ignored him and kept trying to work on the tourniquet. Ford pushed the frazzled medic's chin away.

"Don't fucking touch it."

The medic looked shocked and finally headed toward the back and began working on the commandos. Ford tried to get comfortable. His arm hurt and the flight was taking what he felt was a long time.

As he sat there listening to the rotors beat the wind, Ford started doing the math. It had been several hours since he had been shot. *Shit.* His arm was probably unsalvageable.

When the helicopter finally arrived at Jalalabad, medics from other Special Forces teams and the hospital were there to meet them. The medics swarmed the wounded in the back of the helicopter.

Not as badly hurt as the others, Ford slid off to the side and watched. Spotting a chair near the landing pad, he walked over and sat down, letting out a long exhale. It was as if the world had been lifted off his shoulders. The stress of combat, of fighting for his life and the lives of teammates, had finally melted away.

Steve, a medic and friend from another team, saw him and came over. He thought Ford was in shock.

"Hey, you okay?"

Ford raised up a hand. "Dude, it's good."

Steve started to reach for Ford's kit. His bullet-resistant vest and uniform were covered in blood.

"Do you mind if we start—" Steve began.

"Get this shit off me," Ford said.

Steve started ripping Ford's kit off. Slowly unstrapping the plate carrier, Steve had Ford's sixty-pound vest, covered in ammunition pouches, and other gear undone and on the ground in a few minutes without Ford moving at all. With the equipment off, Steve helped him out of the chair and placed him on a litter. Nurses and doctors were soon at his side.

"Do you need anything?"

"More morphine," Ford said, his arm throbbing from the pain.

But the doctors were afraid to give him more. They didn't know how much he had already had. Ford knew he had had less morphine than the other wounded soldiers. He'd had none since he had taken Wallen's syrette. And that was hours ago.

"I need more morphine."

Steve finally convinced the doctors to get him more, and soon the pain faded away just as they loaded him on another helicopter to Bagram.

72

Wurzbach

While the wounded boarded the helicopters, Wurzbach helped Walton count the soldiers to make certain no one was left behind. It was all part of the routine: The same number of men who came in had to leave. The numbers had to match. Otherwise they would have to come back—and that was something nobody wanted to do.

So Wurzbach began adding up the soldiers. He talked to the sergeants and began counting and adding. He pored over the records. After cross-checking every record, he turned to Walton: "I'm sure we have everybody."

As they waited to get on aircraft, every member of the team began talking about the mission. What they were doing during the firefight. Where they were. Some even took a break and lit up cigarettes, which you're not supposed to do in battle. But they couldn't wait. It was their way of relieving the stress, blowing off steam.

The more Wurzbach heard, the angrier he became. His friends were badly hurt, and he didn't know if any of them would live. And if they lived, he knew their lives would be changed forever.

73

Walton

Over the radio, Walton could hear the pilots talking about the weather. The clouds were closing in again. The cloud depth had dropped five hundred feet in the last ten minutes.

"You have like ten to fifteen minutes to get out of there or we are not going to get you out," the helicopter battalion's commander said. He was flying above.

It had been a huge relief when Walton finally got back to the landing zone. But now the stress was returning. Back at the end of the valley, Apaches, F-15s, and A-10s were pounding the village. Rhyner had a list of the targets and the goal was to bomb them until the helicopters cleared the valley.

With the helicopters inbound, Walton made sure the Afghan captain, Mateen, was ready.

"Do you have accountability of your troops?"

"Yup. We have them all. We're good," the Afghan said through an interpreter.

But Walton wasn't convinced. Mateen had answered too fast and there was no way Walton was going to leave a commando in this valley.

"You count every motherfucker," he shouted. "We're not leaving anyone behind. Every single fucking commando, wounded or not, better be accounted for because we're not leaving because that is your biggest worry."

Everybody was bleeding and exhausted. Their nerves were frayed. Walton's bell was run by the rounds. Howard's eardrums were blown out after shooting the Carl G repeatedly. Commanders had considered leaving the team in place to coordinate air strikes. But they discarded that idea after reports that more than a hundred fighters were moving toward Walton and his men.

Searching the area around the landing zone, Walton knew they didn't have time to get on the high ground to defend themselves. Rhyner had already put in multiple nine-lines to continue bombing. Walton would have happily stayed in the valley for two days in order to bomb them. But his ride was en route and they had nine minutes to go, or the birds would leave them behind.

Just before the helicopters arrived, everybody let loose with their rifles and machine guns in all directions. Nobody shot back.

When the Chinook landed, it was time to leave.

74.

Howard

Howard studied the clouds. He knew that if visibility got bad up there, they would be stuck. He knew the enemy could regroup and they would have to fight through the night. Not a good scenario. At least the wounded had left the valley. While they waited for more helicopters to arrive, the survivors split up into chalks. Howard was with Walton's group.

During that time, Howard had identified HIG fighters moving northwest on the back side of the wadi. Walton was worried that they would threaten the aircraft, so Howard, using his sniper rifle, began firing at them. It was enough to hold them off.

When the Chinook landed, everybody quickly loaded up. He and Walton waited by the ramp to make sure that all the commandos got on board. Soon they were the last two.

"Get on," Walton said.

"No, you get on," Howard said.

Both wanted to be the last to go. Walton won the argument. Climbing up the ramp, Howard tried to pick his way to the front, near the gunners. He hoped to stick his rifle out of the window and get in a few more shots before clearing the valley. But a few steps in—after trying to navigate around a tangled mess of gear and the legs of commandos sitting on the floor in the fuselage—he slammed his shin on a resupply box strapped to the floor.

Nope, I am sitting down now, he thought.

Finding some space on the floor, he could hear the helicopter's engines whine and start to power up. The wheels lifted off the rocks and the helicopter shot into the sky. Howard could see the valley dissolve into clouds.

75

Walton

On the way to Jalalabad, Walton's relief morphed into anger.

He wanted to kill Fletcher.

The major hadn't listened to a single suggestion. Walton knew every mission was dangerous. It's the nature of the job. That's what Special Forces soldiers do. Go on impossible missions. But they always take measures to minimize the risk and casualties. They calculate the best tactics so the mission will be a success. They always ask: What's the best way in? How can they surprise the enemy? What's the best way out?

Then they plan and prepare. Then they practice over and over and over until they get it right.

That was something Walton had learned early in his military career. After he was cut from the football team at West Point, he learned that football was all about learning the plays. Learning about the nuances of the game. That comes by studying and preparing.

His team had prepared hard for this mission. They knew all about the HIG and Haji Ghafour. They knew about the terrain—just how dangerous it was, and how the Soviets—who used brutal battlefield tactics—stayed away from the valley. It just wasn't worth the risk.

But Ghafour was a high-value target, and it seemed that the military believed the benefits outweighed the risks. That's why the team was sent there. Walton understood that. But what he didn't understand was why they didn't let them fast-rope to a position above the village. Why they didn't let them conduct the mission at night, under the cover of darkness. Or why, if they knew the enemy was so strong and entrenched, they allowed a relatively untested commando unit to take part in the mission. Would they have done the same if they'd known where Osama bin Laden was hiding?

The answer was clear: No.

But all throughout the training, the commanders had put so much emphasis on showing off the commandos as this elite fighting force. The commanders thought: *Wouldn't it be great if this force helped capture one of the world's top terrorists?* But the reality was, the Afghan commandos weren't ready. While some performed well under fire, most didn't have a clue. As a result, a Special Forces team came close to being massacred. It was a miracle they had managed to escape.

Now Walton's men were seriously injured. And that image was burned into his memory.

Ford's arm being ripped apart by a bullet and blood spurting everywhere just like in the movies. Walding's leg hanging by a thread after being tagged by a round. His leg was just flopping as he tried to move and fight. The hole in Morales thigh and in his ankle, and Behr's deep pelvic wound. The bullets bouncing off Shurer's helmet. Rhyner's wound. And Wallen's. And of course, CK, who'd felt honored to be wearing a Special Forces uniform, was dead. His head smashed. The final indignity: his body being rolled off the mountain. Everyone was hit. This was hell. Walton had seen a lot of casualties in Fallujah—one of the most vicious battles in Iraq. And he had seen other casualties in his career. But nothing like this.

And that's what was so upsetting. It didn't have to be this way. Defending people who can't help themselves was one of the things that made Walton tick. In this war of shadows, that usually extended to villagers. But today—on this shithole of a mission—it meant protecting his friends.

When the helicopter landed, Fletcher was there waiting for them. If Walton was angry during the helicopter ride, he was now steaming. Look at him? Everyone else in Afghanistan heard the firefight over the radio. They were dressed and ready to help. But Fletcher? Look at him. He was out of uniform and looked like he was ready to work out. Like he didn't give a fuck. A perfect ending to a perfect day. The motherfucker.

Walton bounded off the Chinook. Fletcher started to say something, but Walton cut him off.

"Where the fuck are my men at?" he snapped at the major.

Fletcher was stunned. But Walton didn't care. He knew the wounded were being treated by doctors. He didn't know their conditions. But at that moment he wanted to gather up the remaining members of his team.

When he did, they huddled near the flight lines. He looked at them: Williams, Rhyner, Howard, and the rest. They were all covered in dirt and blood. Their uniforms were torn and there were scratches on their faces. They looked battered and beaten. Walton started to speak, but could hardly get the words out.

"I am sorry I let that happen to you," he said, tears welling in his eyes. "It's fucked up. Fucked up."

[Part 5]

AFTERMATH

76

Wurzbach

Wurzbach was pissed off. The mission had gone to hell—and now at least four of his good friends were seriously injured: Walding, Morales, Behr, and Ford. He had no idea if they were going to make it, and if they did, would they have permanent damage?

With Ford seriously injured, Wurzbach was now the acting team sergeant. He knew he would have to take care of all the paperwork related to the mission. Glancing around the helicopter, he could tell by the soldiers' expressions that everyone was pissed off. He just had to stay in control. Take a deep breath. Remember that they were out of the Shok Valley. Headed back to Jalalabad. And with any luck, everyone would eventually be okay.

When they jumped off the helicopters in Jalalabad, some of the men went back to the barracks and blew off steam. Some were yelling and cussing. They threw their equipment across the room. How could it happen? So many injured on such a fucked-up operation?

Wurzbach understood their anger. He was upset, too. But he had to stay in control. He was the acting team sergeant. He had to file reports, and get those papers ready for commanders.

Before he did anything, he bounded over to the hospital in Jalalabad, where Behr and Morales were being treated. He knew they would be headed quickly to the military hospital at Bagram, which had state-of-the-art equipment and surgeons.

When he walked in and saw his fellow soldiers, he almost broke down. They looked lifeless on the gurneys.

"You guys are going to make it, man," said Wurzbach, fighting back tears. "Everything is good."

But they didn't hear him. They were too sedated. And he made them a promise: he would take care of them. Talk to their families. Take care of all the bullshit paperwork. He told them they were heroes. But he wasn't sure they heard a word he said.

77

Carter

When Carter returned to the base, he asked everyone about the wounded soldiers. *Were they okay? Did they survive?* He was uncomfortable on the entire chopper ride back to Jalalabad. He kept thinking the worst. But when he landed, he quickly discovered that they were still alive and were being transported to Bagram.

He was relieved. Maybe they had a chance.

Then he slowly headed back to his room. He went in and took a long, hot shower. He wanted to wash off the blood and dirt. He was so tired, he propped himself against a wall and just let the water bounce off his body. He had to wash away all reminders of the day. *What just happened?* he thought.

Bits and pieces of the battle flashed in his mind. The blood. The body parts. The bullets. CK's shattered skull. It was almost too much.

After the shower, he called Staff Sergeant Marie Schult, the noncommissioned officer in charge of the public affairs shop in Bagram.

"Hey," Carter said.

"Hey, I heard about your thing," she said. "Are you all right?"

"I'm good," he said, trying to pretend everything was okay. "So I have one question."

"Yes?"

"Do I stay here or do I go back?"

"What are you talking about?"

"Well, I'm not mission capable anymore."

"Are you okay?"

"Yeah, I'm fine. But I have bad news." He paused for a moment. "My camera's been shot. Real bad."

"No way? Serious?"

"Yeah," he said. He knew she couldn't see him, but he was smiling for the first time all day.

She put Dennis, whom Carter had replaced, on the phone. "Hey, you're going to stay a couple of days to iron all this out. You're going to have to give your sworn statement. Then come back."

A few days off. Just what I need, he thought. He prayed that he would be able to sleep.

78

Shurer

When Shurer returned to the base, it looked like he had been shot. Every part of his uniform was covered in blood. His hands were black and dirt was caked in his fingernails.

He took off his uniform and stepped into the shower.

That night, he stayed up with the guys in the team room, talking about the firefight. It was a bullshit session. What they did in the battle. Where they were.

But Shurer's mind kept returning to the wounded.

Trapped on that tiny part of the ledge, he had worked as fast as he could. It was claustrophobic. The ledge—that shitty piece of rock floor in the middle of nowhere—was the size of a tiny room. He turned it into his makeshift emergency room.

He thought he'd performed well under pressure. But he kept second-guessing himself. Could he have done more to help Walding? Did he do enough to save Behr and Morales?

He didn't know. Then he recalled the near misses. Bullets pinging off his helmet. And, of course, CK. Dead. He'd looked at CK's face. This young man. His life gone too soon. To CK, the Americans represented a better future. And really, that's all he ever wanted. A better life for his mother. His relatives. His family and friends.

More importantly, CK had been willing to die for his beliefs. He stood up against the Taliban. He fought against the HIG and all those thugs trying to regain control of Afghanistan.

CK had dreamed of a day when Afghanistan would be free. People would live in peace and harmony. But now he was gone. His body smashed. And that would be one of the enduring images Shurer knew he would carry with him for the rest of his life.

79

Ford

Ford was the first to wake up in the recovery room in Bagram. The first thing he did was look at his arm. His heart raced for a moment—until he saw that it was intact. The doctors had saved it. His biggest fear after being shot was that they would amputate it.

The nurses had him help wake up Morales and Walding. He called from his bed to Walding, who was still asleep.

"If he hears familiar voices, he will come out of it quicker," the nurses told Ford.

"Hey, John. How are you doing? You okay, buddy?" he asked.

"I'm all right," Walding mumbled.

"Okay, cool."

The nurses asked him to do the same for Morales, who wasn't up yet.

"Hey, Luis, hey, Luis," he said.

"Try it a little louder," one of the nurses said.

At this point, Ford was almost screaming. "Hey, Luis! Don't think because you got shot you're not going to have to mow my lawn when you get home!"

It was a running joke with the team, since Morales was part Latino. They always kidded him about being the hired help—an illegal immigrant who just sneaked across the border. Behr got up next, but he was cranky. He was still in a lot of pain and didn't say much.

They stayed up most of the night bullshitting and cracking jokes—just like they were back in the team room. The nurses joined in, and it felt like a party.

"Hey, you guys going to share a pair of boots now?" Ford joked.

"Hey, Scott, can you wipe your own ass?" Morales shot back.

During the night, Lieutenant Colonel Lynn Ashley visited the hospital with Colonel Christopher Haas and Sergeant Major Terry Peters. They told the men how proud they were. They fought hard. They were heroes.

Then Ford broke away for a moment and called his girlfriend. It was the middle of the night in Bagram, but she was in a Target in the Washington, D.C., area. It was early afternoon on April 7, 2008.

He told her what happened. He didn't tell her many of the details. Just that they ran into "bad shit." And that fellow soldiers were wounded. He told her he was shot, but that he would recover. That he would be coming home soon.

"I'm safe. It's going to be okay," he said.

But it would take a long time for Ford to actually believe it.

80

Morales

Morales didn't remember much about his flight to Bagram. Actually, he didn't remember much about anything after he was loaded onto the helicopter in the Shok Valley.

He was in such severe shock—he'd lost so much blood—that he couldn't open his eyes. All he could think was: *Thank God I made it.*

He vaguely recalled those first few hours inside the Bagram hospital. He could hear all sorts of doctors and nurses treating him. One woman grabbed his hand as she was talking to him. She was asking him questions. Every question she asked, he responded to. But for some reason, he thought he was being "kind of a smart-ass" with his answers. He didn't know why.

Morales recalled that they removed his wedding ring and stuck it into his top pocket. Then they cut off his clothes and covered him with a warm blanket, and connected an IV just below his collarbone. He was still shivering after plowing through the cold river. He had hypothermia. Then he was out.

When he awoke, it took a while for his eyes to adjust. It was like peering through a microscope. He had never been in surgery for anything. But then he heard a familiar voice.

It was Ford.

When he spotted Ford, the team sergeant still had his arm. The doctors managed to save it. Morales smiled. It was good news.

As for his own leg, the jury was still out.

It was still attached, but the doctors told Morales that he would have a long, hard road to recovery. That he might never regain full strength in his leg, mainly because of his ankle. At the time, Morales was just happy to be alive. He didn't want to think about it now.

81

Behr

Behr knew it was bad.

He had been complaining about his stomach since he regained consciousness after his operation.

Surgeons had managed to stitch up his pelvis and arm. He was in fair condition, and they were optimistic about his recovery.

How he was still alive, no one really knew. He should have been dead. He had been on that mountain for hours with life-threatening wounds.

No doubt Shurer's care helped. He'd paid close attention to Behr.

Still, when Behr was loaded on the helicopter, he was in severe shock.

Now his stomach hurt.

He had complained for hours, but was told it was probably from the stitches.

But after he ate ice cream, he felt nauseous and nearly passed out.

Concerned, the doctors took X-rays and discovered the problem: His intestines were perforated.

Apparently the rock that hit his stomach on the mountain did more damage than anyone thought. His intestines were infected. So that night, doctors rushed him into emergency surgery to remove part of his intestines. It was an operation that saved his life.

82

Walding

Walding was grateful to be alive. But late that night he began wondering about his future.

Hours earlier, when he was rushed into the hospital, doctors didn't know if he was going to live.

When he arrived in Bagram, his temperature was dropping. Three times on the operating table, his heart stopped beating. But the doctors wouldn't give up. Each time he flatlined on the operating table, they resuscitated him.

Finally, they were able to stabilize him. But they also amputated his badly damaged leg below the knee. On the battlefield, he knew his leg was probably lost. Still, when he woke up, it was shocking to see it was no longer there. He knew his life had changed.

He had worked so hard to join Special Forces. For the first time in his life, he'd felt special. That he was giving back to the country he loved.

Now here he was, in the hospital, without a leg. He'd made a promise on the ledge to keep fighting—and he had. He'd fought to stay alive there. He fought to stay alive in the operating room.

But he knew the hard part was ahead.

For all intents and purposes, his Special Forces career was over. Sure he wouldn't be discharged. He would stay in the Army. But he knew he would probably never go on a mission again.

He was still groggy when Lieutenant Colonel Ashley visited him in the recovery room. Walding's first question was about his career.

"Hey, sir, am I going to have to leave the unit?"

"No, John. You're not. That is not even something you need to be thinking about," Ashley said.

"Well, good. With a name like John Wayne Walding, what else would I do?"

Still, he wondered how his family was going to deal with the injury. How would his wife react? He would need special care—at least for the short term. He would have to be taken care of—a big responsibility.

At the core of his discontent: He didn't want to depend on anyone. It ran counter to his moral code. He was supposed to protect others. That's was his responsibility. Hours removed from the firefight, he was finding it hard to think clearly. But at least he knew he would be there for his wife and children. He would always have his family. And for Walding, that was the most important thing.

And no matter what happened on his journey, he vowed to himself to keep fighting.

83

Morales

Talking to visitors, Morales glanced around the hospital room and spotted two of the team's interpreters.

Blade and Mustafa stood there, looking as if they were afraid to walk inside. Morales quickly waved them in. He wanted to talk to them.

"Hey, how are you doing?" he asked.

They told him they were trying to recover from the battle and wanted to pay their respects to him. They also were in Bagram to pick up CK's body and bring it home for burial.

After the battle, CK's corpse was taken to the morgue at the air base. Now his friends had to claim it. They wanted to make sure he had a proper burial. It was a solemn moment. The terps knew CK's mother would be distraught. Blade had been his best friend and would take care of arrangements. CK took the job to help his family.

CK had tried to become a terp a few years earlier, but was rejected because he looked too young. He was just a teenager, but lied about his age, saying he was in his twenties. His baby face gave him away.

Morales knew CK hadn't been afraid to risk his life. He died fighting alongside Special Forces. He wanted so badly to be a Special Forces soldier. And he might have died because he was wearing an American uniform. A sniper had been targeting soldiers wearing the tan desert camouflage.

Morales could tell the terps were grieving. They talked for a few more minutes about CK. It was a way for everyone to deal with the grief. He told them CK was a great interpreter and that he was in a good place. A place without wars.

A few minutes later, it was time to leave. The terps said good-bye. It would be the last time Morales would see them. The next day he was flown to Germany—the first step in his long recovery.

84.

Lieutenant Colonel Mark Wisdom

Lieutenant Colonel Mark Wisdom walked into his deputy commander's office at Bagram and waited. He was unsure why the deputy commander had requested the meeting. Wisdom only had two weeks left in-country and, after thirty-two years of active duty, was months shy of leaving the military for good. But from the commander's tone, he could tell it was important.

Wisdom was assigned to the Special Operations Command History and Research Office. Deployed to Afghanistan, his job was to move around the country with Special Forces teams documenting their missions and occasionally writing articles.

"Sit down," the commander told Wisdom. He seemed anxious and jumped right to the point. "Whatever you're doing, I want you to stop it."

"I don't understand."

"I want you to go out—and the chain of command wants you to go out—and write this article," the commander said.

He was looking for a positive report about Commando Wrath. Explaining that the operation was a critical success, he described how Special Forces had worked closely with Afghan commandos and Army aviation. He said he wanted an inspired piece that would be published in a "nonclassified magazine extolling the interoperability, the great partnership between Special Forces and the conventional Army."

The assignment was important. Major General John F. Mulholland, then commander of Special Operations Command Central, had requested the report after Colonel Christopher Haas told him that the operation had caused a "significant disruption of a major insurgent sanctuary."

Wisdom wondered, *Why the push?* More importantly: Why him? He only had a short time left in Afghanistan, and had planned to spend it with a Special Forces team in the Orūzgān Province, a starkly beautiful area in the Afghan central highlands. That mission was a big success story, he thought. The SF commander had partnered up with Afghans and "did some real things, things that made a difference." To Wisdom, the big success story overall was the soldiers in Regional Command South—not the operations in Regional Command East, where Operation Commando Wrath took place.

From the deputy commander's tone, Wisdom knew he was expecting a "feel-good article" and there was nothing Wisdom could do. He was stuck and pissed off.

After the meeting, he called his boss, John Partin, to complain. He told him that the commander wanted him to write a story about Operation Commando Wrath. Wisdom said he never heard of the mission. He bitched that the deputy commander knew that military historians usually didn't have time to write and research stories while they were deployed. They were covering too many fighting units. There were too many people pulling them in different directions.

Wisdom knew it also took time and patience to conduct interviews, examine documents. Then he would have to interpret the material and write. It was a time-consuming exercise. How was he going to get all that done in just two weeks? It sounded more like an assignment for a military reporter than a military historian.

After he hung up the phone, he began thinking. If the operation, as the commander suggested, was such a success, maybe he could wrap up the assignment quickly, and still have time to embed with that Special Forces unit in Orūzgān. But he would have to hustle. So Wisdom packed and headed to Jalalabad.

85

Walton

Walton sat in an office staring at his computer screen.

He was supposed to be writing his sworn statement—a paper that would detail every minute of the firefight.

Walton would write a few lines and stop. Maybe it was because he hadn't been able to sleep for more than a few hours a night. This had been going on for a week. He needed Ambien. Every time he closed his eyes, he replayed the battle in his head. The gunfire. His wounded teammates.

He was pissed off more than anything else. Angry that they hadn't been allowed to conduct the operation the "right way." Angry that commanders in Bagram hadn't deployed a quick reaction force to help his team get off the mountain.

A moment later, Fletcher came in.

Walton was still upset at Fletcher but knew enough to hold his tongue. Fletcher was his superior officer. It was one thing to lash out at him when they returned from the mission. Everyone was emotional. It was another to be disrespectful a week later. *Suck it up and keep it inside.*

Fletcher explained that during the battle some of the Afghan commandos had confronted about a dozen armed villagers. The commandos with ODA 3325—nearly a mile from where Walton's team had been pinned down—killed six or seven of them, and the rest surrendered and were taken prisoner. Now the village elders were coming to Jalalabad to try to get them released.

Walton was appalled. He'd had no idea that anyone had been captured. But he was adamant about the prisoners: They should not be released. Not under any circumstances. If they were on the mountain and armed, they were combatants. It was that simple.

Walton exploded. "I will fucking kill them if I see them. They are responsible for the whole thing."

He refused to meet with the elders and resumed trying to write his statement. He wasn't the only one. Everyone on the team had to write statements—and the commanders wanted it "written a certain way to meet the intent of the higher-ups."

He was getting annoyed.

No one knew what happened on that mountain—except the men who were there. And four were still in hospitals.

After some revisions, he finally finished the report and signed his name to it.

Then he put the men in for awards.

In his days as a team commander, Walton rarely put people in for awards. A soldier had to do something special to win one. But this was different. A guy who climbed up a cliff, knowing he could die, just in order to help wounded colleagues deserved a medal. So did the soldier who carried wounded guys down a cliff under fire. Walton knew no one on the team wanted any awards. As one soldier put it, you don't get awards for doing your job. Maybe that was true. But what his team had done was above and beyond heroic. Walton couldn't give a shit if he ever received an award for the Shok Valley mission, but he was going to fight like hell for the others.

Following the battle, the military started to get reports that Gulbuddin Hekmatyar and Commander Kashmir Khan—another major terrorist—had actually been in the village that day to meet with Ghafour. Nothing was confirmed, but the presence of hundreds of well-disciplined and supplied fighters, a large number of radio transmissions in Arabic, Farsi, and Pashto, the latter two languages not commonly spoken in the region, had led commanders to believe that they had stumbled on this meeting by accident.

The day after the battle, newspapers in Pakistan featured stories about how Hekmatyar and Khan had been killed or injured in a raid in Afghanistan. This was one of the indicators that the two had been in the village. It was clear, though, that Ghafour had survived.

The governor of Nuristan held a press conference, without being prompted by the Americans, and talked about a mission targeting Ghafour during a meeting with Hekmatyar and Khan.

Walton wasn't surprised. The fighters he'd faced were well trained and disciplined. And they had one major advantage—they had the high ground.

The captain wasn't sure what happened to the source who tipped off the military that Ghafour was in the village. He had continued to report after the battle started. The source even called headquarters asking why it was taking the SF team so long to get up the mountain. But after a two-thousand-pound bomb was dropped on one of the buildings, he was never heard from again. They believed he was killed.

A few days after Fletcher told Walton about the detainees, the village elders from Shok and Kendal—including a mullah—returned to plead their case. But this time Walton talked to them.

During the meeting, the men adamantly denied playing any role in the attack. "It wasn't us shooting at you," one of them said. "It was twelve men who snuck into our village. We couldn't do anything to stop them. They started shooting."

Then an elder added, "You killed some of our civilians with bombs."

Walton had had enough. He slammed his hand on the table.

"Bullshit. We fucking know your civilians fucking left, which is evident because you're fucking standing here right now. We know exactly what happened. Everybody there was fucking bad. We killed hundreds of their asses and we know that."

Then Walton stared right into the eyes of one of the elders—a short, dark-skinned man with long white hair and a white beard.

"I think you fucking know that we're both experienced fighters sitting at this table," Walton said. "And we both know what it feels like to go up against two hundred of our enemy. And what it feels like to go up against ten of our enemy."

At the end, Walton stormed out of the meeting—but not before issuing them a warning: "The next fucking time you see me will be the last time. Because you are an enemy of Afghanistan and you're an enemy of the United States."

He walked out of the door. He had to leave or he would have killed them. Only days before, the elder had tried to kill Walton and had taken out half of his team. *Now he wants to negotiate to get his detainees back? Really? No fucking way.*

A few days later, though, the detainees were released and, in all likelihood, headed back to the valley.

86

Wisdom

Flying into Jalalabad, Wisdom glanced out the window. The landscape was spectacular. The town was surrounded by a large irrigated plain, producing fruit, almonds, rice, and grain. On the Kabul River, the city had become a major center for U.S. forces. The city was positioned on the key route from Kabul, about 110 miles north-northwest, via the Khyber Pass, of Peshawar, Pakistan, and handled much of Afghanistan's trade with Pakistan and India. The town occupied an important strategic position, commanding the entrances to the Laghman and Kunar valleys.

When Wisdom landed, he watched the organized chaos around him: It was a typical military base with trucks and soldiers everywhere kicking up dust. He was picked up from the airfield and taken to a meeting with leaders of the B team.

Wisdom was at the very beginning of his research and was trying to get a handle on the mission. At the meeting, Mark Guzman, the B team's warrant officer, and others on the team told him they would fill him in on the entire mission. It was a multimedia presentation. For an hour, they told him what happened, handed him documents, and revealed even more details through a PowerPoint:

> MISSION: 201st Commandos and ANP 03, combat advised by AOB 3310 and ODAs 3336, 3325, 3312, conducts a cordon and search of Shok (OBJ Panther) and Kendal (OBJ Patriot) villages IOT Capture/Kill . . . vetted target Haji Ghafour (A high-ranking HIG commander)

The plan seemed straightforward enough. It was divided into phases, with an air assault into the vicinity of the target compound, followed by a move into the village. Then they would begin their search for Haji Ghafour, starting with "known INS targets." The teams would then conduct "tactical site exploitation" and remove the troops by helicopters back to the base.

The objective was clear. By capturing or killing Haji Ghafour, the SF teams would be able to "greatly" disrupt the HIG ability to "fund the insurgency." In addition, they would "deny enemy sanctuary." Again, all good goals—on paper.

But Wisdom was unsure if planners had taken all of the factors into consideration. It seemed that the planners had predicted a short fight, and thought that the teams could wrap up the operation fairly quickly. But Wisdom later determined that, based on the information in front of him, this was a bad assumption.

According to intelligence, Ghafour claimed to have three thousand fighters—possibly one thousand in the Shok Valley—and had been threatening military-aged males with conscription. The extremist had been stockpiling weapons, including surface-to-air missiles, PKM machine guns, DSHK and DPU antiaircraft guns, and RPGs.

Ghafour had distributed the weapons to HIG commanders in the valley. He also told supporters southwest of Kendal and at the mouth of Shok Valley to provide early warning of approaching U.S. forces and to fight all troops attempting to enter the valley. HIG subcommanders lived in nearly a dozen compounds in the mountains.

And then there was the terrain.

The Shok Valley was an insurgent stronghold. The area was "extremely rugged and mountainous." Not to mention isolated. There was no Coalition presence. In the Kendal village, the population was loyal to the insurgents. And soldiers would have trouble reaching the village. Aircraft would be unable to fully touch down in the HLZ because of jagged rocks and the fast-moving water that covered the landscape. Soldiers would have to jump up to ten feet off aircraft in the HLZ.

There were multiple wadis in the vicinity of objective, and soldiers would be surrounded 360 degrees by structures with enemy fighting positions. The ground had intermittent ice and snow, and there was a "myriad of structures not previously identified by imagery."

The intelligence said that stepped terrain led up to target buildings. There were thirty to forty buildings on multiple mountainsides, and there were sniper holes in the structures. Soldiers would have little to no cover or concealment. And the entire mission would be conducted at an altitude of ten thousand feet in forty-degree temperatures with descending cloud cover.

It took at least a week before Wisdom had a basic grasp of what happened. But after Wisdom examined some of the information from the actual battle, he concluded that the men had walked into a hornets' nest.

Not only was the enemy numerically superior, they were highly disciplined and well trained and fought until death. This was not some ragtag unit. They had some degree of command and control and utilized fire and maneuver tactics. The enemy soldiers were extremely effective with their sniper and machine-gun positions. They had large-caliber sniper weapons systems. They had men stationed on flat roofs and shooting out of windows, firing with deadly accuracy. And they had a high number of reinforcements throughout the Shok Valley that were alerted—they would do everything to protect Ghafour and his gem-smuggling operation.

During the battle, Ghafour was in the village, according to a source. The military had intercepted communication in the firefight showing that Ghafour was in the Shok Valley and had been staying at Mullah Habibullah's house. In fact, he was apparently heard saying, "Thank God. I have the rockets and binoculars." At one point, a source inside the village told the U.S. teams that they had reached Ghafour's compound, but hadn't gotten to "the proper building yet."

As Wisdom thumbed through the mission documents, he discovered that Army aviation had played a major role in the mission. Aircraft were riddled with bullets. One pilot was shot during the evacuation. Black Hawk medevacs landed under heavy fire. All told, the battle raged for six and a half hours and there were nearly seventy danger-close air strikes. Two Afghan commandos were killed, and fifteen U.S. and Afghan soldiers were wounded, many of them seriously.

At some point, Wisdom realized that this was the battle he had listened to a week earlier in Kandahar—along with seemingly all military person-nel in Afghanistan. The contact between the soldiers and pilots was being piped to the radio network at the bases. It was riveting. Everyone was clus-tered around the speakers. They could tell something bad was going down. Special Forces soldiers were talking about casualties, possibly being overrun. Bombs were exploding in the background. It seemed that every fighting unit in Afghanistan was getting ready to rescue the SF team.

So here Wisdom was, reading about the mission and ensuing battle, and expected to write a glowing story about the operation. He took a deep breath and turned to one of the B-team members. "This thing was operationally unsound."

The silence only confirmed his suspicions: The mission had been a tacti-cal disaster.

87

Morales

At first, things didn't go well for Morales at the U.S. military hospital in Ramstein, Germany.

At the Landstuhl Regional Medical Center, where nearly thirteen thousand wounded U.S. service personnel have been evacuated since 2004, he was placed in a room and started complaining about being hot. No matter what the nurses did, it didn't matter. He was sweating.

It was still winter in Germany. There was snow on the ground, but it felt like Morales was in the middle of the desert.

Finally, the doctors discovered what was wrong: Morales had developed prickly heat—a condition in which pores get clogged with sand or dirt or salt.

He had spent days scratching. He itched so badly, he felt like ants were biting him.

He was pissed off and cranky.

He couldn't move his leg. The pain was intense. And he was anxious to see his family. He had talked to Katherine and his parents on the phone. They were all worried about him. He told them he was doing better and would be home soon. They wanted to fly to Germany to visit, but he said he would be returning soon to Walter Reed Army Medical Center in Washington, D.C.

They were worried about that. They had read about a scandal at Walter Reed. In February 2007, the *Washington Post* published a series of investigative articles outlining cases of neglect and poor hospital conditions. Morales assured them that conditions had changed for the better. That's what friends had told him.

Besides, he knew he would need more surgeries and physical rehabilitation in order to get back on his feet. He was going to try to do everything to save his leg.

Still, he was down—until he heard that Major General David Rodriguez, the commander in charge of Coalition forces in eastern Afghanistan, was visiting the hospital in order to see him. When the general arrived, he pinned a Purple Heart on Morales in his hospital bed. It was one of the proudest days of Morales's life. His grandfather had received a Purple Heart after he was wounded in the Korean War. Now Morales was the recipient of one for his wounds in Operation Enduring Freedom.

In a way, he had come full circle. He was carrying on the family tradition. He only hoped that, with his wounds, he would be able continue his military service.

88

Wisdom

Wisdom had a lot of work to do in a short time. He wanted to interview everyone associated with the firefight before he headed back to the United States. But he was realistic. He knew that being able to wrap up the report while he was still in Afghanistan was unlikely, and that much of his work would probably continue when he returned home. But he was driven to get as much done while he was in-country as possible.

Interviews with the B team and others at Jalalabad helped. The documents and the after-action reports were critical. When he began interviewing Walton's team, he found answers to some of his questions. Some of the soldiers were at the base, including Walton, Sanders, Howard, and Wurzbach. He also interviewed soldiers from the other ODAs and began talking to the helicopter pilots.

He learned from Walton and team members that there had been real concerns about the mission from the start. He discovered that Walton's team didn't play much of a role in the planning. The mission was basically handed to them.

But the inherent dangers were clear to Wisdom. Fighting uphill was dangerous. The village was well defended, and any element of surprise was lost when the troops landed in daylight. If anyone was wounded in combat, it would be a logistical nightmare for helicopters to swoop into position and extract him. And the planners didn't seem to take into account the area's dangerous history. That, Wisdom thought, was a too common practice in both Afghanistan and Iraq.

If the commanders had studied the area, they would have understood the dangers facing the teams. Up until the late nineteenth century, many Nuristanis practiced a primitive form of Hinduism. It was the last area in Afghanistan to convert to Islam—and the conversion was accomplished by the sword. When the Nuristanis adopted Islam, they embraced its most conservative form. Wisdom knew that no one else in Afghanistan practiced Islam like the Nuristanis. Every law was taken literally; there were amputations for stealing, and women were stoned to death for adultery. In fact, the Islamic Republic was founded in Nuristan during the Soviet War. And Haji Ghafour was the first commander of the revolution, and he was particularly brutal. He interpreted religious law so narrowly that he offended even ultraconservative Muslims in the area. The Nuristanis were also fiercely anti-American.

So it was no surprise that Ghafour's followers were involved in ambushes against U.S. troops in September and October 2007. The province was a brutal hot spot. There was speculation that Haji Ghafour was behind the attacks. Indeed, the Shok Valley itself was a place where Ghafour felt safe. It was a remote valley where no Americans had ventured. Genghis Khan? He had avoided the valley nearly nine hundred years earlier. So did Alexander the Great. The Soviets? They didn't even try to go there. Surely the Americans would bypass the valley.

But Ghafour figured wrong, and Wisdom, after studying the battle plans, concluded that the U.S. military approach to the operation was extremely risky. Commanders had put not only the soldiers, but helicopters at great risk.

Wisdom knew the two biggest fears of the Army's chain of command in Afghanistan: a U.S. soldier being taken hostage, or a large helicopter, like a Chinook, being shot down. These were rarities, but when they happen, the command structure has to scramble for damage control. The negative publicity is intense.

So to ask Army aviation to go down into these valleys where they would be sitting ducks took a lot of balls, he thought. In effect, the commanders were putting aircraft down into a position where they were utterly defenseless. Anyone who has ever been in a helicopter with door gunners knows they can only shoot down. They can't shoot up—they can't shoot through the rotors. So once they start dropping below ridges, the door gunners are pretty useless. The Afghans know that. The insurgents' fathers passed down to their sons the tactics they used to defeat Russian helicopters. They would lure the helicopters down in the valleys where the aircraft was defenseless.

American and Coalition pilots were extremely conscious of this fact. They were one of the few groups that took seriously the lessons learned from the Soviet experience in Afghanistan.

When Wisdom interviewed Ford, the team sergeant told him he'd had a similar reaction to Wisdom's about landing in the valley. Ford believed it was an operationally untenable plan. You don't land guys in a valley and ask them to fight uphill or go uphill. Ford told Wisdom that his team did look seriously at the alternatives to landing on the low ground—including fast-roping to an area above the compounds.

But by landing in daylight in the middle of the valley, the enemy knew they were coming. Their men were in position on the high ground for the ambush. As Wisdom listened to Ford, he concluded that Walton's team and the pilots—and possibly members of the other ODAs—could have been massacred. And if that had happened, the publicity in the United States would have been overwhelmingly negative. The antiwar folks would again focus on Afghanistan—and push hard to bring home the troops that were stationed there. The pressure could have turned the tide of the war—or at least public sentiment, which still favored the U.S. presence in Afghanistan because of the country's role in planning the 9/11 terrorist attacks.

One of the things that helped save lives was that ODA 3312 had been in a similar ambush a few months earlier. Wisdom talked to members of ODA 3312 and discovered that they had been on a reconnaissance patrol near

Gowardesh in the mountains. Their mission was to clear the valley of insurgents who had been attacking Coalition forces. But while on patrol in January 2008, they were attacked. It was a brutal firefight, and one of the Green Berets, Staff Sergeant Robert Miller, was killed providing fire for his men to escape. Members of ODA 3312 said that the Shok Valley's landscape—and the mission—reminded them of the earlier operation. Uneasy, they moved cautiously as they headed to their positions to support Walton's team. They weren't surprised by the Shok Valley ambush and knew all the insurgents' tactics. They stood their ground and were able to hold them off so they couldn't overrun Walton's team.

With most of the material in hand, Wisdom called his boss. He explained to him that Commando Wrath had the potential to be a massacre—and the potential to have the "entire chain of command relieved."

Wisdom didn't know what his commander would say. But after a brief pause, he told Wisdom the words Wisdom had hoped to hear: "Go ahead. Write the report."

89

Wurzbach

Wurzbach took his role as the interim team sergeant seriously.

He began collecting the sworn statements from the soldiers, and handling paperwork—something Ford would normally have taken care of.

But Wurzbach also had concerns about the future of the team. They were so badly shot up. Would they go home? Would they stay in Afghanistan? What was next for the team?

After waiting for a while, he decided it was time to speak to his commander.

He told the commander that there was a rumor that the team would be going back to their original firebase outside of Kabul and would switch out early. He paused before adding, "Having just heard of this—but I'm pretty certain that I speak for everyone on our team—if you do that you'll have a real big problem on your hands. We're not done. We're still the mission company. We're still combat effective. We can conduct missions and we're ready to go. Let's start working our next target. We may need a little help. But let's get ready to roll. Let's get back on the horse. We're not going to put our tail between our legs and go home. It's not going to work that way."

The commander said he'd figured that would be the sentiment.

And so the team—sans Ford, Morales, Behr, and Walding—stayed in Afghanistan and conducted a few missions. They were mostly minor operations, and a few months after the Shok Valley battle, the team was redeployed to the United States.

90

Wisdom

Flying back to the United States, Wisdom realized his research was leading him in an entirely different direction. There was no question that the soldiers reacted heroically under fire. But Wisdom questioned the thinking behind the entire mission.

When he returned to the United States, he began discussing the mission with several historians at United States Special Operations Command among others. He sought their input and perspective. What he found was disturbing. Reviewing the information—and everything he knew from all his years in the military—he realized that Operation Commando Wrath was more than a failed mission. It represented many of the operational failures in Afghanistan.

You had a special operations community "hell-bent to validate this whole man-hunting concept." Even though it had never been shown to be effective, the military's infatuation with network analysis and net-centric warfare had become part of the eventual replacement of sound operations and tactics.

The mission had had a high potential for aircraft full of troops going down. The Green Berets were extracted because of aircrews that were willing to assume an extraordinarily high degree of risk. When you're an infantry-man, you can get down the rocks. You can't do that in a Chinook. You can't do that in a Black Hawk. They still have a lot of weight and balance issues. The air quality definitely affects Apaches and Black Hawks.

At the command level, it was believed that the mission had been planned out meticulously. But one question Wisdom was unable to answer was: Who pushed this plan? He knew Walton's team was given the plan but had little input into its details. Planning is a critical part of any operation—and plans have to be approved down the line. You develop a plan and it has to be approved from above until it reaches the final "seven or eight guys who are going to execute it."

As a student of history, Wisdom knew that this was an issue in Special Forces. Traditionally in Special Forces, especially in the 1950s and well into the 1960s, SF teams, had large companies commanded by lieutenant colonels. You had companies and teams, and the teams were often out in the middle of nowhere. The teams would develop their own plans and execute them, and they would resource them all the way back to the top so they had aircraft and air cover and air support.

The Green Berets were independent operators in many ways. By the 1970s, the Regular Army wanted little to do with Special Forces. The Army didn't want anything to do with counterinsurgency warfare. These were simply not discussed, not talked about in the Regular Army.

"In fact, Special Forces practically went away," Wisdom recalled. "It was on life support. There was a lot of resentment toward Special Forces in Viet-nam as well as [toward] Army aviation. Those were the only two branches that came out with their heads held high."

So Wisdom watched the shift from the Vietnam-era concept of Special Forces—according to which Green Berets lived in the boonies and worked with host-nation forces and tribes—to a more conventional unit.

Wisdom noticed just how conventionalized Special Forces had become in Afghanistan. In his view, Operation Commando Wrath illustrated this change. The mission was a conventional operation. Just because it was led by

Special Forces didn't make it a special operation. He concluded: It was an operation that a good infantry company could have handled.

Fortified with his information, he wanted to write a report that could stand for twenty years—the military could learn from its mistakes.

To do that, he needed to collect more information, and to his surprise, it came from unlikely sources. Many NCOs and officers who knew he was writing the report started slipping him information "under the table." To Wisdom, this was another indication that there was more to Commando Wrath than just a fight that went bad. Fights do go bad, he knew. Some days you get the bear and some days the bear gets you. But here he had soldiers giving him material that no one else had been willing to turn over. It was always: "Hey, you need to look at this."

He had to put together a time line, which he did in part by listening to the radio traffic.

One of the problems with Commando Wrath—and it helped illustrate the many problems in the war—was that many of the operations were driven by sources. Everyone seemed to be running their own sources. *Even Grandma has her own network,* he thought. So who was working for whom? How much circular reporting was going around? With Commando Wrath, they had a source telling them Haji Ghafour was in the Shok Valley and that, for the most part, he could be easily taken.

Easily taken? That was flat-out wrong—and it was something he would hint at in his report.

91

Behr

It seemed like the entire team was at Walter Reed.

In the months following the mission, Behr saw Ford, Morales, and Walding. They were all on different floors.

A steady stream of people visited them. For Behr, his time at the hospital was filled with reflection—and great physical pain.

Just like Walding, he knew he had died on the operating table in Bagram. The infection was so bad, that doctors didn't know whether they would be able to save him.

He underwent eight operations. For the first six months, he had to stay in bed because most of his hip was gone. Doctors had to wait for the wound to heal completely before performing hip replacement surgery. He began walking again only after massive rehabilitation. It was a struggle.

Whenever old friends visited, they would tell him they'd heard the battle over the network radio. That they were angry and had wanted to head to the Shok Valley to help. The U.S. military was like that. Everyone was truly a band of brothers. They might argue. They might bitch and moan. But when the shit hit the fan and one of their own was in trouble, they joined forces and discarded all the bullshit. That's just the way it was.

Behr's family visited. Even his wife, Amanda. They had separated long before he was deployed to Afghanistan, but she wanted to make sure he was okay. He knew their marriage was over. The two of them had too many issues. It was difficult being married to a Special Forces soldier. They work long hours when they are in the United States, and are always deployed, most of the time to secret locations in war zones. They carry a lot of stress because they deal with life-and-death issues.

Behr was wrestling with his future. What he was going to do once he was released. One day when a friend was visiting, he spotted a nurse, Mary Elizabeth Just, a volunteer with the American Red Cross, leaving the hospital. Pretty, she had visited Behr's room several times to help. Behr's friend glanced at Mary and asked her to have lunch with them. Behr was embarrassed. He liked the nurse and thought his friend was making a move.

In her midtwenties, she seemed smart and perky, with a bright, friendly smile. Every time she came into Behr's room, it snapped him out of his funk. The three had lunch that day. By the end of the meal, just before she got up to leave, Behr said he wanted to see her again. She said yes.

Now, sitting in the hospital room, Behr didn't know what his future would hold with the Army—he had been thinking about getting out—but he hoped it would involve Mary. He smiled for a moment. It was another ironic twist. He had found someone he liked under the worst possible circumstances. He knew he wouldn't have met her if he hadn't been wounded on the worst day of his life.

92

Wisdom

Wisdom became consumed with the report. He wanted to know every last detail. For example, the role of joint tactical air controllers (JTACs) is critical in any battle. They are the pilot's eyes on the ground, leading them to targets and, in many cases, away from civilians. But Walton had an inexperienced JTAC on his team. And when the shooting started, they had to turn to the JTAC on ODA 3312, Robert Guttierez, to help call in the danger-close strikes.

As Wisdom examined the course of the battle, he discovered other mistakes: The command structure, for example, had downplayed the intelligence. Walton, the mission's ground force commander, was too close to the front lines.

It was a case where you had one ground force commander leading three ODAs, and you had two-thirds of an Afghan commando company spread out over four locations, over extremely rough terrain. How do you maintain command and control? Walton was leading the charge. And when the ambush occurred, he found himself immediately cut off. He became, for the most part, combat ineffective. He had to rely on the radio, and that's not something you want to have to do in that type of terrain.

Finally, Wisdom completed a draft of the report, which detailed every aspect of the mission. What went right? What went wrong and how had they avoided a complete disaster? Luck played a major role.

Then he presented his findings to his deputy commander.

"Tell me what really happened?" the man asked.

It was an open invitation to be candid, and Wisdom took advantage of it. The deputy commander listened intently as Wisdom spent an hour talking about the mission. He noted the lack of enthusiasm the soldiers had felt about the operational soundness of the mission.

"Well, when things finally get to our level, they have been so sanitized, so whitewashed, we often don't know really what happened," the commander said.

He added that the operation had come across as a huge success. Wisdom was shocked. "The team didn't get the objective of the operation," he told the commander. The deputy commander told Wisdom that while they didn't catch the bad guy, they "disrupted the enemy." He took a deep breath. "You're not going to change the report, right?"

Wisdom was worried. He knew that the soldiers were pretty upset and some had expressed concern that he was going to whitewash the mission.

The deputy commander looked Wisdom in the eye and said, "Write it up. Warts and all."

And that was what Wisdom did.

93

Final Report

Wisdom worked on the report up until the day he left active duty. He started writing it ten months before, and he completed his second draft on April 23, 2009, and was discharged a day later. It took that long.

When he finished, he filed the report—all 298 pages of it. Based on dozens of interviews and hundreds of documents, it went to commanders for review.

It was the real inside story about what happened—not the version that had been presented to the media. The Army had awarded ten Silver Stars to the men trapped on the mountain—the most to any fighting unit since the Vietnam War. The publicity surrounding Commando Wrath was widespread. Every major news organization from the *Washington Post* to the Associated Press had recounted the tale to a wide audience. It was always the same, how a Special Forces team scaled a mountain to reach a top unnamed terrorist and inflicted heavy casualties on insurgents. There were exciting details about how the trapped soldiers escaped, scaling down the side of a mountain under heavy fire. It was a made-for-Hollywood movie. But there were no details about the origin of the mission—or the tactical problems the soldiers had faced.

None of this mattered to Wisdom. He wrote it so that someone in twenty years could examine the battle and understand what happened. They could examine all the mistakes. And maybe someone could learn from it. So it wouldn't happen again.

But unknown to Wisdom, his report was never published. The Special Operations Command's History and Research Office said Wisdom's report "contained weaknesses in its historical methodology" and the draft would need revisions.

EPILOGUE

On a cold December day at the end of 2008, the team was finally reunited at Fort Bragg, North Carolina.

Under the glare of television cameras, Walton, Ford, Morales, Walding, Behr, Howard, Sanders, Shurer, Williams, and Carter were about to receive Silver Stars—the military's third highest combat decoration. It was the most Silver Stars awarded to a single fighting unit since Vietnam.

Their families arrived early in the John F. Kennedy Special Warfare Center and School auditorium as the men made their way to a stage. In a few minutes, their prerecorded voices would recount the daring feats of each soldier. Carter was the only recipient who was not in Special Forces. But he held a special place at the ceremony—he was the only combat cameraman in U.S. military history to win a Silver Star.

The audience was spellbound as the narrators told their story—complete with video. How they were trapped on a mountain. How some were seriously wounded. How they had risked their lives to drag fellow soldiers out of the line of fire. How they'd had to find a path down the side of a cliff to carry the wounded to safety.

Lieutenant General John F. Mulholland, commander of Special Forces Command, told the audience that day that he was awed by their actions.

"Alone and unafraid, working with their counterparts, they took on a tenacious and dedicated enemy in his homeland, in his own backyard. Imagine the Taliban commander thinking, 'What the hell do I have to do to defeat these guys?'" Mulholland said.

He continued:

"As we have listened to these incredible tales, I am truly at a loss for words to do justice to what we have heard here. Where do we get such men? . . . There is no finer fighting man on the face of the earth than the American soldier. And there is no finer American soldier than our Green Berets."

Mulholland was confident that many people simply wouldn't believe the courage displayed by the men arrayed before him.

"If you saw what you heard today in a movie, you would shake your head and say, 'That didn't happen.' But it does, every day," he said.

With that, he pinned medals on the men's chest.

In March 2009, Rhyner was awarded the Air Force Cross—the service's second highest award for heroism, after the Medal of Honor.

It was the culmination of months of publicity surrounding the mission.

The story captured the public's imagination. A daring early-morning raid into the heart of an insurgent stronghold. A small force trapped on a mountain, but still able to kill nearly two hundred enemy fighters before escaping after a six-and-a-half- hour battle.

The soldiers were interviewed by dozens of local and national news organizations. They were hailed as heroes. The story was powerful and compelling.

The ceremony took place shortly after Democratic Illinois senator Barack Obama was elected president. As a candidate, he promised that America would shift its defense resources from Iraq to Afghanistan, which he called ground zero for any war on terrorism. He vowed to remove one or two brigades a month from Iraq, and get all combat troops out within sixteen months. In Afghanistan, he said he would ramp up the American military effort, particularly on the Pakistani border, and said that if America received intelligence about suspected Al Qaeda operations in Afghanistan and Pakistan, he was prepared to act on it.

It was clear that the newly elected president's foreign policy focus would be on Afghanistan.

If anything, the Shok Valley battle helped illustrate the problems facing American troops in that nation. There weren't enough ground forces to combat the rising influence of Al Qaeda and its supporters, mainly the Taliban and the HIG. In some areas, like the Shok Valley in Nuristan, the insurgents operated openly and without fear.

Since the lights faded that day at Fort Bragg, the soldiers have moved on with their lives. So it was no surprise that they initially balked when they were approached in April 2010 about being interviewed for a book about Commando Wrath. They said they would have to think about it. They didn't want any more publicity. Finally, they said they would cooperate—but only if the authors "told the truth" about the mission.

Yes, it was a dangerous mission. Yes, they risked their lives to do their job. But they wanted the entire story told.

So, for a year, the team reluctantly talked to Mitch Weiss and Kevin Maurer about Commando Wrath, their loyalty torn at times between the Army they loved and telling the truth about a battle that has dominated their lives.

To get the full picture, the authors interviewed more than sixty people and reviewed hundreds of pages of documents, including detailed maps and after-action reports of the mission. (The Army refused to release Wisdom's final report because it was still in draft form.) Kevin Maurer, who has been embedded nearly two dozen times with Army troops and Special Forces soldiers in Iraq and Afghanistan, visited Afghanistan in 2009 and 2010 and talked to some of the Afghans who fought that day. (The authors wanted to visit the Shok Valley, but it was too dangerous.)

In interviews, it was clear that the soldiers were proud of how they banded together to get off the mountain. How they overcame overwhelming odds to survive. But it was also evident that they still carried the deep scars of that day.

Since April 2008, Walton, twenty-nine, has been deployed to Afghanistan several times.

He still enjoys military service. When he's not deployed, he is a volunteer firefighter with a department on the outskirts of Fort Bragg.

Reflecting on the mission, he was proud of the way his men handled themselves. But he hates the notoriety, and he is particularly hard on himself.

"I don't feel like a hero," Walton said. "I feel like I led a mission that went to shit and we all fought to the death to save our buddies and survive. Did we accomplish our fucking mission? No. Those fuckers are still alive. Granted, two hundred of their closest associates are blown all over the fucking mountain right now. And I am thankful every day we killed them. But that doesn't make up for losses that we took."

He recalled Wurzbach once telling him that he didn't want to be defined by one battle.

But he already has been.

"That battle was a definitive fucking moment in everyone's lives," Walton said. "Will there be more? Potentially. But maybe not. But up until that moment in our lives, nothing like that had ever happened."

As much as he tries to put it behind him, he can't.

"Is it right to put it behind you and completely forget about it? No. That is probably not the right thing to do. Do you want to think about it? No. It was weeks before I could sleep. I could not fucking sleep. It was not because of PTSD [post-traumatic stress disorder]. I wasn't having nightmares and flashbacks. I was just so fucking pissed off that I could not relieve the stress. No amount of cigarettes worked at the time. I went to the medic and got Ambien," he said.

Walton has seen subtle changes in his personality. Bright and ambitious, he was always driven to success. He still is.

"But I have a lot shorter fuse than I used to. You can only take so much stress before you snap. The stress came from all the other bullshit. There is a guy missing a leg. One guy has a fucked-up arm. Several guys got out of the Army . . . So there is a lot of aftermath there. A lot of this stuff is really never going away."

The thirty-one-year-old Morales has tried to move forward with his life. He is still in Special Forces, even though he has undergone twenty-four operations and has had his leg amputated. But there are times when he stops and thinks about the Shok Valley.

He recalled the day he arrived at Walter Reed Army Medical Center. He was in a case-assessment room with Ford and Behr. As usual, they were all being obnoxious. But when they wheeled Morales to his room, Morales's parents and his wife, Katherine, walked in. It was a tearful reunion.

"Katherine is crying and hugging me. My dad is emotional and my mom is, too. They were all crying, and in that sort of situation, I deflect emotion. I didn't break down crying. I try to stay calm in those kinds of situations when other people are losing it," Morales said.

But when he was alone with Katherine later, it all caught up with him. He broke down. He told her about everything he had been through. About losing CK. They hugged for most of the night.

And he began a desperate fight to save his leg.

He could barely move it—and it hurt like hell. Doctors told him he would eventually develop arthritis. "[They] told me that most of the guys will have their legs amputated when it gets this bad."

Morales wanted to prove them wrong.

"At that time, I wanted to fight it," he said.

One surgery, they tried to fill the hole in his ankle. They surgically removed the skin and an artery from his calf. Then they tried to fit them into his ankle to get the blood vessels to connect. It didn't work.

They also used two vats of leeches to suck out the coagulated blood underneath the skin flap. It was creepy. The leeches usually stayed on the wounds. A few times, though, they crawled up his body. The doctors did this for two weeks.

Over time, surgeons performed more surgery to shave down the skin in order to increase the flow of blood. Along the way, there was hope. He was doing physical therapy.

"I was working my ass off. I was working through pain. I was taking a lot of medication. My goal was to be able to try to play golf," he said.

Morales was an avid golfer. But now he could barely stand up. In April 2009, a year after Shok Valley, he headed to Duke University Medical Center for a second opinion. He wanted to see if they could do ankle replacement surgery. But the doctors told him he didn't have enough bone to work with, and ruled him out as a candidate.

Walking to the car from the hospital, Morales became upset. He realized the ankle wasn't going to get any better unless he had it fused. So he did. He had three pins screwed into his ankle at a ninety-degree angle. But he found it was hard to walk with a fused ankle. So he had to find shoes with a curved sole.

He did that for a while. He even walked with a cane. But it still hurt. In November 2009, he went with Ford and other wounded warriors on a hunting trip in South Dakota. But he couldn't go hunting. His leg hurt too much. He saw other soldiers with amputated legs, like Walding, moving around fine. So he decided to have his leg amputated so he could have a somewhat normal life.

Katherine wasn't happy with the decision. She wondered if there were any other options. "I was determined. I was tired of being in pain. I wanted to be able to get around and do other things again without pain," Morales said.

He had the surgery on January 14, 2010. "I didn't make it a big deal. It's another surgery that needed to be done so I could start another part of my life so I could get around."

For the most part, since the amputation, he has been pain-free. Sometimes he has phantom nerve pain. But now, with a prosthetic leg, he can walk. Play golf. And he was waiting to get a running prosthetic leg. And he was about to start a family. Katherine was pregnant and expecting their first child in late 2011.

He plans to stay in the Army—at least for the next six years. Then he will have twenty years and can retire.

Still, he wants to continue doing intelligence work and hopes to deploy again to Afghanistan.

"For me, I'm helping my buddies. I can't see being away from the military."

But there are triggers that take him back to the Shok Valley.

While he was at Walter Reed, Morales attended a Major League Baseball game with his father. At the end of the game, there was a crescendo of fireworks. Morales turned to his father: "Dad, that's what my firefight sounded like." Both father and son "teared up."

Walding made a remarkable recovery and was running again. Before the injury, he averaged about fifty miles a week.

He still believed he could do the job, and proved it when he trained to be a sniper instructor.

While recuperating, Walding worked as an assistant instructor at 3rd Special Forces Group's sniper detachment. But to become a full-time instructor, he had to complete a sniper course. The seven-week Special Forces Sniper Course teaches sniper marksmanship, semiautomatic shooting, ballistics theory, and tactical movement. During the course, many of Walding's classmates didn't even know about his injury and prosthetic leg.

When he was finished in the summer of 2010, he hoped to work his way back to an ODA—maybe even deploying to Afghanistan.

Not anymore.

He realized that physically, he would never be the soldier he was the morning of the Shok Valley mission. While he enjoyed being an instructor, he joined Special Forces to "hunt down and kill the bad guys."

He still loved Special Forces. But he said it was time for his family to head to southeast Texas to be around their aunts and uncles and grandmother. (His grandfather—the inspiration of his life—died two days before Christmas in 2008.)

It was a difficult decision.

"I prayed about it a lot. I feel that God has a plan and the best thing for me to do is try something in the civilian market. Move back to Texas. Be close to home. I want to contribute to the fight. That's what I've done for the last ten years—protect our country. And if I can't do it in the Green Berets, I'd still like to contribute somehow," Walding said.

Walding is proud of how Americans have come together to support Iraq and Afghanistan veterans, especially wounded warriors.

Everywhere he goes there are special nonprofit groups waiting to lend a hand. Some organizations were set up just to help wounded warriors get back on their feet. It's a far cry from Vietnam, when returning veterans were shunned by the public.

Because of those groups, Walding is going back to school. He was accepted in a special program that pays for living expenses while veterans go to college. And there is another organization that is helping him build a house in Texas.

As far as the mission is concerned, his missing leg is a constant reminder of everything that went wrong.

He said that sometimes it's hard for him to get up in the morning. He doesn't have the energy he used to have—and this is not uncommon for someone who suffered injuries like his. He said Ford told him he had the same symptoms.

"This is something I'm going to face for the rest of my life," he said.

On his youngest daughter's first birthday, he knew he had to get the house ready for the party. But he had to force himself to get out of bed. "You know, I'm hardworking. I have a great work ethic. I used to go days without stopping. Once I get up, I'm okay. It's just getting started."

He recalled that the first time he told his aunt about the mission. He showed her pictures of the Shok Valley. She was stunned.

"To kind of prove the point about how tactically flawed this was, I showed her the video of the Shok Valley and showed her the ground and how we went up the mountain and everything. And my freaking little hippie aunt looked at me and said: 'Why were you all charging a hill? Isn't that tactically not a good thing to do?'

"If my hippie aunt could realize that this was a stupid mission, that should say something how obvious [it was that] this was not the right way to do it. It was basically this one guy who wanted to do this mission and it didn't matter why and this was going to happen. And that's what happens whenever you stop listening to the five principles of patrolling, and the last one is common sense," he said.

Behr, thirty, left the military in June 2010 and is back in college—this time at Georgetown University in Washington, D.C. He is enrolled in the security studies program with a concentration in technology and security.

He divorced his wife, Amanda, and is dating Mary Elizabeth Just. They are planning a life together. "She is the one," he said.

Behr's road to recovery was difficult. He underwent eight operations. His wounds resulted in severe intestinal damage and a hip replacement. He was on his back for six months, and spent the next six in rehabilitation trying to walk. It was a grueling process, but he can now walk without help.

Now he is employed by a small technology consulting firm and began cycling in order to rehab his injury in 2009. He fell in love with mountain biking, which he learned to do with the aid of two friends at Walter Reed.

Behr said he had been thinking about leaving the military before his last mission. But after the Shok Valley, he knew he had to leave. He could no longer physically perform at Special Forces level.

"It was a tough decision. I loved Special Forces. But I'm entering the next phase of my life," he said.

He paused for a moment to collect his thoughts.

"But I think about it," he said about the mission. "Sometimes it just comes up. Those guys saved my life. I wouldn't be here without them. They saved my life. "

Shurer also left the Army and is employed with a government agency. His first son was born shortly before the Shok Valley mission, and his second son, Tyler, was born in April 2011.

While he loved the military, he is happy with his new life. He tries not to think about what happened in the Shok Valley. He believes he took the right measures on the mountain. But at first, it was difficult to come to grips with everything that happened.

"That day was rough for a while. I spent a fair amount of time beating myself up. You go back and look at stuff and you say: 'Could I have done that a little bit faster? Should I have wasted so much time trying to do that?' "

But over time, he has learned to live with the decisions he made during the firefight.

"What ended up helping me with that was when you talk to surgeons who worked on everyone and they're all like: 'What you did saved his life. Don't beat yourself up. You did what you had to do. Every one of them—all four of them—had life-threatening wounds. Every one of them would have died without treatment.'"

He stopped and took a deep breath.

"It took a while to really kind of process that and not keep going over it. I got them out alive," he said.

But there are days when he is haunted by the images.

"There are some days it pops in your head," he said.

And there are triggers. He can't watch war movies.

"You just have to come to grips with it. Once you do, it gets better," he said.

For Ford, it was a long, hard journey. He spent months in rehabilitation. There were days when he felt like giving up.

But he is back doing what he loves best: training snipers. The 3rd Special Forces Group asked him to take over their sniper committee.

In the years since the Shok Valley mission, he has gotten married and had a daughter. He tries not to think about the battle.

"I have my confidence back. I am shooting all the time. In the last six months, I came back out of my shell. I am really just enjoying my career. We'll find out in the next few months if I can go back and take a team. I think they are going to let me take a team. I am just really happy. Cher and I had a baby last summer. I've never been closer to a family or the family I have now."

The same can't be said about the team. They've all drifted away from one another. Some to pursue other career opportunities. Others because of rifts among teammates. A Special Forces team, more than almost any other unit in the military, is a family. And as is the case with even the best families, there is always some drama. But Ford knows that over time the bonds they formed in that valley will last.

"I wanted that team to stick together for the rest of their lives. Keeping in contact every five years. Ten years," Ford said. "Always having that brotherhood from being on that team."

Many of the soldiers, like Carter, Sanders, Howard, Williams, Rhyner, and Wurzbach, are still in the Army. And in 2011, Sanders, Williams, Wallen, and Wurzbach returned to Afghanistan for another deployment.

Sanders said he was embarrassed by the attention.

"We certainly weren't the first guys to get in a firefight and we won't be the last, and as far as that goes for me, don't take this wrong, even with the book, I kind of feel sort of awkward. It's almost kind of embarrassing really."

Carter tries to downplay his role. Yet it's hard to ignore. A combat cameraman, he ran into the line of fire to pull wounded soldiers to safety. He tended to the wounded. He climbed down a mountain to help find a path off the mountain. Then he carried the wounded down that dangerous trail.

Now stationed in Hawaii, he works with an Army forensic team trying to find the remains of missing soldiers from earlier wars. "It's pretty much what Indiana Jones does. We use archaeology to help identify remains of missing soldiers. We look for the remains of POW and MIAs," he said.

It usually starts with tips. Then the investigation team tracks down possible witnesses.

"They'll get the information from them and mark the site and they come back and let them know where they need to go, and that's when the recovery teams will go out and dig the site," he said.

Still, the Shok Valley mission creeps into his memory when he least expects it. It could be late at night. Or when he's out with friends. Or when he's on assignment. In a flash, the images return, and he feels like he's back on the mountain.

"I fight it," he said. "But sometimes it's hard."

Carter's experience is a typical one for the soldiers in the Shok Valley that day. They experienced things that most Americans will never see—their friends blown apart in a mission that nearly wiped out their team. They faced serious injury and death. And pinned on a mountain in that remote, hellish valley, they overcame their own fears and fought overwhelming odds to save one another.

Years after the battle, one thread connects them: In conversations, they emphasized over and over that they did what they had to do. They were always quick to add that other soldiers, facing similar circumstances, would have done the same.

We'll never know if other soldiers would have performed the same way.

We only know what they did on April 6, 2008, and it was remarkable. Trapped in a brutal firefight on a narrow ledge with a terrorist group, a team of Special Forces soldiers carried their wounded comrades to safety. They battled hard to return to their families. They received Silver Stars. They were called heroes.

But if you dig deeper, this mission serves as a cautionary tale for politicians sitting in the comfort of their living rooms—the ones who are so quick to send our troops to war. The soldiers didn't want to undertake this mission. They knew the plan was flawed. But in the end, they went. They overcame near-freezing weather. They exposed themselves to protect their teammates and climbed through machine-gun fire to save every man. So be careful what you ask soldiers to do because they will die trying to accomplish their mission.

They won't fight and die for just the flag or the other lofty goals of freedom and democracy plastered over recruitment posters and commercials.

They fight and die for each other.

ACKNOWLEDGMENTS

This book grew out of a story written by Kevin Maurer for The Associated Press. The piece focused on the dangerous mission—and how the Special Forces team was awarded ten Silver Stars for bravery in the Shok Valley firefight.

Turning the story into a book was a long journey, and we want to thank a number of people who helped us along the way. We would like to thank the entire team—ODA 3336 and Michael Carter—for allowing us to write the book. We spent countless hours on the telephone—sometimes several time zones apart—and in their living rooms asking endless questions about the mission, and details of their childhood and personal lives. It gave us incredible insight and allowed us to write with authority.

At the beginning of the journey, we made the men a promise: We would pull no punches. We would write a compelling book about the mission. And that happened because of their cooperation.

Special thanks to Scott Ford and Luis Morales, the team's unofficial historian. Ford was instrumental in getting the story to the page and gave his time generously to make sure we understood what his team accomplished against some staggering odds. Whenever we needed information or a contact, Morales was always there. A true hero, Morales wanted no credit. He downplayed his role and always gave credit to his fellow soldiers.

We'd also like to express our gratitude to Kyle Walton, Dillon Behr, Ron Shurer, Karl Wurzbach, Carter, Seth Howard, and David Sanders for their support and time. Another special thanks to John Wayne Walding, an incredibly brave and tough soldier. We wish him—and the other team members— only the best as they move forward in their lives. They truly are the quiet professionals.

We would like to recognize Carol Darby, Major Manny Ortiz, and Staff Sergeant Jeremy Crisp and the rest of the USASOC and USSOCOM public affairs office who made this book possible. And we would also like to express our gratitude to Major General Michael Repass for his advice.

We'd also like to thank our agent Scott Miller of Trident Media Group who recognized the value of the story, and we would also like to express our gratitude to the team at Penguin Group for their editorial support, including Natalee Rosenstein, our book editor, who truly understood the importance of the story and pushed us to greater heights.